ACADEMIC
OUTLAWS

More Praise for Academic Outlaws . . .

"William G. Tierney is a practicing *outlaw*, crisscrossing the horizon where cultural studies meets the academy. One of our premier critics of higher education, Tierney reveals how cultural distinctions shape our relation to key dimensions of everyday life: sexuality, ethnicity, gender, and social class. *Academic Outlaws* works at the intersections of cultural studies and queer theory by forcing us to reflect on how authors/readers reflect and interact with one another in the construction of a text. The book has a theoretical sophistication and elegance of style that is rare in academic writing. A thought-provoking work that is as courageous as it is provocative."

—Peter McLaren, Professor of Education
and Cultural Studies, UCLA

"Simultaneously autobiographical, fictional, and theoretical, this powerful and accessible exposition is essential reading for all interested in cultural studies and politics."

—William F. Pinar,
St. Bernard Parish Alumni Endowed Professor,
Louisiana State University

"William G. Tierney provides a provocative contemporary look into queer scholarship and queer scholars. There is certainly a need for this book as many academic units are currently struggling with issues on the role of gay and lesbian scholars and scholarship in their respective disciplines. The book should definitely make a significant contribution to the field of gay and lesbian studies."

—Larry D. Icard, School of Social Work,
University of Washington, Seattle

ACADEMIC OUTLAWS

Queer Theory and Cultural Studies
in the Academy

William G. Tierney

SAGE Publications
International Educational and Professional Publisher
Thousand Oaks   London   New Delhi

For information address:

SAGE Publications, Inc.
2455 Teller Road
Thousand Oaks, California 91320
E-mail: order@sagepub.com

SAGE Publications Ltd.
6 Bonhill Street
London EC2A 4PU
United Kingdom

SAGE Publications India Pvt. Ltd.
M-32 Market
Greater Kailash I
New Delhi 110 048 India

Printed in the United States of America

Library of Congress Cataloging-in-Publication Data

Tierney, William G.
  Academic outlaws : queer theory and cultural studies in the academy / Author, William G. Tierney.
    p. cm.
  Includes bibliographical references and index.
  ISBN 0-7619-0682-7 (cloth : acid-free paper). — ISBN 0-7619-0683-5 (pbk. : acid-free paper)
  1. Gay and lesbian studies. 2. Culture—Study and teaching (Higher) 3. Gay teachers. 4. Gays—Identity. I. Title.
  HQ75.15.T54 1997
  306.76'6'071—dc21   96-45823

97 98 99 00 01 02 03 10 9 8 7 6 5 4 3 2 1

Acquiring Editor:	C. Terry Hendrix
Editorial Assistant:	Dale Grenfell
Production Editor:	Sherrise M. Purdum
Production Assistant:	Denise Santoyo
Typesetter/Designer:	Tina Hill
Cover Designer:	Ravi Balasuriya

Contents

*For Barry Weiss, without whose love
and friendship I would have
completed this six months sooner.*

Introduction
Setting the Record "Straight"

Readers approach scholarly texts in manifold ways. Some individuals first check the table of contents to gain an idea of what is in the text. Readers who are faculty members often turn to the bibliography to see which authors and books have been cited and, frequently, to determine if the author has cited them. Acknowledgments increasingly provide the reader with a sense of who the author's friends are and whether those friends are among the academic cognoscenti. As Henry Giroux (1993) notes, "Acknowledgments have become the new markers indicating webs of association that place one in the pantheon of 'respected' company" (p. xi). For example, to cite Camille Paglia presumably provides the reader with one insight, while acknowledging that Cornel West is a "true friend" (hooks, 1990) tells us something else. The reader needs to know the likes of West and Paglia, but often the invocation of such names on the acknowledgments page presumes such knowledge in much the same way that a baseball aficionado is supposed to nod in understanding when a rookie pitcher says he grew up in awe of Tom Seaver or Sandy Koufax.

Dedications are a different matter. A dedication most often humanizes the author and lets the reader know that the individual is a member of the human family. "The thoughts expressed in this book," writes John Guillory (1993), "represent my part in an ongoing conversation with Jennifer Wicke. For that conversation and so much else, I will always be grateful. This book is for her" (p. xv). Vincent Crapanzano (1992) simply says, "For

Jane Kramer" on one page and at the end of his acknowledgments adds, "To my daughter, Wicky, and my wife, Jane Kramer, I owe my greatest thanks, for they have had to live with me as I wrote and propounded" (p. viii). Comments like these tell us a great deal. The author is often married and frequently has children, and the spouse and family members have sacrificed for the author; the author appreciates the support to such an extent that the book is dedicated to the individual's wife or husband and often includes the children. Sometimes an author's parents receive kind words, but most often we read about the individual's immediate family. Implicit in the dedication are two points: We learn not only that the author is a human being but also that the individual makes an implicit claim of heterosexuality.

Such knowledge, however, is so commonsensical, so matter-of-fact, that it most often is hidden from us. We do not explicitly pause over a dedication and think, "Gee, Crapanzano is straight. That's interesting." An orthodoxy exists with dedications that enables the reader to continue reading; the names may change, but the structure is set. The dedication may have a tone that is humorous or serious, touching or bland, but underneath the commentary is what I will define in this text as "heterosexual privilege" (Harbeck, 1992, p. 132). When someone dedicates a text to one's husband or wife, we usually do not pause. The narrative portrait we have created for our authors may not be a specific picture of an individual, but as with societal portraits, such images contain certain characteristics; heterosexuality is one of them. However, in a text such as this one where the male author not only dedicates the book to a man but also mentions the love between those two persons, the reader pauses and any number of comments become plausible. "Huh, he's gay," one reader might think, and another one, "How inappropriate!" A third might be unsure why one's sexual orientation needs to be brought up in this fashion, and a fourth reader may simply stop and ponder the revelation. My assumption is that very few readers will read a gay dedication in the same manner as they read a heterosexual one.

To be sure, same-sex dedications are possible that will not raise the issue of one's sexual orientation. T. S. Eliot, for example, dedicated *The Waste Land* to Ezra Pound, and Melville dedicated a text to Hawthorne. However, love was not mentioned. The point is that the dedication of a text between two men or two women in a manner that is commonplace for a man and a woman becomes an explicit political and social act, whereas we most often do not think of all other forms of dedications in such a way.

What alternatives exist and what are the implications for an author and the reader?

To Dedicate or Not to Dedicate: The Politics of Invisibility. Until recently, the overwhelming response by homosexual authors has been to avoid marking oneself as gay or lesbian. Dedications might have been oblique—"to RK"—or consciously studious: "I'd like to thank my colleagues in the department." The consequences of such omissions are multiple for the reader. Again, heterosexual readers may think nothing in particular; although it is true that the reader may not have a family like the rest of us, one does not pause over any explicit revelation. Readers still assume the author is heterosexual. The image that readers have in their heads has not been disturbed. Some individuals may think that the author believes that any personal characteristics of a writer should be bracketed because a text should be a purely intellectual undertaking. In this light, a sharp distinction has been made between the life of the mind and one's daily life. With whom one sleeps is irrelevant.

Much as all authors are not heterosexual, all readers are not either. The lesbian or gay reader also learns lessons from such dedications. Just as George Chauncey (1994) has pointed out that gay men in the early 20th century in New York looked for physical manifestations in other men to discover if they were gay, gay and lesbian academics also look for clues about the nature of one's colleagues. A gay or lesbian reader, then, might assume that a dedication to RK is a dedication to the author's lover. The response, again, may be manifold. One gay reader may enjoy knowing a secret that others do not; a second reader may think that even the use of initials is bold; a third might consider the use of initials cowardly or evasive. One overriding lesson learned is that the disclosure of one's sexual identity would be a mistake. Some gay readers may think that it is inappropriate to reveal one's sexual identity in a scholarly text, but the vast majority of individuals will point out that it would be foolhardy and professionally suicidal. Thirty years ago the revelation of such a fact in a book's dedication would have had ramifications for an author well beyond the worth of his or her text. The simple phrase "To my friend and lover, Barry Weiss" would have been grounds for ostracizing or dismissing the author at the vast majority of colleges and universities.

Thus, the avoidance of a gay dedication may seem to sidestep a difficult circumstance in someone's life, but when it is framed within the scope of all other academic texts and academic life, what such avoidance accomplishes is to render not only the author but all other gay and lesbian academics invisible. We learn that it is important to keep one's sexual orientation—if one is homosexual—a secret in our professional lives. How is someone's personal life compromised if the most important individual in the author's life must be an absent figure or reduced to initials? What does it say about the definition and parameters of the academic community if an individual's longtime companion is rendered invisible in the text? Thus, heterosexual authors can combine their professional and personal personae whereas lesbian and gay authors have to keep their professional personae distinct from their private lives. What are the consequences?

Similarly, it is also plausible that a naive reader may think nothing at all about a male author's dedication to a man. The reader reinforces heterosexism by assuming, perhaps, that the two men are brothers, cousins, or close friends. Although the author and the individual to whom the book is dedicated will have a different last name, the idea of homosexuality is so distant from the reader that the author's sexual orientation is nonexistent; in effect, heterosexuality is such a structured norm that any other possibility is inconceivable.

Dedication and Rejection: A Personal Response. Increasingly over the past decade, gay and lesbian academics have revealed their sexual orientation to their colleagues and readers, although the vast majority of gay academe remains closeted and invisible. Gay or lesbian authors who have decided to dedicate a text to their partners vary from their heterosexual counterparts in significant ways. The gay author has made an explicit decision that may have taken up a great amount of thought, whereas the heterosexual writer may spend no more than what it takes to write the dedication thinking about what to inscribe.

Many heterosexual authors, of course, may care a great deal about those to whom they dedicate their text—a dying relative, an inspirational colleague, a cherished spouse. And yet the thought that goes into such a dedication is entirely different from that of the lesbian or gay author who makes an explicitly gay reference to that same dying relative, inspirational colleague or cherished partner. To say that you are gay or lesbian is inescapably an explicitly political act in the late 20th century. What we often do not realize is that if the comment is political, then logically the absence of the comment is equally political. We either disturb the image in the reader's mind, or we reinforce it. Second, the author's comment is often a conscious public affirmation of his or her identity. The implicit nature of the heterosexual dedication is a public affirmation, but it usually is not conscious. Ironically, a conscious heterosexual dedication often is used by a closeted individual who hopes to hide his or her sexual orientation.

One response of heterosexist readers to such a dedication is personal: They want nothing to do with anything homosexual; or rather, they want nothing to do with anything explicitly homosexual. Obviously, if the author had hidden his or her identity, the reader would have read the text and the text still would have been written by a gay or lesbian individual. The problem for the reader is that the author proclaimed his or her sexual orientation. If an individual has been raised in a fundamentalist religion, for example, or has grown up in a socially conservative family, then merely the realization that someone is gay or lesbian would be grounds for rejection. What is interesting in this response is the inability of the reader to distinguish a writer's background from the work that he or she does. In a curious way, then, the rejection on a personal level highlights what closeted academics most fear: Their ideas are discarded out of hand not because of what they have said but because of who they are. If a reader were to put down a book before turning to page one of Chapter 1, the message transmitted is that one's background counts. In effect, the closeted author has correctly read the audience. At a minimum, for the heterosexist reader the structured heterosexist image changes; the hand that wrote the text, the mind that developed the ideas, belongs to a homosexual.

The lesbian or gay reader will also have personal responses, but curiously, they will be simultaneously self-referential and external. On the one hand, if the reader is closeted, she or he may be forced to consider why this particular author could, or would, come out. On the other hand, the reader will look for clues in the response of other readers about the safety of coming out. The heterosexual readers who reject such a dedication confirm the gay reader's fears.

Conversely, as I discuss below, the straight reader who has lesbian or gay friends or family and has thought about bias and heterosexism offers a different reading and commentary. My point here is that the context for the gay reader is decidedly different from that of the heterosexual. Straight readers who take offense neither need to question themselves nor look to others for their response. Such a dedication is wrong because it states something that is immoral in the belief system of the heterosexist reader.

Dedication and Rejection: An Intellectual Response. Some readers may cloak their response in the guise of the disengaged intellectual. One's sexual orientation, assumes a proponent of this stance, should have nothing to do with the work under investigation. To disclose personal aspects of one's life is at least unnecessary and at worst, politically charged and potentially damaging. If the writer feels compelled to tell us about his or her personal life, goes this line of thought, how might the text itself be compromised to fit the author's personal agenda? The answer is often in the question itself, for why ought one to bother reading a text that appears jaded from the outset?

Individuals who speak from this perspective often have personal beliefs akin to those heterosexist readers in the first category, but they may also accept basic notions of science framed from a positivist perspective. In this light, the role of the intellectual is to advance knowledge from a disinterested perspective in an empirical manner. Ideas such as objectivity and external validity, reliability and the traditions of Durkheim and Comte argue that the scientist conducts work that ought to matter little whether one is male or female, French or German, gay or straight. When the scientist enters the laboratory, she or he leaves personal characteristics behind. The scientist tests hypotheses that ultimately may be generalized. Thus, any individual who chooses to mention such information as sexual orientation in any text raises serious doubts about the trustworthiness of his or her data.

The concerns of these readers are twofold. On the one hand, the mathematician who says he is gay at the front of a mathematical treatise seems to use objective data to advance a personal agenda. In effect, the reader is suggesting that the author keep his personal politics out of the equation. Even more harmfully, the sociologist who writes that she is "a lesbian in a committed relationship" in a text about deviance, could inadvertently imply to her readers that she may have skewed her data to further her political beliefs. According to this line of reasoning, at a minimum the data are compromised and questionable, and, at worst, the author has been self-serving and unethical. In either case, the reader rejects the text because the author is biased or does not want a distorted account of a particular scientific investigation, or both.

An analysis of this response reveals the norms that the reader believes exist. The invoking of heterosexual privilege assumes that the heterosexual married individual has no personal agenda when one's spouse appears in a scientific text. Presumably, that we learn an individual has been happily married for twenty years at the start of a book about homosexuality and deviance also has no implications. The concern raised here, however, is precisely such a differentiation: The reader is unable to distinguish that whatever one's sexual orientation, proclaiming that one is gay or straight makes similar points. To accept such an analysis, however, brings some of the most fundamental assumptions about the scientific method into question. If any author who offers a dedication to a spouse is either framing societal norms or approaching a research topic from a particular subjective position, or both, then at a minimum we must bring into question, if not reject, notions such as objectivity and reliability. Curiously, the intellectual rejection of such a dedication, then, does little to disturb the mental imagery of the heterosexual reader. The reader's stance is that she or he is not concerned with the author's background, but at the same time, the author's lesbian background is precisely why the text has a greater likelihood of being discarded than if it were written by a straight author who begins with a dedication to her husband.

The lesbian or gay reader may have a similar response. As there are feminists who subscribe to a feminism that rejects notions of traditional science because they are patriarchal, there are also feminists who consider themselves positivists. From this perspective, feminism concerns equal rights but it does not necessarily bring into question the scientific method. Similarly, there are gay and lesbian researchers who assume that their sexual orientation should play no role in their research. They, too, may wonder about the necessity of proclaiming one's sexual orientation. One difference, however, is that most lesbian and gay readers who make this claim will also be aware of their mental imagery. Because they are different, they realize the meanings and consequences of straight and gay dedications. Nevertheless, they hold to notions of distancing objectivity and may intellectually reject any perceived or intended authorial bias.

In many respects, the logic of this position is stretched to the limit in literary texts. Those who reject the so-called flaunting of one's sexual orientation readily agree that to understand T. S. Eliot, for example, we must examine his conversion to Catholicism, or to comprehend the work of Richard Wright we should know that he was African American. And yet the sexual orientation of Henry James, Walt Whitman, or Willa Cather often escapes scrutiny because such information is presumably irrelevant. One wonders by what stretch of the literary imagination the race or religion of an individual is important, but sexual orientation is not?

Dedication and Acceptance: The Personal Liberal. As increasing numbers of gay and lesbian academics and individuals beyond the academy come out of the closet, more heterosexual individuals learn that a relative, friend or colleague is gay or lesbian. When they read a text and discover that the author has dedicated the book to a same-sex partner, the response may be of mild acceptance. This group of individuals holds to dualistic thinking. On the one hand, they are not disturbed that someone should dedicate a book to her or his longtime companion. The attitude is one of both, "Who cares?" and, "That's nice." On the other hand, the easy assumption that it does not matter who receives the dedication in a book leaves unquestioned the political implications of a basic mental imagery with which we construct social, cultural and academic relations. The reader will still gloss over a dedication "To my loving wife" without pause but will stop to acknowledge the male writer's tribute "To Bob."

This form of response goes one step beyond the reader who reads a homosexual dedication but thinks nothing of it. That individual's mental imagery is so structured that lesbian and gay people are invisible even when there is evidence to the contrary. Liberal readers acknowledge that homosexuality exists and that homosexuals should not be persecuted but have accepted the idea that sexual orientation is relatively unimportant. Readers may also acknowledge that someone is Latino/Latina, Protestant or Pakistani; what matters, however, is the text. One's experiences and background are not incorporated into a reordering of the inherent structure of identity that exists. The reader does not acknowledge that a structure exists; we are autonomous individuals and our autonomy should be celebrated.

Gay and lesbian readers' responses are helpful here because even before they open the text, they have been forced to consider the mental imagery of sexual orientation. In the late 20th century, it is nearly impossible for even the extremely closeted queer academic not to know other lesbian and gay individuals. Consequently, a dedication for this group is an affirmation of the structure they have created for themselves: There are straight authors and queer authors. However, the explicit comment is also a personal affirmation. The gay liberal hope is that the day will come when one's sexual orientation is irrelevant and lesbian and gay people may offer dedications without fear or recrimination and in the same manner as their heterosexual counterparts.

Dedication and Acceptance: The Critical Intellectual. The reader who accepts a gay dedication from what I will call a "critical intellectual" standpoint rejects the stance of the positivist and also moves beyond the personal acceptance of the liberal. Critical intellectuals realize something is up when they read a queer dedication. The scientific method already will have been brought into question by this individual, and, in consequence, the implicit structures that readers have in their minds will be questioned. When the individual reads the female author's comment about "the support received from my friend and lover, Beth," the response goes beyond mere acceptance. From this perspective, if we think that such a dedication is political, we also bring into question those dedications that previously have not been seen as political (i.e., heterosexual ones).

Similarly, the male math professor has every right to dedicate a text to a spouse or a partner and both comments are equally political/nonpolitical. The female sociologist who is lesbian or straight and studies deviance exists in a political web from which she cannot extract herself. Gay or straight novelists create fiction in historical and social contexts where their sexuality inevitably influences the text. The challenge for any researcher or reader is to develop standards of trustworthiness that will be quite distinct from positivism's beliefs about objectivity or literary criticism's modernist assumptions about how to read a text. As McLaren (1989) has noted, the critical intellectual's task is partly in developing a language of representation and hope that enables those of us on the margins to "speak outside the terms and frames of reference provided by the colonizer" (p. 52). Thus, rather than merely proclaiming a gay dedication to be "nice" or "innocuous," the reader's categories are disrupted as they undoubtedly have been in other areas of their lives.

Oddly, the gay reader may stand in sharpest contrast to his or her counterpart who accepts a gay dedication from a personal perspective. The gay critical intellectual may think that a dedication that enables lesbian and gay people to be accepted like everyone else is an assimilationist strategy that is fundamentally flawed. The point is not assimilation; such acceptance has never worked for us or other colonized peoples such as Native Americans in the United States. The gay critical intellectual seeks to reframe the structural categories. An individual's ability to dedicate a book to his or her partner is not merely nice; it is essential if the underlying cultural and societal norms are to be brought into question, challenged, and ultimately overthrown.

Queer Theory and Cultural Studies

I began this text on a Monday in September, 1994, framed by an odd confluence of events. Barry's birthday was the day before, Sunday, September 25th, and it was also a day in Los Angeles when 30,000 people had participated in an AIDS Walk to raise money for AIDS. We had arrived in Los Angeles the previous month because I had accepted a faculty position at the University of Southern California (USC). Barry, my partner for the past decade, accompanied me with the expectation that he would find employment in his field of computer science. Indeed, part of the bargaining that took place to get me here was the Dean's willingness to help Barry find employment. Like the fictional institution I will discuss in Chapter 6, USC has no domestic partners' agreement that enables me to cover Barry on my health insurance policy if we so choose. Although both in excellent health, as we walked that Sunday, we were reminded once again of the kind of chaos and tragedy that can befall individuals who are sick, not simply because they are ill but because medical benefits for lesbian and gay partners are nonexistent; we live in a society where adequate health care is a privilege, not a right.

This text, then, is about the reframing of the university. It is about nonexistent medical benefits and a research enterprise that has studiously avoided studies of lesbian and gay people. It is about the dedication of books by authors to their long-time companions and the invisibility of lesbian and gay academics. At first glance it may appear self-indulgent to have gone on at length about the dedication of a text to the fellow whom I have loved and lived with for the past decade. Yet a goal of this book is to outline how the lives we live and the matter of with whom we live help determine what counts for knowledge, which in turn becomes tied to institutional policies and framed as parameters of power.

I argue here that the manner in which we have constructed gay identity in research has helped frame the way lesbian and gay people get defined in the daily life of the university. Conversely, societal constructions of homosexuality also influence the ontological parameters of one's research. To argue in this manner rejects the notion that we are able to conduct research in the pristine conditions of the laboratory, or to believe that the university itself is an ivory tower removed from the daily life of society.

The idea of the advancement of knowledge is a central purpose of the university. When one teaches doctoral candidates about how to conduct research, or when undergraduate students partake of general education courses, they engage in the acquisition and accumulation of knowledge. From this vantage point individuals enter the institution without much knowledge and they learn facts and ideas; to use Paulo Freire's (1970) well-worn phrase, such an idea is a "banking concept of education" (p. 58).

Students pay to get something, and the payment is wisdom; at times, the dividend is also a job. Thus, teaching is one primary area of the university where knowledge advances. Obviously, the idea itself does not advance—as if it is an autonomous agent marching down an intellectual avenue; instead, an individual's understanding of the idea increases. The distinction is important if we are to decode and come to terms with how knowledge gets created and advanced.

The advancement of knowledge—rather than the individual's understanding of knowledge—primarily occurs through the work of the faculty in their laboratories and studies. Research has become the raison d'etre of faculty life in the late 20th century. No more direct example exists of an individual advancing knowledge than that of the scientist in a laboratory struggling to gain insights about a phenomenon. The reward system, promotion and tenure, institutional totems such as academic freedom, all revolve around the ability of the professorate to advance thought and create intellectual breakthroughs in a particular area of inquiry. Such developments become known through academic representations of the intellect: journals, professional conferences, scholarly books, and, to an increasing degree, film and other multimedia approaches.

When we speak of the advancement of knowledge and use the academy as the vehicle to move forward, two unstated assumptions take place. First, we assume that knowledge advances. Such an assumption is based on modernist notions of progress. The researcher knows more today than yesterday. Knowledge is accretionary. Second, knowledge production is an intellectual activity that is best discussed with like-minded peers. The judges and arbiters of whether one has actually advanced knowledge are those individuals who have become leaders in the creation and maintenance of a particular field of study. The consequence is that in large part other audiences are excluded from debates about whether a particular idea has merit. Students acquire knowledge, but because they do not have the requisite skills to begin with, they most often are not deemed worthy of knowing anything about a particular topic. The common citizenry often is deemed to know even less than the students. The result is a portrait of the university faculty as an intellectual vanguard who protect and advance an understanding of the world. Others may try to grapple with ideas, but their own particular backgrounds and social contexts are not equal to the task.

Throughout this text, I take issue with these assumptions and I elaborate an alternative way of reading—and acting—in academe. I argue that knowledge does not advance one step after another; the idea that as academics we are divorced from society is historically mistaken and intellectually foolish. The root of the analysis derives from postmodernism, but I pay particular attention to two postmodern derivatives—cultural studies and queer theory—in the analysis of sexual orientation and knowledge production in the academy. As I discuss throughout the text, postmodernism's critique of identity, rationality and the idea of objective progress is of enormous benefit for those who study sexual orientation. My purpose is not to become enmeshed in academic Ping-Pong about what postmodernism is and is not; rather, I hope to outline what I mean by cultural studies and queer theory in order to develop strategies for change.

I have laid out the text in two parts. Part I expands on the theoretical ramifications of what I am suggesting. In Part II, I consider the consequences of these theoretical notions for life in the academy. To unite theory with the academic life, I first offer portraits of what it means to be gay in academe; I then offer suggestions for change.

Specifically, in Chapter 1, I expand on the notion of culture. Chapter 2 outlines the implications for academe with regard to structural and disciplinary issues if we work from a framework that uses queer studies and cultural studies. I pay particular attention to the idea of postmodernism and how it frames queer theory and cultural studies. Is queer studies merely a topic in search of departmental acceptance and graduate students? The answer to the question incorporates how we think about sexual identity and cultural studies.

In Chapter 3, I turn to a discussion of how norms get defined and consider the implications of queer theory for how we think about popular culture and the academy. This chapter uses the theoretical focus of the text in order to analyze mainstream attempts to define sexual identity in a particular way. The specific focus of the chapter returns to the question outlined above pertaining to those who work from an assimilationist perspective and seek to define gay and lesbian people as no different from the mainstream.

Part I closes with a chapter that pertains to oppression and difference. Far too often words such as *oppression* get used, but they are not interrogated for authorial intent. We hear that different groups are oppressed or that different situations are oppressive. What I attempt to outline in Chapter 4 is how oppression gets played out in the lives of lesbian and gay individuals and how our oppression is similar and different from the oppression of other groups such as African Americans. The goal of the chapter is to consider individualism and community and how alliances might be created that maintain integrity and distinctiveness.

In Part II, I begin by offering an overview of how gay identity has been framed in college and university life. Chapter 5 combines interviews from closeted gay academics today with life history interviews of older gay academics. Chapter 6 takes into account how language is used, hidden and framed about gay and lesbian issues in academe by way of a piece of ethnographic fiction that portrays the dilemmas that members of an academic community face when one of its members has AIDS. In Chapter 7, discussions revolve around real-world issues such as domestic partner benefits and sexual-orientation clauses. The final chapter considers what a postsecondary institution would look like that uses queer studies and cultural studies. I conclude by arguing that the acceptance of sexual identity will inevitably disrupt academic life as we currently know it, and I offer a rationale and strategies for creating such a changed institution.

I should offer a comment on the use of data in Part II. In many respects Chapter 5 calls on what we have come to think of as standard interview data. I have used interviews from previous studies that I have done and have also interviewed a group of senior gay academics to bolster the second part of the chapter. The interviews followed standard interview protocols and lasted at least one hour in length, although at times I conducted multiple interviews with one individual. If Chapter 5's data are standard, Chapter 6's data are not. Increasingly, I am convinced that social scientists need to expand their repertoire in portraying particular situations (Tierney, 1995a; Tierney & Lincoln, 1997). We rely far too heavily on interviews and case studies; as an author, I recognize that there are times when such interviews or case studies—such as in Chapter 5—are helpful and useful. However, we also need to consider how else we might present portraits of those whom we study. This point is particularly germane with people who are closeted and whose actions or reactions only occur off the record. Chapter 6, then, is an attempt at another venue; I have used ethnographic fiction with the hope that its narrative structure would give me greater leeway to present life in the academy than other textual techniques might afford.

Finally, if I have outlined what this text is about, I should also mention two major issues that I do not consider here. Namely, I do not take up the topic of bisexuality at any length. I also do not discuss in depth the economics of privilege and how it permeates white, gay male identity in particular. Both topics—bisexuality and issues of class—are significant enough to demand more discussion than I would have been able to give to them here; these areas of inquiry await further research and investigation with regard to how they either conflict with or are in agreement with the ideas I develop pertaining to cultural studies, queer theory and knowledge production.

Acknowledgments

I would like to acknowledge the feedback of Sage's external reviewers—Larry Icard, John Longres, Clyde Hendrick and Peter McLaren. Their comments on a draft of the text were most helpful to me. I am also grateful for the support of my editor at Sage, Terry Hendrix, and the senior editorial assistant, Dale Grenfell. Everyone at Sage has been great to work with on this project. Clive Leeman has been an invaluable copyeditor. At USC, I appreciate the support of the Center's secretary, Syan Ekwegh, and my research assistant, Patrick Dilley. Roger Platizky offered excellent advice and support on an early draft. Agapito Diaz deserves credit for the cover photograph.

PART I

THEORETICAL INTERSECTIONS OF CULTURAL STUDIES AND QUEER THEORY

The queer is the artistic arbiter of our age, chum.

—*Raymond Chandler*
The Long Goodbye *(1953)*

Chapter 1

A Cartography of Culture

Personals

I had ended graduate school and a sad relationship simultaneously, and soon thereafter, I landed in a new job in Boulder, Colorado. As I drove to Boulder, I wondered how I might meet gay men in places other than the bars. I have nothing against drinking or the bar scene, but I tend to think that taverns are not the healthiest of environments to reside in on a regular basis. I devised a plan. I felt somewhat silly then and still do today, when we tell friends how Barry and I met:

GWM, 32, 6 ft. 160 lbs. desires positive relationship with a guy who's not especially into bars or baths. My interests are: running, camping, writing, movies, theater, music, good food, quiet times, gardening. I'm new to the area and involved in leftist politics, the nuclear freeze and gay rights. I'm

3

an honest, shy, sensitive, funny man in search of someone similar. If you
desire an intimate, fun, steady relationship write to—

I received more than fifty letters. One of them was from a handsome,
redheaded fellow who lived in Denver. He had lived in Colorado for a
dozen years and loved to hike. We arranged to meet on the weekend and
go for a walk. Barry knocked on my door on a cold Sunday, and the rest,
as they say, is history.

As with any story, how Barry and I met offers multiple readings.
Although times have changed rapidly over the past dozen years, lesbian
and gay people still often need to use safe havens such as bars as our main
meeting places. Because of homophobia and the parameters of the closet,
we are denied access to multiple venues for meeting other lesbian and gay
people. How two gay or lesbian people meet and our coming-out stories
are staples of our discursive notions of our culture. Invariably, lesbian and
gay people have stories about growing up, coming out, and how we
experience the world in ways different from the mainstream. Such experiences and the language we use to express them go to the heart of how I
think about cultural studies and queer theory.

Indeed, in large part this book will be a delineation of the intersections
of cultural studies and queer theory in academe and the implications for
college and university life. The view of cultural studies and queer theory
that I call on derives from critical postmodernism. Peter McLaren (1995)
has noted that critical postmodernism "takes into account both the macro-
political level of structural organization and the micropolitical level of
different and contradictory manifestations of oppression as a means of
analyzing global relations of oppression" (p. 209). Critical postmodernism
is a blend of critical theory and postmodern analysis of social life.

Broadly stated, critical theory is an attempt to understand the oppressive aspects of society in order to generate the conditions for change and
empowerment of those who have been silenced and invisible. Critical
theorists assert that all knowledge is socially and historically determined
and a consequence of power. Given such assumptions about knowledge,
the concept of power becomes infused with a concern for empowerment.
Theory is not simply the quest to understand life but to change it.

Postmodernism, from the perspective employed here, challenges modernist notions of rationality, norms, and identity. The idea of reason comes
in for critique so that we seek to decode and understand how ideas such

as truth or deviance have been constructed, defined, and employed. "Postmodernism," suggests Bloland (1995), "points out that totalization hides contradictions, ambiguities, and oppositions and is a means for generating power and control" (p. 525). The struggle from a postmodern stance is to highlight the multiple representative practices that exist within society. In particular, we analyze how norms come into being and what it means for those groups and individuals on the margins. How marginality is constructed and maintained becomes a central point of investigation.

Critical postmodernism seeks to unite both theoretical formulations. Critical theory's advocacy for empowerment and the development of voice for oppressed peoples becomes fused with the postmodern notion of difference and the deconstruction of norms. Thus, I will argue that all individuals, but lesbian and gay people in particular, are both objects and subjects in history. We are neither incapable of resistance nor are we sole determiners of our destinies. Instead, action and meaning are enacted on a cultural terrain that is contested, redefined, and resisted.

Critical postmodernism also concerns itself with praxis. By praxis, I mean a strategic approach to academic life that seeks to disrupt norms that silence individuals and groups so that we are able to create the conditions for enablement and voice. I use the idea of agape as the core for disrupting norms so that we are able to develop voice and resistance. *Agape* is the Greek word referred to in the New Testament and used by philosophers to speak of a specific form of love. In Greek, we find three kinds of love—eros or romantic love, philia or brotherly love, and agape. Agape refers to selfless love. Martin Luther King, Jr. (1958) spoke of such love as a "love seeking to preserve and create community" (p. 87). Agape involves the explicit search for community.

Community is not merely a pleasant attribute but a core value. That is, rather than think of the idea of community as a list of things or qualities—parks, recreation centers, safe streets—we think of community as a fundamental value that speaks to the worth and importance of every individual. We honor the unique talents individuals bring, and we work to use and develop such attributes instead of seeking to smother and assimilate them. The underlying tenet here is to search for connectedness while we maintain difference.

"A critical notion of community," writes Jeffrey Weeks (1995), "is the precondition of a radical humanism, for it questions what is and opens the possibility of thinking what could be" (p. 80). Community, then, is defined not by what exists but by what we might be able to build. Our ability to question taken-for-granted assumptions about our community is a starting point for action. In this light, the focus of this book seeks to understand what we mean by a queer identity while at the same time we try to develop the notion of relationships within the academy that honor a community that acknowledges difference as an organizing concept.

Because both ideas—cultural studies and queer theory—are relatively new, one should not be surprised that the terms are unclear and often contested. Insofar as the idea of culture is central to an understanding of how I analyze the academy and knowledge production, I focus in this chapter on the interpretation of culture. My purpose is not to offer a simpleminded checklist about what constitutes culture but, rather, to outline a provisional cartography that enables us to think about how sexual identity operates in the academy as a part of culture.

As opposed to modernist versions, then, culture is not simply the sum of the tasks of a group or organization; culture is not the understanding of the real function of a particular task or object. To the contrary, as McDermott and Varenne (1995) note, "Being in the world requires dealing with indefinite and unbounded tasks while struggling with the particular manner in which they have been shaped by the cultural process" (p. 337). Culture is the multiple interpretations an organization's participants give to ostensibly neutral or real facts. We receive a portrait, then, where identity is much less determined than a modernist version. In effect, culture is up for grabs or, at the least, contestable. To be sure, constraints exist by way of historical and social forces, but multiple possibilities exist to reinscribe culture with alternative interpretations and possibilities. As McDermott and Varenne remind us,

> Life in culture is polyphonous and multivocalic; it is made of the voices of many, each one brought to life and made significant by the other, only sometimes by being the same, more often by being different, more dramatically by being contradictory. Culture is not so much a product of sharing, as a product of people hammering each other into shape with the well-structured tools already available. We need to think of culture as this very process of hammering a world. (p. 326)

In what follows, I offer seven ideas that expand on such a notion of culture and in consequence outline my assumptions about cultural studies, sexual identity and queer theory, as well as the theoretical geography of this book.

Culture as Mediation. Cultural studies and queer theory in large part have come out of the humanities. In a relatively short time, proponents of both theoretical concepts have created their own canon of authors who are considered essential reading. It is not my purpose here to enter into a historical exegesis on these authors or the various schools of thought that have produced cultural studies and queer theory, but it is important to point out how I incorporate the idea of culture in the text. Perhaps we should not be surprised that some individuals in humanities departments have spoken of cultural studies only in terms of high culture. Others have suggested that we need to look at all of culture rather than only those writers whose ideas have been transmitted through the ages and defined as masterpieces. Indeed, one not only studies popular culture but critically investigates how texts become masterpieces and are immortalized.

When we define culture in terms of masterpieces, or we attack cultural masterpieces and argue that we must include popular culture in our analysis, we have, in effect, developed a dichotomized, referential view of culture. Culture either gets defined as the analysis of Tolstoy, Shakespeare, and Proust, or it does not. We thus develop alternative readings to show how different individuals and groups have been excluded and to gain an understanding of their lives. For example, we may read about the life of Rigoberta Menchú, the Mayan activist and Nobel laureate in Guatemala, and we may read a history of the Navajo. Or we might point out how popular culture—television shows, movies—has an impact on the daily lives of individuals and society as much as, if not more than, so-called literary masterpieces.

Although one undoubtedly needs to move away from the idea that culture is a compilation of literary artifacts, the problem is that simply rejecting the idea does not push the definition of culture far enough. For the purposes of this text it is more helpful to call on anthropology rather than the humanities. My concern is not only with general education requirements or the role that television plays in a technological society. Instead, I am trying to delineate how our definitions of sexual identity may intersect with, fragment, confirm or contradict our notions of what counts for knowledge. Cultural analysis is neither high nor low; it is all-pervasive. As Renato Rosaldo (1994) contends,

> Mediation is the keyword. Rather than being a separate domain, like icing on a cake, culture in this sense mediates all human conduct. It has to do with everyday life; material, economic, and institutional realms; politics,

romance, religion, and spirituality. To perceive cultural dimensions, one
need only ask: Could things human be otherwise? Compare with Nuer
politics, Balinese romance, Navajo religion, and Huichol spirituality. Now
explore the tacit and explicit assumptions that guide local social relations
and institutional forms. (p. 526)

The anthropological concept of culture, then, investigates the interpretive aspects of society in all its manifold shapes and forms. If culture is
no longer a hermetically sealed object for analysis, it is also not merely the
study of popular society. Thus, the role of culture as a realm of representation and a provoker of meaning is recognized within cultural studies
as central to understanding how the dynamics of power, privilege, and
social agency structure the daily life of a society. However, if a sea change
in the development and reception of what we think knowledge to be has
taken place, it has been coupled with an understanding of how we define
and apprehend the range of texts that are open to critical interrogation and
analysis. Instead of connecting culture exclusively to the technology of
print and the book as the only legitimate artifact, for example, we investigate how textual, visual, and social representations are produced, organized, and distributed through a variety of cultural forms such as the media,
popular culture, film, advertising, mass communication, large-scale and
alternative publishing houses. The challenge thus becomes to develop new
theoretical models and methodologies that address the production, consumption, structure and exchange of knowledge.

The implications for how one analyzes gay and lesbian issues are vast.
Whereas the conservative argument would propose that there is no place
in high culture to include aberrations such as homosexuality, a proponent
of a dichotomized, referential view of culture would disagree. Thus,
authors investigate historical texts to point out that a gay presence has
always existed in society (Boswell, 1981). The backgrounds of famous
writers are studied in order to point out, for example, that a poem by Walt
Whitman or W. H. Auden about a woman was actually encoded to disguise
their love for a man. Others investigate the popular realms of society to
show how gay and lesbian people have been portrayed. Analyses of
televisions shows such as *I Love Lucy* or *Laverne and Shirley* (Doty, 1993)
will point out how lesbian and gay people either are excluded or portrayed
in a particular light.

Although there is much to applaud with both approaches, it is not the
direction I follow in this book. Neither am I content with creating a new

canon that includes a representation of queer texts nor am I satisfied to demonstrate the shortcomings of network TV. I do not doubt that in a heterosexist society it is extremely educational to point out that men loved men many centuries ago, or that popular culture promotes images of lesbian and gay people that are derogatory and stereotypical. But ultimately such analyses do not seek to reorder the basic structures of knowledge and power. The logical extension of such projects is that when we study a poem, we should know if the poet was gay and was using a code word in his or her work, and we should lobby the entertainment industry to become more inclusive.

As I shall elaborate in Chapters 2 and 3, the problem with such an approach is that it calls on a static concept of personality that seeks to define the gay, lesbian or straight identity as an accomplished social fact (Seidman, 1993). Culture is not an undifferentiated system that serves to integrate society. When we work from such a position, the struggle of gay and lesbian people—and that of other oppressed groups—becomes conflated with assimilationist strategies that only serve to reproduce the existing social order. In effect, the liberal acceptance of the dedication that I outlined in the Introduction is the result of such a strategy; the individual reader allows for a certain degree of inclusion, but the mental map with which she or he navigates society remains unchanged.

The purpose of this text, however, is not to serve and reinforce the social order but, in keeping with the idea of agape, to change it. I am working from the assumption that assimilationist strategies have never worked for colonized or oppressed peoples, and ultimately, as I discuss in Chapter 4, such strategies seek to constrict, marginalize and silence those who are different. The basis for analysis here is the opposite: We interrogate identity and community as a site of ongoing contestation, regulation, and reformulation. Individuals and groups neither exist through autonomous will, nor do they reside entirely within the construct of culture. As Agger (1992) notes, "Cultural studies in its best sense is an activity of critical theory that directly decodes the hegemonizing messages of the culture industry permeating every nook and cranny of lived experience, from entertainment to education" (p. 5). The investigation of culture thus becomes a search for meaning and identity throughout the multiple temporal and social contexts in which humans live.

The Grammar of Culture. In the perspective advanced here, we place a particular emphasis on the study of language. The analysis is not a technical and developmental issue; rather, we focus on the relationship of language and discourse to power and the production, organization, and circulation of diverse texts and institutions. That is, instead of connecting culture exclusively to the technology of print and treating the book as the only legitimate academic artifact, we study how textual and visual representations get produced through cultural forms such as advertising, mass communication, electronic mail, film, and other modes of cultural production. In effect, we read culture as a text. In doing so, we take into account the status of the reader, author, and the situation under study. As opposed to a scientific investigation conducted by a disembodied observer irrespective of time and place, the study becomes an interpretive project that seeks to make meaning out of what is studied.

From an academic standpoint, cultural studies studies itself. I am not suggesting that proponents of cultural studies are simply navel gazers fascinated with their own area of inquiry. On the contrary, students of cultural studies seek to ramify areas of investigation as well as highlight individual and group subject positions. In doing so, the potential for a quite different reading of knowledge production and academic structures exists. Does the evolution of cultural studies in academe mean that its proponents grasp onto traditional disciplinary grammars—conferences, journals, courses, and tenure lines—or is cultural studies an alternative format that seeks to infuse a political reality into its project? In large part, the answer to such a question helps frame and define the purpose of Part I. If we first come to terms with how an institution's or discipline's participants speak about gay and lesbian issues, we will have come a long way toward understanding how policies become encoded and how knowledge gets defined. Indeed, who speaks, with whom someone speaks, and under what conditions, become critical aspects to analyze.

An investigation of academic discourse, then, looks at grand symbolic markers, but it also looks at the more microscopic aspects of day-to-day discourse. We consider not only what is said but what is not said. Again, if we return to the Introduction, we consider not only if an analysis of lesbian and gay lives is published as a topic under the rubric of "deviance," but we also consider seemingly inconsequential aspects, such as an author's dedication. How words and phrases are used or suppressed becomes key.

Accordingly, it is appropriate to mention how I use a queer lexicon in this text. I once wrote a book (Tierney, 1993) that occasionally discussed sexual orientation. Throughout the chapters, I often used the words *gay, lesbian,* and *bisexual.* The text came back from the copy editor with the note that she found the constant use of gay, lesbian, and bisexual redundant and wordy and had reduced the words to the term *homosexual* whenever she came across them. I changed it back to gay, lesbian, and bisexual, and the copy editor acceded to my wishes. In the late 20th century, the word homosexual has a medical connotation that conjures up all the wrong imagery. The copy editor obviously did not understand the political ramifications of using the word homosexual in the same manner as I. In this text, I tend to use homosexual when I am writing as if I were speaking from a conservative or clinical vantage point.

At the same time, as a gay male, I am also uncomfortable speaking for women in general and lesbians in particular—as if I were a gay everyperson who could speak for all. It would be most peculiar in a text that is concerned with developing voice if I spoke unproblematically for all queer people. However, as I mention in Chapter 4, by not discussing lesbians, I also run the risk of omission—as if I somehow absolve myself of discussing people different from myself. I also have friends who are lesbian who prefer to be called gay and other lesbian friends who resent the overarching term gay because they believe it makes women invisible. The patriarchy does not simply vanish because we are queers.

Indeed, there are those who will say that one reason we should opt for the use of queer is that it is more inclusive; the use of the word gay, they argue, automatically excludes lesbians and bisexuals. Yet *queer* is a word like any other word, and how society defines it provides no preordained inclusiveness or exclusiveness. In a similar vein, the mass media seems to have defined family with a particular eye toward what connoted a middle-class white family in the 1950s. This text is in part about bringing such taken-for-granted definitions into question. When I use queer I speak about a theoretical notion of difference that gets defined in the text. My point is that language is contested and one ought not to accept an author's words without some degree of self-reflection. In essence, this is the key task of interpreting the grammar of culture.

Decentering Norms. In related fashion, the work of cultural studies is to interrogate assumptions that are accepted as fact. History exists not as a linear narrative of progress but as a series of ruptures and displacements. Questions turn on how a specific issue might be understood as a historical construction related to economic, social, and political events that are produced in and through specific historical and social contexts. Of consequence, ideas such as family, race and ethnicity come in for critical investigation.

Cultural analyses often have ranged between one of two theoretical formations: Either the world is entirely socially constructed and therefore up for grabs; or alternatively, a concept has been statically handed down through the ages and what we see today is merely a slight reformulation of what existed yesterday. The study of homosexuality is but one example of critics from different persuasions arguing from similar theoretical standpoints. There are those, for example, who will say that homosexuality has always been viewed as deviant behavior and others who seek to show that gay and lesbian people have existed sometimes with less or more acceptance throughout the ages. Some critics will say that one's sexual orientation is entirely a matter of choice, and others will argue that sexual identity is a result of immediate social contexts. We hear that individuals who are gay are congenitally ill—as if one had no choice whatsoever—and simultaneously listen to individuals state that children can be recruited to the "homosexual lifestyle." We read about the breaking of a genetic code that explains the biological foundations for homosexuality, and we also find treatises that argue that certain societies do not have homosexuals. Steven Epstein (1987) has nicely summarized this debate:

> "Essentialists" treat sexuality as a biological force and consider sexual identities to be cognitive realizations of genuine, underlying differences; "constructionists" stress that sexuality and sexual identities are social constructions, and belong to the world of culture and meaning, not biology. In the first case, there is considered to be some "essence" within homosexuals that makes them homosexual—some gay core of their being, or their psyche, or their genetic makeup. In the second case, "homosexual," "gay" and "lesbian," are just labels, created by cultures and applied to the self. (p. 11)

The work of cultural studies and queer theory that I am advancing seeks a middle ground where we refuse to reduce complex concepts such as sexual orientation to an either-or analysis. Omi and Winant (1993, 1994) have argued from a similar position with regard to the study of racial identity. Such analyses, argue Omi and Winant (1994), "must be explicitly historicist. It must recognize the importance of historical context and contingency in the framing of racial categories and the social construction of racially defined experiences" (p. 6). Thus, to understand sexual orientation, we must situate our work in present social contexts and analyze how sexual identity has been institutionalized. We need to come to terms with how sexual identity gets defined and how such definitions vary or are in congruence with previous definitions so that we do not merely accept a transparent gay identity. And we must question the modernist idea of progress. George Chauncey's (1994) historical work about gay New York in the 1920s is a helpful example here because he makes a compelling argument that life in the early part of the 20th century was immeasurably better for gay men than life in the 40s or 50s.

If we decenter the norms that exist in culture in this manner then the idea of knowledge in the academy becomes much more a question of understanding not the objective nature of a study but, instead, the epistemological relationships of the study to larger social issues. We investigate how lesbian and gay people are situated in the academy in their present contexts and how these contexts have evolved. We look at the study of homosexuality and try to come to terms with how it was investigated, what ideological norms existed, and how they might change. Thus, by decentering norms, we move away from a politics of identity that situates analyses within individuals and we struggle to move toward an understanding of institutional and cultural practices that frame sexual orientation in a particular manner.

Cultural Production and Cultural Policy. The study of culture and its mediating influences and the investigation of representational practices implies that political struggle occurs in arenas that heretofore were seen as nonpolitical. As noted, how women are portrayed on television, how people of color are defined in literature, how lesbians appear in movies, and a multitude of other significations, have become battlegrounds over meaning, identity, power, and knowledge. Representation becomes a political vehicle that encodes imageries of how to act and how we think of specific groups. When we suggest, for example, that Black youth drop out of the mainstream at much higher levels than their Anglo peers and that we need to develop plans to get them into the pipeline, we develop distinct portraits of minority youth. To drop out is an act—he or she falls. To drop out of the mainstream is presumably not a positive act, and yet, what does the mainstream image imply for one's cultural integrity? Similarly, what kind of economic imagery is conjured up with that of a pipeline? In this light, the aim of cultural studies is to develop the linkages between an analysis of culture and the political economy.

The point is not that individuals mechanistically fit the images that television and the media place on them; they are also not free subjects who are able to disregard societal portraits—especially when those portraits are promoted and regulated by the dominant culture. Rather, the struggle and challenge of cultural studies is to come to terms with how individuals and groups are simultaneously subjects and objects in culture. Individuals and groups create and are created by the cultures in which they live and work. The work of Pierre Bourdieu is helpful when he writes about cultural capital. Cultural capital refers to the sets of linguistic and cultural competencies individuals inherit because of their class, racial and gender identities (Bourdieu, 1977). Thus, we investigate the cultural capital of individuals and groups in much the same way that an economic analysis would study the structure and flow of the economy. The shortcoming of Bourdieu's analysis is that although some form of cultural capital exists, we ought not to think of it simply as a mechanistic process that is banked. The cultural capital that individuals and groups accumulate is more than a symbolic object that is acquired. Culture is a fluid, ever-changing process of production, circulation and consumption; it is this production that we need to analyze.

I am suggesting that the ideology of cultural studies is not simply the objects—real or symbolic—that exist in life but that ideology exists in the interstices of daily life so that we must investigate the minutiae of existence as well as the macrosociopolitical structures of life. Such an argument is particularly important when we study groups such as gay men and lesbians or institutions such as schools and colleges. Lesbians and gay men who struggle to hide their lives for fear of discrimination are trying to develop the symbolic capital necessary to succeed in a culture that denies their existence. Conversely, the larger society frequently appropriates gay artifacts but is able to maintain a stabilizing structure so that lesbians and gays remain marginalized. Singers such as Boy George, Melissa Etheridge, Elton John or k.d. lang may be welcomed around the world for their musical exploits and passively accepted as homosexual, but policies are not linked with how to approve of their identities as gay people, rather than as gay performers.

From an organizational standpoint, no greater battleground exists than educational institutions for an analysis of cultural capital. What is taught, who is taught and who teaches the curriculum are all areas that speak to cultural capital and the struggle over meaning. Debates about the canon, for example, speak to identity formation as well as the need to understand what has been defined as high culture. From the argument advanced here, what needs to be studied is not simply who teaches what to whom but how these discussions get framed, carried out, and challenged. Thus, what we really need to concern ourselves with is the production of culture—how capital gets produced, who produces, and what are the mechanisms of power that enable such production to take place, or not to take place.

The suggestion that we use cultural studies in this manner also demands that we move one step further. The rigidification of cultural studies or gay and lesbian studies into academic departments and the like seems to be in direct opposition to the framework I am trying to develop. Cultural studies should naturally translate into cultural policies aimed at reform and renewal. The divorce of theoretical studies from policy analyses is a flaw that must be overcome. As Tony Bennett (1992) has recently suggested, "Policy and governmental conditions and processes should be thought of as constitutive of different forms and fields of culture" (p. 25). What we then examine is not simply the theoretical stitchwork across the fabric of culture, but we turn instead to understanding those seams and thinking about how to develop a plan to change the more oppressive elements.

Education: Pedagogy and Voice. Although a variety of debates within the cultural studies field have taken place over the past decade about the curriculum in higher education, there has been relatively little discussion about the nature of pedagogy or the structure of academe. "Educational theorists demonstrate as little interest in cultural studies," observes Henry Giroux (1994), "as cultural studies scholars do in the critical theories of schooling and pedagogy" (p. 279). Such lack of interest is unfortunate and needs to be remedied. Education is a primary means for the acquisition of economic and cultural capital; even more important, it is a central component in helping us understand the intersections of power and knowledge. Cultural studies not only attempts to broaden the terms of learning, it also raises questions about what knowledge needs to be produced in the university in order to be consequential for extending and deepening the possibilities for democratic public life.

By making culture a central construct, cultural studies focuses the terms of learning around issues relating to differences and diversity to extend the possibility for dialogue and debate about the quality of democratic public life. In this instance, both the construction of curricular knowledge and pedagogy are organized around providing narrative space for understanding and critically analyzing pluralistic histories, experiences and cultures. Furthermore, cultural studies places a strong emphasis on linking the curriculum to the experiences that students bring to their encounter with institutionally legitimated knowledge. This suggests that texts cannot be fully understood outside the context of their historical and social production. They also cannot be removed from the experiences and narratives of the students who engage them. Thus, an analysis of education is committed to studying the production, reception, and varied use of texts and their relationship to power in terms of how they are used to define social relations, values, ideas of community, and definition of the self.

From this perspective, education and pedagogy become one of the defining principles of cultural studies and the analysis of culture. Questions such as what one does for students who are less self-literate than others become central. If we broaden the definition of pedagogy so as to move beyond a limited emphasis on the mastery of techniques and methodologies, students would be concerned with comprehending pedagogy as a configuration of textual, verbal, and visual practice that seeks to engage the processes through which people understand themselves and the possible ways in which they engage others and their environment. Pedagogy thus represents one of the clearest forms of cultural production; it examines how power and meaning are employed in the construction, organization and dissemination of knowledge, desires, values and identities. As Giroux (1994) notes,

> Cultural studies also rejects the traditional notion of teaching as a technique or set of neutral skills and argues that teaching is a social practice that can only be understood through considerations of history, politics, power and culture. Given its concern with everyday life, its pluralization of cultural communities, and its emphasis on multidisciplinary knowledge, cultural studies is less concerned with issues of certification and testing than it is with how knowledge, texts, and cultural products are produced, circulated and used. (p. 280)

The implications for queer theory are vast. Coming to terms with how homosexuality has been defined and changed in the academy becomes a central topic. We look to teaching and the curriculum by way of cultural analysis in order to understand how and why gay curricula have been absent from colleges and universities and, as I discuss in Part II, why teachers who see themselves as gay have been denied voice.

Dedisciplining: Knowledge and Location. Many writers speak of cultural studies as inherently interdisciplinary: If we are to study culture, the thinking goes, then we need a variety of disciplinary tools to study it (Giroux, 1993, 1994). Queer studies is the most recent interdisciplinary example of an area of knowledge that seeks to assert its importance in the academy. One way to seek prominence is traditional. Thus, we have seen the creation of conferences, journals, and departments, or concentrations within departments, where faculty say they do cultural studies or queer theory. Tenure lines are vied for, and a canon of authors whom we all quote is produced. Within these conferences, departments or journals we will indeed find interdisciplinary studies. A political economist may write one article and a sociologist the next one; two faculty members in the same area may study gay and lesbian issues from a psychological perspective and a literary one. My concern is not that such work is interdisciplinary. In one respect, we merely state the obvious when we acknowledge that more than one discipline is at work on a particular topic. However, from the perspective advanced here, I will suggest that rather than be interdisciplinary, our work needs to transcend disciplines, or at least not be limited to a traditional disciplinary paradigm. We need to think of the structure of academe and how knowledge gets located in particular arenas. I will save until a later chapter a more complete discussion of academic structure and cultural studies, but I note here the challenge raised by Agger (1992): "Cultural studies refuses to become a rigid program; its diversity and flexibility are its epistemological hallmarks" (p. 19).

Such a commentary raises a variety of intriguing and fundamental questions: Is the logical next step for proponents of cultural studies or queer theory to form a department? What should be the requirements for tenure? Are journals peer reviewed? What should be the role of the faculty? I discuss the parameters of these questions at length in Chapter 2 and then return to them in the final chapter.

Critical Intellectuals and Public Discourse. Cultural studies not only attempts to broaden the terms of learning, it also views educators as public intellectuals who actually generate knowledge and power. Proponents of cultural studies strongly reject the assumption that teachers are simply transmitters of existing configurations of knowledge. As public intellectuals, academics are viewed as agents who produce knowledge and assume responsibility for its effects in the larger public culture. Hence, cultural studies raises questions about how knowledge gets produced and who produces it in order to extend and to deepen the possibilities for democratic public life.

In opposition to the current drive to vocationalize colleges and universities and the increasing technicalization of curriculum and the training of prospective teachers, cultural studies offers the possibility for defining and providing the institutional space and practices for education teachers and administrators to be public intellectuals. Broadly conceived, cultural studies becomes the theoretical matrix for producing individuals who are on the forefront of transdisciplinary, intellectual and theoretical work, especially around language, culture (including popular culture), gender, and race.

Faculty should move beyond the narrow confines of their discipline or institution and out into the public to engage the citizenry in specific ideas, knowledge or debate. There is a certain irony that those who engage in the study of popular culture often do so by using the most obtuse and abstract language. The use of cultural studies in the manner suggested here demands of necessity that individuals become engaged in the cultural politics of everyday life in their communities and in society at large. As Agger (1992) notes, "For cultural studies to remain entombed in the theoretical libraries of rarefied intellectual critics denies it political efficacy, which is one of the hallmarks of an engaged, relevant version of cultural studies" (p. 186). In contrast, I am arguing for our vernacular to be stripped down and usable by the public and for an engagement that is usually absent in the academy. The point is not to use grade school language, because to do so makes a mockery of our ideas and denigrates the intelligence of our readers; rather, I am suggesting that a public language of critique needs to be built that enables those of us inside and outside the academy to come together in dialogue to envision and build the kind of community we seek.

Arguably, nowhere is the drive to create such a community clearer than in discussions surrounding queer theory. To academicize the study of homosexuality and divorce ourselves from the daily struggles that happen to lesbian, gay and bisexual individuals, is a temptation to which we ought not to succumb. At the same time, to suggest changes that are theoretically void of any historical, social or cultural understanding risks repeating failures of the past. The challenge, then, is to map out a cartography of our lives that accounts for previous interpretations and creates the conditions for a reformulation of the academy.

Chapter 2

Queer Theory as Cultural Politics

Framing Gay Men

Many years ago, when I was still in the closet and struggling with my sexual orientation, I brought home a college friend who I found out a decade later was gay. When we were classmates, neither he nor I discussed being gay, and we never did anything remotely physical, but there was a certain bond of friendship that enabled us to enjoy one another's company even though we were quite different. He was an engineer and I was an English major; he liked team sports and I liked the solitude of running. He appreciated rock and roll, and I opted for folk music.

One of the first times he left our home my mother commented, "That Donald seems queer." I remember my heart racing so hard that the blood rushing to my head made my temples feel like they were about to burst. I could hardly stammer out, "What do you mean?" I was so afraid that my mother had voiced something that I knew instinctively but was too scared to mention. But, of course, my mom was no forerunner—this was the

1970s—for Queer Nation. "He just seems weird," she said, "not like your other friends."

It turns out that Donald actually was like some other friends; he's "queer" in the gay sense, not in the way my mom used it. He was also like countless men who put personal advertisements in gay and increasingly, in straight newspapers every week and hope to hide their sexual orientation. On any given day in the United States, we can turn to a newspaper and find a personal ad such as the following: "GWM, 31, straight acting and appearing, seeks same for friendship and possibly more. Likes romantic evenings, long drives in the mountains, and skiing. Not into drugs or femmes." What makes a person gay? Why do we think one person is straight and another queer? What does it mean for someone to be "not like a normal man?"

I work out in a gym in downtown Los Angeles that reflects the diversity—and tension—of the city. The gym is in a part of LA that has a high number of gay men, but it is not in an exclusively gay area, like West Hollywood. The gym also has reasonable rates, so it is crowded; a large proportion of young working-class men go there to lift weights, and older men and women use the pool and sauna. It is common to hear Chinese, English, Japanese, and Spanish. Men from throughout North, Central and South America are in particular evidence. There is a certain unspoken tension in the locker room that I have never experienced in a gym before. I have been in gay athletic clubs and in university gyms. To be sure, the camaraderie and atmosphere are different from locale to locale—chummy in the gay gym and pretentious in the university athletic center—but in my present gym the differences in race, class, and in particular, sexual orientation, account for a tension that is usually unspoken and yet visible.

The unease is most palpable in the men's locker room. Some men wrap towels around themselves en route to the showers; some even shower in their underwear. Some will disrobe and dress with a towel that covers their genitals and rear end so that others may not see their bodies. A policeman always stands quietly in the locker room. One of the more ironic aspects of the locker room is that frequently those same presumably heterosexual men who seek to shield their bodies from sight are also the fellows who take the longest to dress after a shower. They use oils and talcum powder for their skin, they comb their hair with explicit attention and they carefully put on their jewelry. In contrast, most of the fellows who I think of as gay (by their T-shirts? Their earrings? Their eyes?) seem to go through a quick routine of showering, dressing, and running a comb through their hair as they exit.

Sometimes I wonder if we were able to make a silent movie of the locker room how we would be able to tell who is gay and who is straight. Who comes across as straight acting and who would my mother say is queer? Who acts like a normal man? In this chapter, I take up these questions not to answer them but, rather, to consider how we have framed them. I first discuss what I mean by the terms *cultural politics* and *queer studies,* and I then consider the ideological, existential and strategic challenges that a queer view of the world presents to the academy. Throughout the chapter, I use the scaffolding developed in Chapter 1 to focus on the indeterminacy of language, "the pressure of the unspeakable," to use Foucault's phrase, and the hidden norms that exist to frame sexual orientation.

Cultural Politics

In daily life we commonly divorce what we think of as culture from politics. As noted in Chapter 1, from one perspective, culture is art and politics pertains to the battles in state houses and in Congress. Some art, defined as propaganda by conservatives and agitprop by liberals, is accepted as political. If one is conservative, such art has no place in the public domain; a liberal will disagree and argue that agitprop is a historically recognized artistic genre that has every right to a public showing and, conceivably, to public funding. Thus, a storm of controversy has erupted during the last decade over a handful of decisions made by public agencies such as the National Endowment for the Arts that decides to fund a show arguing for gay rights, or a museum that displays photographs such as Mapplethorpe's gay iconography. The assumption of those of us who subscribe to cultural studies is that all art has a political nature, and indeed, culture is more than simply what painters, dancers, and playwrights create.

In Chapter 1, I offered a sevenfold scaffolding for what I think about culture. But before I build on this concept of culture, I need to outline three points about what culture is not:

1. Culture does not simply consist of the artifacts that exist in a given tribe, society or organization.

2. Culture is neither inherited by groups nor discovered by researchers.
3. What we think of as culture and politics cannot be divorced from one another.

From the perspective of those who propose cultural studies, culture is a signifying system and a system of material production. That is, culture exists by way of constant interpretation by individuals and groups of the myriad of ideas, practices, institutions, acts, norms, rules, literary and artistic expressions that get worked out in daily life. Culture is a process of production, circulation and consumption rather than an object to be studied or inherited. As a signifying system, cultures have built into them ideological components that get played out in the interstices of everyday life. When ideology goes unquestioned, it is hegemonic and enforces hidden norms; when we investigate microscopic aspects of society and relate them to larger social forces, we bring into question how ideology operates and how it constrains or empowers different individuals and groups. As a signifying system and a system of material production, culture operates in a feedback manner in which symbols support production and vice versa. How images are developed, disseminated, and carried become key points of analysis. If we can understand how signifying systems operate, we have the potential to disrupt the system and provide a voice for those who are silenced by the norm.

Such an analysis of culture moves us dramatically away from the three points raised above and toward an analysis based on cultural studies. I do not study culture merely as a set of things such as clothes, works of art, or ceremonial acts. One mistake that many researchers of organizational culture have made is to envision that a central task of their work is to build a taxonomy of what they perceive to be organizational culture; a handful of years ago, management by walking around, or keeping one's door open, by definition were described as cultural acts. The flaw with such examples is twofold. On the one hand, the assumption is that culture is like water in a tap, and a manager is able to turn it on or off. When we walk around a building, we are acting in a cultural frame, but presumably when the budget is built, the work is not cultural. Some researchers describe as cultural acts managers' having open doors to indicate they are approachable or college presidents' making speeches to the faculty on the importance of teaching, thus highlighting that the leader values teaching. Presumably, having an open door or presenting a speech is a cultural act. What such researchers fail to see is that all such acts are open to different kinds of interpretation.

An open door may mean accessibility to some people, or, to others, it may be overridden by other acts, or, to still others, it may not connote accessibility at all. A speech about the importance of something may achieve its intended purpose, or it may be ignored or even discounted.

Culture becomes, then, a creation to be interpreted rather than objects to be discovered. We cannot decontextualize acts from their social, historical and economic situations. All acts, ideas, institutions, and the like have histories that frame how they get presented and interpreted, but we are also able to provide our own interpretations. It is at this point that the term *cultural politics* enters the discussion. For if all parts of our lives are open to interpretation, then individuals and groups will have competing and contested definitions of reality. If culture is not simply the 18th-century piece of art that hangs in the museum, then we need to ask not only what an individual's view is of that particular painting but also why only that piece hangs in the gallery and not others, who sees the painting and who does not, and what such a painting says not only about the time in which it was created but also about its implications for society and our own lives today. We need to come to terms with the world beyond the painting and recognize that a museum piece that presents a particular view of society helps frame or challenge norms and relations of conduct moving far beyond the museum piece itself.

The struggle, then, is not simply to replace one picture with another or to substitute one set of authors in a college curriculum with a second set. Instead, we need to consider what canons represent, how they get defined, who enjoys the power of choosing and defining, and who does not, and what the relationship is between the canons and the larger social structures. As Patton (1993) notes, "The crucial battle now for 'minorities' and resistant subalterns is not achieving democratic representation but wrestling control over the discourses concerning identity construction" (p. 173). Hence the need for cultural politics.

Cultural politics seeks to accentuate difference and understand the invisible norms at work that account for our thinking of one group as mainstream and another as odd. All of the examples at the chapter's outset accentuate the need for a cultural politics that deconstructs how it is that we have come to think and act in a particular manner. What does it mean for someone to say he is "straight acting" and, more important, why does he feel the need to mention it? When we say that we are "not into drugs and femmes," are we equating similarities? Do we wrap ourselves in towels because we fear a specific action—a pass, a come-on—in a public arena?

Is the concern that a man may think of me as a sexual object and, if so, that the towel will mask my sexuality? How does such thinking support or stand in contrast to those who say someone could be gay but offer only emotive reasons—he's sensitive, funny—and nothing overtly sexual? Are all acts—the removal or placement of a towel—conscious acts, and what are the implications if they are or are not?

Proponents of cultural politics seek to interrogate and uproot certainty. Indeed, we are uprooting ideas built on our collective social constructions rather than unearthing difficult truths we already know. Representation thus becomes a battleground for understanding how individual and collective identities are shaped or reshaped. Our identities exist somewhere between the cheery, radical essentialism that asserts that we can become whatever we want to become as long as we try hard and the dour straitjacket of orthodox Marxism or Freudianism that believes individuals and groups have little possibility for controlling their lives.

As with Agger (1992), I am arguing for a cultural politics based on a postmodern interpretation of cultural studies, acknowledging the strengths and weaknesses of modernity. I reject a postmodernism that analyzes issues without a political project in mind. The conservative postmodern belief that struggle is useless, that little matters other than irony and wordplay, overlooks the practical strengths of democracy and collective action. Of necessity, then, a postmodern cultural studies of the kind I am suggesting begins by asserting the primacy of cultural politics in society, in institutions, and in groups. Again, critical postmodernism emphasizes that the point is not merely to study the world but to change it. Our aim is to assemble new practices, languages and ways of seeing and hence acting in the world so that individuals and groups will not of necessity need to subsume their identities into a homogeneous mass. Proponents of cultural politics struggle to come to terms, then, with the interdependent and relational nature of identities and how they are shaped, formed, mangled and enabled by the conditions at work in society.

In particular, we investigate those institutions and industries that play central roles in the development of culture. Schools, for example, have long been thought of as transmitters of culture. Colleges and universities play a critical role in defining knowledge. Museums, libraries and cultural centers such as theaters afford an opportunity for understanding what society deems as worthy of representation. Indeed, how we define cultural centers such as theater—Broadway, community theater, gay theater—are critical sites for investigation. And the rise of the communications industry during the last generation stands as a crucial area for investigation. What we see on nightly television is not merely funny or sad, interesting or boring. Television, movies, MTV, now play an overwhelming role in legitimating certain aspects of life and not others. Theaters, museums, television, and other cultural terrains are not merely surface phenomena that keep a well-oiled machine functioning. They do not act simply as breaks from the workaday world as if a sharp delineation existed between the world of work and the world of leisure. Instead, cultural centers act to modify, constrain, define and support the world of work and, in turn, feed back images to schools.

The shape of the argument pertaining to cultural politics is important for any number of investigative arenas, but at this point in U.S. society perhaps in no area can we better analyze the politics of culture than with regard to sexual orientation and the development of identity. Chandra Mohanty (1989-90) has commented that the development of a public culture based on cultural politics is "fundamentally about making the axes of power transparent. . . . It is about taking the politics of everyday life seriously [so that] culture itself is thus redefined as incorporating individual and collective memories, dreams, and history that are contested and transformed through the political praxis of day-to-day living" (p. 207). What does it mean if we are to make the "axes of power transparent" with regard to sexual orientation? If we are interested in a public culture that is inclusive of lesbian and gay people, what takes place in the "politics of everyday life" so that societal "memories, dreams and history" are contested and ultimately transformed? The answer to such questions involves investigations of signification based on historically specific social relations. Identity becomes not something taken as a given but as something that is up for grabs.

The power of the norm turns on the need for society to define heterosexuality as the only acceptable identity and relationship. Those who are not heterosexual are perceived as individuals in need of fixing and, more important, in need of labeling. A cultural identity from this perspective is possible, notes Stuart Hall (1990), because we think of culture "in terms of one, shared culture, a sort of collective 'one true self,' hiding inside of the many other, more superficial or artificially imposed 'selves' which people with a shared history and ancestry hold in common" (p. 223). Thus, from this perspective, heterosexuality is one unstated common code that we all share and it is an unchanging, static attribute of our individual and collective selves.

On the other hand, the view of cultural identity that I am suggesting here works from the perspective of a cultural politics of difference (Tierney, 1995b). We do not look at identity as fixed and unchanging; we see it as in a constant state of flux and redefinition while norms and borders become destabilized. Identities are not static, but they are also not simply the sum of past experiences, as if sexual mores naturally evolve from a perceived prim Victorian age to a more liberal one. Cultural identities exist in sociohistorical contexts and they undergo constant transformation and redefinition.

The implications for how one studies gay and lesbian people are quite significant. The investigation of sexual orientation is not a linear analysis of the past to understand how we have gotten to where we are today but, rather, we study the indeterminacy of past and present language and action to make sense of where we might go tomorrow.

Until the 1970s, however, the literature about homosexuality and its relationship to society was framed in one of two ways: either by absence, or by defining the topic as deviant. That is, up until a generation ago, not a great deal of social science research existed on homosexuality. When authors did write about the topic, they usually came from psychology or sociology and they looked on the subject population as either deviant or in need of repair, or both (Tierney & Dilley, in press). Willard Waller's classic, *The Sociology of Teaching,* for example, pointed out the dangers of allowing homosexuals to teach. As homosexuality was a disease infecting homosexuals, Waller (1961) suggested that homosexual teachers would be able to contaminate students and spread the illness. "Nothing seems more certain," wrote Waller, "than that homosexuality is contagious" (p. 147). Such assumptions exemplify the initial line of research about homosexuality. Scientists studied a subject population either to highlight their danger to the general society, or to suggest ways to cure them of their illness. Researchers in other disciplinary areas such as literature or philosophy had little to say about the topic.

Academic Outlaws:
The Advent of Queer Studies

The 1970s saw a rise in a second, more intensive and prolonged burst of research that looked at lesbian and gay people not as deviants but as normal or almost normal. This line of research primarily began after a professional organization, the American Psychiatric Association, decided in 1973 that homosexuality was no longer a mental illness, and the Stonewall Riots in a New York gay bar in 1969 publicized to the world that lesbian and gay people were going to fight harassment and intimidation. Obviously, no single event marks a change in the manner in which individuals and groups study topics, but both events mirror the general thrust of research since that time.

The scientific term *homosexual* gave way to *lesbian* and *gay*. As opposed to degenerates in need of imprisonment or a cure, lesbians and gays were studied as another minority group in need of rights and understanding. Research mushroomed in multiple areas rather than only in psychology and sociology. In large part, we might think of this research as assimilationist. The underlying assumptions were that discrimination existed; if we outlined the mistakes and misunderstandings of the larger population, we would be able to develop legal, political and social solutions.

Most recently, we have seen a new development—queer theory. I use the word *queer* with hesitation. Words and phrases gain an academic trendiness that rob them of their original intent and power. *Empowerment* is an example of a word that had a specific meaning pertaining to civil rights and social justice only fifteen years ago, but subsequently, a multitude of individuals and groups appropriated the word for their own use so that credit card companies and conservative politicians sought to empower us. Even though *postmodernism* is an openly contested term, it has achieved a cachet so that I now sit in conference sessions with titles such as "Postmodern Theories of Leadership" or "The Postmodern Organization," but the presenters are not able to articulate the difference between postmodern concepts of leadership or organizations and modern (or even romantic) notions. Frequently, I read studies that make claims to be critical or feminist, but the only evidence that can be presented is that the studies might investigate women or people of color.

My point is not that I have knowledge that others do not share but, rather, that scholars and the general public as well far too often appropriate terminology when they have no theoretical or epistemological understanding of the terms or no investment in the theory. As Agger (1992) notes, "This is the fate of all theory in an age of instantaneity: It functions as embellishment, not as substantive social thought and rigorous criticism" (p. 112). I am also not claiming that only a select priesthood should use these words. There is obviously a middle ground between someone like the right-winger Oliver North, of Iran-Contra fame, saying he wants to "empower" the voters and assuming that only Lyotard and Baudrillard have the right to write about postmodernism.

In many respects, I use queer because of its embattled nature, its indeterminacy, and the manner in which it has been appropriated and in my view, misappropriated. In an important article on queer theory, De Lauretis (1991) writes in her introduction,

> The term "queer," juxtaposed to the "lesbian and gay" of the subtitle, is intended to mark a certain critical distance from the latter. . . . The phrase "lesbian and gay" or "gay and lesbian" has become the standard way of referring to what only a few years ago used to be simply "gay" (e.g. the gay community, the gay liberation movement) or just a few years earlier still, "homosexual." (p. iv)

In Alexander Doty's (1993) book, *Making Things Perfectly Queer,* he moves well beyond the idea that queer is an umbrella term for gay and lesbian by claiming, "When I use the term 'queer'. . . I do so to suggest a range of nonstraight expression in, or in response to, mass culture. This range includes specifically gay, lesbian, and bisexual expressions; but it also includes all other potential (and potentially unclassifiable) nonstraight positions" (p. xvi). In a nearly 700-page text about lesbian and gay studies, the authors tell us that they did not use queer—although they like the word—because "The names lesbian and gay are probably more widely preferred than is the name queer. And the names lesbian and gay are not assimilationist" (Abelove, Barale, & Halperin, 1993, p. xvii). In his book, Bruce Bawer (1993) takes their statement one step further: "I've chosen not to use the word 'queer,' which is favored by some gay activists and academics but turns off almost everybody else, gay and straight" (p. 14). Miguel Gutierrez has troubles with queer but from a completely different perspective; he sees the term as unproblematically inclusive so that it does not take into account issues such as race and class: "There are people who cannot afford to be nonassimilationist; they are fighting just to eat and live" (quoted in Cosson, 1991, p. 16). Queer Nation's chant, "We're queer, we're here, get used to it," was explicitly confrontational and used as a synonym for lesbian and gay individuals and people who were out and proud. Whereas only a handful of years ago, queer meant lesbian and gay, in the late 1990s queer now also includes bisexuals and transgendered people. There are those who will say that simply using the coupling lesbian and gay, or writing about queers and defining them in binary fashion, is false and misleading. From this perspective, queer should seek to unhinge sexual identity so that a person does not get defined as lesbian or gay. Instead, gender construction is a floating definition that constantly undergoes reconfiguration.

What's in a name? Quite a lot, evidently, or individuals would not be arguing over whether to use the term. Somewhat disconcertingly, I have trouble with and am in agreement with virtually every definition that has been cited. Doty's willingness to use queer on anything that is nonstraight is so open ended that the term can become used in whatever way an author desires; at the same time, his desire to emphasize that straight norms exist is helpful for the argument I develop. Bawer is probably correct that the vast majority of individuals who think of themselves as gay or lesbian reject the term queer, but I wonder if terminology should be decided simply by popularity contests? I find his unwillingness to think more concretely about the nature of language troubling, but on the other hand, those academics who also do not think about the masses are equally worrisome. We might reject binary definitions, but we should at least recognize that the world is recognized in such a fashion and it will take more than our rejection to move beyond binarism. Gutierrez's point is well-taken. As noted in Chapter 1, if language is contested, then we cannot claim that simply because we opt for one word—queer, fruitcake, faggot—it will be any more inclusive or exclusive than another. At the same time, it appears that queer has been called on with an explicit objective to be more inclusive. The reappropriation of the term has also changed a discursive sign from a stigma into a badge of solidarity. Again, we have brought language into question. The point of saying, "We're queer," is that it highlights difference in an effort to expose norms. In effect, we are outlaws—socially, intellectually, and linguistically.

Doty (1993) offers a helpful point about how I conceive of the word queer: "Queerness should challenge and confuse our understanding and uses of sexual and gender categories" (p. xvii). In scholarly work such as I am attempting here, we should challenge commonly accepted notions of reality; by doing so, we become academic outlaws.

At the same time, because the word is so explicitly confrontational, there are also moments when the need to confront may be outweighed by other factors. These other factors have to do with questions of situation and audience and return us to the organizing notion of agape. To work from the idea of agape demands that at times we will confront one another.

Queer theory helps members of the community—straight and queer—to realize that points of view in a truly multicultural group will exist that may be different from their own. We struggle with the idea of what it is like to live a life where one is beyond the norm. Again, the critical intellectual is one who does not simply pass over a dedication from a woman to her life-long partner but realizes that the structural categories that exist that frame such commentaries need to be radically reconfigured. At the same time, confrontation does not occur at every turn, with every comment. Too often we fear that confrontation carries with it an implicit or explicit threat that if the individual does not agree with us, then that individual must conform or leave. Agape works from the opposite perspective. We accept confrontation because we realize that differences will exist in a community of multiple identities, but we advocate neither assimilation nor banishment; we recognize instead the authenticity of those multiple identities.

Language is a central component for working out the parameters of community and agape. When Barry and I attended a Mahler concert with a handful of friends recently and I said, "There sure are a lot of queers here," the comment was decidedly nonconfrontational. All of us were gay, and the use of the word queer in this context was (a) nonpolitical—a statement of fact; (b) humorous—gay men love their Mahler; and (c) a sign of camaraderie—the comment was made only to people who understood the term. But even in this nonpolitical context, there are political ramifications: I noted that the comment was intended to be funny "because gay men love their Mahler," which equates queer with gay male. I am not certain that if we had gone to a women's softball game, the comment would have been that there were a lot of queers instead of lesbians at the event. So much for inclusiveness.

Conversely, if someone innocently did not know my sexual orientation and made the same comment, I would take it as an insult, just as I would if a speaker were to make the same comment confrontationally, knowing that I was queer. "He's queer," or the objectifying "He's a queer," are used in this manner to deride, insult or isolate. Even if I turn the speaker's words on their head and assume a challenging stance, "Yeah, I'm queer, too. What about it?" I may be justifying my use of the term, but not the speaker's. I am trying to compensate, and the speaker is trying to denigrate. We are involved in a linguistic, ultimately cultural battle. Such an example is what I mean by cultural politics where, as Patton (1993) noted above, we are "wrestling control over discourse" (p. 173). We are not content to be named and defined by those who seek to marginalize us or render us voiceless. There are, then, individuals who have the right to use the word queer and others who do not.

And, of course, we have my mom's use of the term in a nonsexualized way that implies neither support for nor denigration of an individual's sexual orientation. Her usage also highlights one way I will not use the word: In one way or another, queer is related to sexual orientation. A queer person is not simply odd. The maddening part of such a comment is that once I offer the statement, we immediately need to contextualize the meaning. We run the risk of defining sexual orientation as merely sexual activity when we call on sexually explicit imagery to define what we mean by queer. That is, Queer Nation's posters of two men kissing, or two women locked in a passionate embrace, offer simultaneous images of confrontation—"We are here"—and sexuality—"We are sexual beings." Rosemary Hennessy (1995) helpfully points out, "To the extent that queer tends to advance a subjectivity that is primarily sexual, it can threaten to erase the intersections of sexuality with class as well as the gender and racial histories that still situate queer men and women differently" (p. 145). Our challenge is an intellectual and symbolic tightrope—we demand acceptance as ourselves. We do not want to be reduced to merely sexual objects, but we also do not want to become sexless in our quest for equal rights and protection.

As with other words, today's trendiness enables an individual to say, "I'm queer." I am most uncomfortable with this usage because it rips any political meaning from the term other than the speaker's adopting the false voice of authority. I am arguing that we must be constantly aware of the contextualized nature of all language and that as long as speakers use the term queer in a socially and theoretically conscious manner, I support them. Bawer's easy dismissal of the term, the homophobe's use of the word as a weapon to hurt, and the liberal's use of the word to show that he or she is sophisticated, must be rejected as retarding our understanding of gender and sexual orientation.

I have little doubt that a generation from now, we will not use the word queer as we use it today. Possibly, the confrontational edge that it has in the waning days of the 20th century will have eroded, or conceivably the word will be seen as too moderate. Perhaps we will no longer be seen or think of ourselves as outlaws on the periphery. In my parents' youth, they spoke of colored people, and, in my own youth, we first said Negro and then Black. Today, we debate over whether African American or person of color is more appropriate. Again, notice my language. In reality, we do not debate. As a white man, I generally call people of color what they want to be called; at a minimum, I do not have the right to label—and this is the core of my point. Language is contested; language helps create reality. I use queer because I want to highlight our difference. To be different, to view the world not as a monolith, to hope not for consensus but for disagreement, frames reality in a way fundamentally alternative to modernist assumptions. Because I accept our difference does not imply that we have little in common with others, or that we always must confront. Theoretical notions about difference do not automatically translate into political confrontation between queers and straights. I am suggesting that because someone is different does not mean that the creation and maintenance of community is impossible. Ultimately, to form community around notions of difference and agape is our greatest danger because it can cause groups to isolate themselves, but it is also our greatest hope. Much as we must not renounce our individual identities in our engagements with one another, we also ought not to fall prey to facile thinking that suggests we have nothing in common with one another. I use queer studies and cultural politics, then, as an analytical and political tool for first understanding the world and then trying to change it.

As Jonathan Rutherford (1990) has noted, what I am suggesting is that our struggle is "to turn those sites of oppression and discrimination into spaces of resistance" (p. 12). The manner in which we do so is by reconceptualizing how we talk about and think of sexual identity. The debate between proponents of essentialism and social constructionism has helped us think through why someone is queer; however, in my view the debate has pretty much run its course. We have learned about as much as we can. Diana Fuss (1989) nicely summarizes essentialism as "a belief in the real, true essence of things, the invariable and fixed properties which define a given entity" (p. xi). Social constructionism is its opposite. Supporters of both sides have offered helpful analyses. John Boswell's (1981) work, for example, offers significant evidence that we always have existed. Foucault (1977, 1980), more than anyone else, has proposed that we study sexual identity as subjective meaning. Sexual acts have no inherent meaning, he argues, but rather, society gives meaning to them. A differentiation is made between homosexual behavior and someone who is homosexual. Thus, whereas essentialists assume that all societies can be reduced to groups who are heterosexual and homosexual (and perhaps bisexual), constructionists assume that the homosexual is a sociocultural phenomenon.

Following the stunning theoretical work of Goldberg (1993), and Omi and Winant (1993, 1994) on race, I offer a middle ground that seeks to incorporate both views so that we are not forced to accept that queers always have been here or that we are an invention. The analysis hinges on a critique of modernism. Modernism's project has been to use science in order to categorize and label. Concurrently, liberalism's concern has been to ensure individual liberties that are based on universal principles. The assumption that we are all members of the human family who can work out differences through universal appeals to truth and reason are hallmarks of the modernist project. The concern here is that universal principles inevitably create norms that mark some people as normal and others as not. When race, for example, is assumed to be irrelevant, one can only define racism as an individual flaw, an irrational action. But, as Goldberg (1993) argues, "Racism is not a singular transhistorical expression but transforms in relation to significant changes in the field of discourse" (p. 42). Racism needs to be studied not as a singular identity flaw in the individual racist but instead as a construct embedded in societal practices. Thus, rather than rationalist appeals for individuals to improve, we need to question how and why racialized expression changes over time. When we ask this question we force ourselves to look at racism not as an isolated act but, rather, as inextricably woven into the fabric of society and culture. To ask such a question moves us away from thinking of constructs such as race and sexual orientation as essences that are fixed and objective. It also moves us from the position that race and sexual orientation are simply cultural constructs that a modernist utopia would eliminate. Omi and Winant (1994) offer an alternative definition:

> The effort must be made to understand race as an unstable and "decentered" complex of social meanings constantly being transformed by political struggle. *Race is a concept which signifies and symbolizes social conflicts and interests by referring to different types of human bodies.* Although the concept of race invokes biologically based human characteristics, selection of these particular human features for purposes of racial signification is always and necessarily a social and historical process. (p. 55)

The implications for how we think about and study sexual orientation are clear: Boswell and others are obviously correct that homosexuals existed in other ages, but what that meant can be understand only within the context of the time. Sexual orientation is in a continual process of formation and it is a result of historical and culturally situated projects in which individuals, groups, and social structures act and react with and against one another. The challenge is to question our taken-for-granted notions of the world—in this case, heterosexuality—and see how they have been constructed and defined. As Seidman (1995) notes, "The point of departure for queer theory is not the figure of homosexual repression and the struggle for personal and collective expression or the making of homosexual/gay/lesbian identities, but the hetero/homosexual discursive or epistemological figure" (p. 130). Thus, the need arises for a cultural politics that decodes large and small events and actions and a queer studies that actively provokes us to think about the discourse and structures that create norms and differences. The analysis, then, seeks to break heterosexuality's hegemony of the norm.

The little previous work on homosexuality in academe in large part used the psychological perspective of deviance. Homosexuals were mentally ill creatures in need of either reform or condemnation. Although any intellectual area does not change abruptly, when the American Psychiatric Association in 1973 acclaimed that homosexuality was not a mental illness, research in large part followed suit. More recently scholars have employed a framework of liberation that, notes Slagle (1995), "sought to allow gay men, lesbians, and bisexuals participation within the dominant system" (p. 86). Thus, Crew's (1978) work, *The Gay Academic* or Chesebro's (1981) text about how social scientists studied homosexuality tried to create a place for the academic within the existing social order. I want to emphasize that I am not criticizing work that for its time was a dramatic step in offering visibility to an otherwise invisible topic. Crew's text, in particular, was among the first of its kind and made possible alternative configurations of how we might think about homosexuality.

Nevertheless, queer theory seeks to break disciplinary boundaries, rather than work from within them. Deborah Britzman (1995) points out how queer theory, "is an attempt to move away from psychological explanations like homophobia, which individualizes heterosexual fear and/or loathing toward gay and lesbian subjects at the expense of examining how heterosexuality becomes normalized as natural" (p. 153). Whereas previous studies of homosexuality looked on gay and lesbian people as deviant, or mentally ill, recent work such as Crew's sought to reframe the dialogue and point out that we were just like everyone else. Queer theory, however, seeks to understand why we have developed binary categories such as homo/hetero and how such terms have gotten developed in popular and disciplinary culture. The strategy of queer theorists, then, is to surface the unmarked criterion that scorns some and honors others. And within academe, we investigate how disciplines and regimes of thought have helped define and marginalize queer identity.

The implications for political action are also clear. Whereas liberal heterosexuals tend to think of homophobia as an individual flaw that needs to be eradicated, proponents of queer theory and cultural studies see homophobia as the product of a system of structural power where heterosexuality is encoded throughout daily life. The liberal flaw is that they only see homophobia as consisting of isolated, explicit acts—teenage boys beat up a man because he "acts gay." The idea suggested here seeks to understand what it means that television cannot present two women kissing one another, for example, even though the presentation of heterosexual affection is commonplace. Queer studies as cultural politics can be summarized as follows:

1. It is historicist in that it seeks to understand sexual identity over time.
2. It seeks to uncover norms and decode ideological practices.
3. It is confrontational and disruptive rather than consensual.
4. It understands sexual identity in terms more significant than simply a sexual act.
5. It sees all of culture as interpretive and political.

Cultural Politics, Queer Studies, and Difference

If we accept the propositions listed above, what are the implications for queer theory? We face three levels of challenges that, following Cornel West (1990), I will define as (a) intellectual, (b) existential, and (c) strategic. The intellectual challenge pertains to how to think about representational practices. In effect, if we agree that sexual identity is more than simply a sexual act and is to be understood as historicist, ideological and interpretative, how do we then understand and analyze sexual identity today? The answer to this question goes to the core of this book's purpose. If we accept the theoretical propositions about cultural studies and queer theory that I have discussed, then what does that mean for how we think about sexual identity within academe?

The Intellectual Challenge

When we use cultural studies as an analytical tool, sexual identity becomes directly engaged with the political functions of academe. We develop a definition that seeks not merely an academic reconfiguration of what we mean by sexual identity, but we also investigate those practices that define, restrain, and encode sexual orientation within the organization and system. That is, the study of lesbian and gay issues ramifies in various directions. Individual scholars and academic departments develop ways alternative to those in which knowledge has traditionally been constructed and presented; transdisciplinary configurations are built. Global comparative analyses occur so that we are able to comprehend how ethnicity, class, nationalism and religion, for example, influence sexual formation. Local politics investigates how those who have been silenced might be ensured voice and empowerment.

"Queer theory," notes Seidman (1995), "can be viewed as a response to the development in the postwar United States of the university as a chief site in the production and validation of knowledge" (p. 138). How we determine what we define as knowledge becomes a key arena for struggle and debate because the outcome—knowledge's definition—is viewed as related to power. Seen in this way, sexual orientation becomes a transitory point for thinking about what we mean by social institutions such as the family and schools, as well as such ideas as individual freedom, censorship, and civil rights. Of consequence, the university is no longer merely a purveyor of objective concepts but, rather, a central determiner of how society seeks to maintain, or disrupt, the status quo.

In saying this, I am offering an explicitly different formulation from not only how knowledge about sexual orientation has been configured but also what is currently taking place in the burgeoning field of queer theory. Over the past few years, we have seen lesbian and gay studies develop in ways that are entirely expected. Courses first have been offered and they are followed by programs and centers. Journals have been developed, special interest groups in major associations have started, and we now even have our own national conference as well as a panoply of special institutional and regional conferences. All of these actions are logical as a field begins to develop; in effect, we are professionalizing queer studies in exactly the same manner that any area of knowledge has developed in the U.S. academy in the past century. If we looked at any fairly new field—biochemistry, women's studies, American studies—we would see that the same pattern of professionalization has occurred. I am suggesting, however, that we ought to be wary of the rigidification of structures such as departments, journals and conferences. From the perspective advanced here, it is those very same structures that have created and reinforced hidden norms of privilege for heterosexuals.

Therein lies a paradox. To advance our understanding of sexual orientation, we need to unmask and understand how hidden norms operate, and we need sensitive investigations about heterosexism and homophobia. But we ought not to unthinkingly undertake these studies within a framework that has supported and sustained heterosexism. Audre Lorde's (1984) well noted comment that "The master's tools will never dismantle the master's house" (p. 112) is an apt observation. How is it possible to use scientific understanding and rational scrutiny to change the logic on which heterosexist ideas have been built? At the same time, by deconstructing heterosexism and struggling to decenter norms we find that we have used those tools—logic, rational persuasion, academic structures—to build our case. As Epstein (1987) asks, "How do you protest a socially imposed categorization, except by organizing around the category? (p. 19). We have come together as queers to protest the exclusion and discrimination that queers have faced.

Although such actions are understandable, if we accept the framework advanced here, then we must work against the institutionalization of queer studies in the academy. Instead, we develop strategies through queer studies that will help transform the ways in which all of us experience the cultural world, changing the way we communicate and interact with one another. I am not content, then, simply to work for acceptance by adding queers as an ingredient in the academic stew. The kind of queer theory I am arguing for here seeks to interrogate terms such as gender and race so that the norms of our lives are reconfigured. William Haver's (in press) rhetorical questions are helpful here:

> What if queer research were to be something other than a banal reproduction of academic business as usual? . . . What if queer research were to be something more essentially disturbing than the stories we tell ourselves of our oppressions in order precisely to confirm our victimized subjectivity, our wounded identity? . . . What if queer research were actively to refuse epistemological respectability? (p. 2)

Haver's questions seek answers that disturb norms rather than reconfirm them, albeit from a slightly more inclusive and liberal angle.

Proponents of queer studies acknowledge the agitational role that they play and will seek to unite their theoretical propositions to popular and civic positions that serve as a force for demystification. We become change agents from within rather than dispassionate observers from without. Given this passion, we acknowledge our role as situated observers. We develop analytic ways not only to decode culture but also to offer a self-criticism and referentiality that ordinarily does not exist in academe. In arguing in this manner, I am rejecting the role for ourselves as advocates of special interest group politics and little more. To be sure, we must be change agents on our campuses and at state and federal levels. However, if we were simply to accept our role as that of lobbying for specific policies, it would be inconsistent with the propositions of cultural studies. I am not seeking tolerance but, rather, a redrawing of intellectual, hence institutional, boundaries so that how we configure what is normal is changed. Again, the use of queer comes into play because at this moment in our history it is harder for us to slip into assimilationism when we use the word. We are transformational. As Michael Warner (1993) has aptly noted,

> People want to make theory queer, not just to have a theory about queers. For both academics and activists, "queer" gets a critical edge by defining itself against the normal rather than the heterosexual, and normal includes normal business in the academy. (p. xxvi)

This point raises challenges for those who are now at the forefront of academic queer studies. We are in the initial stages of acceptance—academic, social, and personal—after generations of exclusion and disdain. Scholars who may have feared studying lesbian and gay issues now find their work is in demand. Authors who could not get their work published in mainstream journals now find publishing houses vying for their texts. The accolades of academic glory, then, are beginning to appear, and just as individuals are beginning to reap the benefits of their efforts, I am suggesting that we resist them. A queer studies that invokes a cultural politics such as has been discussed here ought not to re-create the reality that we are so fiercely criticizing. How, then, do we position ourselves and what do we build? This leads us to the existential and strategic challenges.

The Existential Challenge

When we speak from the position of a cultural politics of difference an existential question arises that Cornel West (1990) asks:

> How does one acquire the resources to survive and the cultural capital to thrive as a critic or artist? By cultural capital I mean not only the high-quality skills required to engage in critical practices, but more important, the self-confidence, discipline, and perseverance necessary for success without an undue reliance on the mainstream for approval and acceptance. (p. 106)

Although West made his comment in reference to people of color, it holds true for queers as well. The widespread notion that heterosexuality is normal and everything that is not heterosexual is somehow aberrant has placed queers in a constant existential state of questioning ourselves, our identity, and how we should act. If we are in the closet, our angst may even be worse because we have no support whatsoever; if we have friends who know we are queer, we still must face a daily barrage of images, acts, and structures that favor heterosexuals. Up until twenty years ago, society defined homosexuality as an illness; gay people were sick and society wanted to cure us, understand us, or condemn us. Times have changed somewhat, but there is still a broad majority outside and within academe who think of homosexuality as aberrant behavior. What are the implications?

Clearly, this is a structural issue and not simply an individual one. To encourage individuals to "be strong" or "be proud" are helpful comments, but they are insufficient. To be sure, we must end the self-hatred that has long pervaded queer lives framed by societal mores, but we must also assume a collective stance toward society—this is what is meant by the existential challenge; it fits nicely with the ideas developed earlier about sexual formation. Homophobia is not just an individual issue but a construction that needs to be dealt with on a macrolevel; if this is true, then we must also develop a collective response rather than one that tells individuals how to cope. There are four cultural stances available to us (West, 1990). That is, if we look at the organization as a culture and wish to think about our own and others' representation in this culture, how might we act?

Passers. First, there is the position that I will elaborate on in Part II that concerns itself with assimilating into the mainstream. Most of us work hard at passing—the ad at the start of the chapter is a typical example of someone who wants to act straight and desires someone else who is similarly normal. Proponents of this position disdain flamboyant clothes, actions, or positions. Gay Pride parades with contingents such as drag queens and dykes on bikes, ACT-UP demonstrations at churches, or Queer Nation zaps at shopping malls are anathema to passers. Instead, passers seek to blend into the mainstream. We want acceptance, to be like everyone else, this line of thinking goes, so we must try to act like everyone else. Although some individuals may be "out" in the sense that individuals know the person is gay or lesbian, degrees of outness are always consciously managed.

The primary stance here is one of hoping to hide sexuality. These individuals believe that their sexual orientation ought to be irrelevant to their work life, so no mention need be made about partners, lovers, companions. They often have developed such ideas through experiences in which they have seen others lose jobs because they are gay. In this sense, their beliefs derive from rational fears—to come out involves danger. Others may argue that society should know they are gay (never queer), but most often such individuals come across as sexless human beings. Straight society knows that the individual is different, but the difference is nonthreatening. No open displays of affection occur, and anything overtly sexual is avoided.

The problem with this stance is that the norms of heterosexuality are never challenged, and many individuals live lives of loneliness and desperation. In effect, we have changed, but society has not. We have changed from fully functioning, explicitly sexual human beings (albeit deviant), to implicitly sexless individuals who look and act the way dominant society supposedly looks and acts. Those individuals who cannot or will not fit into the mainstream are either derided or left by the wayside. This stance places us in a suppliant position in which we seek acceptance from the mainstream even though everyone knows we are not and cannot be the same. We seek membership in an exclusive club with the hope that if we behave ourselves, our membership will be renewed. Because we are not charter members of the club, we must constantly seek member renewals. The power of the norm goes unchecked, and we are forever off balance trying to ensure that we speak and act in the proper manner.

Castro Clones. When I was a graduate student at Stanford in the early 1980s, I visited the Castro in San Francisco for the first time and discovered an area that was exclusively gay. Most major cities have such enclaves. To live in such an area does not demand that the individual be overtly political or think of him or herself as queer as opposed to lesbian or gay. However, the overriding emphasis in the ghetto is toward a life that is exclusively gay. Individuals shop at gay stores, attend gay events, have gay friends, and frequently work in gay businesses. When we speak of sexual orientation as an ethnicity, Castro clones offer an example of an ethnic enclave akin to those of other minorities (e.g., the Chinese community in San Francisco, or the Italian community in the North End of Boston).

It is also possible that individuals do not live within a specific geographic area, but they live the life of a Castro clone. Individuals segregate themselves from the mainstream even though they live within it. Such an individual lives with other lesbian or gay individuals, works in a business or department with other gay people, frequents restaurants or bars that are gay, and goes to gay cinemas, plays and other gay cultural events. They dress or act in a manner that many would interpret as gay, but they in general do not need to consider—for one reason or another—what the mainstream thinks about such actions. Individuals assume such a stance as a way to cope with the norms of society and to enjoy life. West (1990) argues that this stance is usually transitional, and if it is permanent, "it is self-defeating in that it usually reinforces the very inferiority complexes promoted by the mainstream" (p. 108). I have no empirical data to support the argument that this stance is transitional, although a common assumption amongst many of us in the gay community is that when individuals first come out they frequently adopt consciously gay habits and gradually may change. At the same time, I have known many individuals who have lived in gay ghettos for years and are contented with their lives.

However, such a stance is also in reaction to the dominant mores of society in a manner akin to that of passers. Neither group seeks to disturb the normalizing relations of society and they both see themselves as apolitical. One group seeks acceptance, and the other simply wants to be left with its own kind. The desire to have nothing to do with mainstream society is not by definition self-defeating, but it is entirely possible that the desire to sidestep the power of the norm does not promote a sense of empowerment or the kind of self-analysis that proponents of cultural studies seek. It is also true that these people might enjoy their privileges at the expense of others who cannot afford them. This position, then, is one of coping within inequity in an unfair world.

Queer Nationalism. Cultural separatism subscribes to the idea that different groups have distinct identities and the differences are so great that we have little in common with mainstream identities such as those of heterosexuals. The idea of separatist aesthetics and politics is lodged in areas that seek to build ingroup solidarity and destroy norms that are seen as privileged. In some respects, this cultural stance is related to Castro clones, but it is also the inverse. Rather than apolitical, it is decidedly political. The group does not seek toleration as the passers desire, and queer nationalists are not content with merely finding a space for themselves. Instead, queers in this area seek—demand—acceptance.

This stance is much more confrontational, unwilling to accept that we can survive and thrive in a world of heterosexism. Architects of this persuasion focus on the symbols and communicative vehicles of institutions and society in order to point out how different groups are relegated to the border zones of the academy. The critique of queers who are coping by either passing or living an apolitical life is that they are simply reaffirming a life on the fringes. Queer nationalists seek to redefine the structures of society, emphasizing their difference: "No one can speak for us." Heterosexuals who study queers are viewed with suspicion if not rejection. Queer nationalists maintain that a queer agenda will only be derived through discussion with other queers.

My concern with a vision of separatism is that it denies the possibility for human agency, hope or agape (Tierney, 1993). There is a certain stridency to this voice, so that even other lesbian and gay people may be criticized for living lives that are seen either as passing or coping. Condemnation often falls on those of us who are viewed as not being as enlightened or as courageous as others. Individual and group constraints are seen as so overwhelming as to deny any chance of collective, pluralist action across diverse constituencies. The desire for understanding the Other and the oppression of different groups becomes subsumed or lost by the postmodern assumption that we cannot bridge differences. The argument that the queer position is unique and so different that no one else can possibly understand it or engage in dialogue with others denies voice to everyone but the speaker and those who think like him or her. Cultural separatists often appear to mirror the idea that because they cannot understand a reality different from their own, they are absolved of further action with others who have problems different from their own. In effect, we are denied the voice of solidarity.

Cultural Citizenship. Here we have a view of culture as contested terrain that involves a politics of difference and coalition building. The idea of cultural citizenship is one that seeks to reconfigure borders. Proponents of this view struggle to redefine the same structures as queer nationalists do. The difference is not so much in the critique of what must change but in what should replace those oppressive structures. We try to understand cultural difference. We honor one another's identities not by assuming we can amalgamate differences but by engaging in dialogues of respect and understanding across groups.

West (1990) speaks of such people as "cultural workers who simultaneously position themselves within the mainstream while clearly aligned with groups who vow to keep alive potent traditions of critique and resistance" (p. 108). Cultural citizenship implies that discussions are needed aimed at reformulating norms so that individuals and groups are neither isolated nor silenced. The idea that we must simply appear in mainstream society as sexless beings is rejected out of hand, but so is the life that forces us to live in ghettos either as a mechanism for survival or rejection. Instead, we do not deny ourselves the benefits of what mainstream society has to offer, but we also honor the differences that a multicultural society will have. We thrive on a culture that incorporates rather than excludes. Cultural citizenship's need for historical and social understanding and critique addresses the intellectual challenge. We do not simply think of cultural capital as a passive object to be accumulated. Instead, the existential challenge enables us to think of cultural capital as malleable and open to interpretation and change.

The Strategic Challenge

If we are able to work through the intellectual and existential issues of sexual orientation, then ultimately we must act. A cultural politics of difference suggests that strategy consists of forging alliances with marginalized groups and developing reciprocal relationships with individuals who are guided by a vision of democracy. The challenge before us lies in the development of an active politics that takes seriously the notions we have discussed about cultural studies and queer theory. As Steven Seidman (1993) notes, "The present condition of communities organized around affirmative gay/lesbian identities yet exhibiting heightened conflicts around those very identities should be the starting point of contemporary gay theory and politics" (p. 129). Thus, we decenter norms and bring into question sexual identity so that differences of ethnicity, race, class, nation, and a multitude of other possible formations, come in for question, analysis and consideration. The strategic challenge thus becomes how to articulate a cultural politics of difference that bases itself not on a single or binary notion of identity but on the multiplication of identities.

Strategy becomes a protean attempt at dialogue whose goal is change. We assume that consensus is not an aim. Different individuals and groups will have competing interests. As I explain in Chapter 7, the challenge is to ensure that people's voices are heard and that our work centers around acts of respect and understanding. We struggle, then, to enact a community of difference where dialogues and conversations occur across borders. Sexual identity becomes an ongoing site of contestation and redefinition rather than a Durkheimian social fact.

Before turning to Chapter 3, a brief review is in order. Although I do not want us to get lost in the far corners of postmodernism's myriad debates, in order to comprehend fully how I analyze the data of Part II and how I develop the suggestions for academic change, it is important first to develop a comprehensive theoretical critique. My interpretation of cultural studies and queer theory is informed by what I have called "critical postmodernism." I reject the more nihilistic interpretations of postmodernism and accept "post" modernism's relationship to modernism.

For the purpose of this text, a critical postmodern view of culture drives my understanding of cultural studies and queer theory and forms what I have called "cultural politics." The importance of understanding academic institutions is threefold. First, I want to change the more oppressive aspects of the academy that silence and make invisible many lesbian and gay people. Second, I want to emphasize that the academy is a critical social institution involved in the production of knowledge and how sexual orientation gets defined. If we are able to employ cultural studies and queer theory in our analysis of knowledge production, then we will be better able to uproot the structures that entangle societal understanding of what it means to be queer. Third, I want to show how academic communities offer us the opportunity to come to terms with the interrelationships between individuals and community and intellectuals and society. On the one hand, then, we are able to investigate how identities and communities are molded and shaped by one another and, on the other hand, to reflect on the public responsibility and ability of intellectuals to effect change. I have summarized these points by using West's ideas of intellectual, existential, and strategic challenges. In the next chapter, I will extend the analysis in relation to intellectual and existential challenges. What makes for a norm? How do those of us who do not fit within the norm adapt, react, and gain voice?

Chapter 3

Dining at the Table
of the Norm

Tricks and Treats

As we sped to West Hollywood on Halloween, we took our usual positions. Barry was behind the wheel and I sat next to him, absentmindedly channel surfing on the radio. West Hollywood, a gay enclave in Southern California, reportedly was one of the better places to be on Halloween night. The larger-than-normal traffic jam in which we soon became enmeshed made it apparent that others thought as we did. Eventually we parked the car and walked to the parade route as did thousands of other individuals.

Not everyone had a costume, but more than half of the 40,000 or so people wore some kind of outfit. The O.J. Simpson affair had covered the news for the past six months, so there were a fair number of garish costumes that revolved around the murders. Some individuals also came dressed as famous personalities from the murder trial—from Judge Ito to the lawyers, Marcia Clark and Robert Shapiro. The typical number of drag queens were on hand, as were sets of groups—the Supremes; Bill, Hillary, and Chelsea

Clinton; Jerry Falwell and the devil; Michael Jackson; Elizabeth Taylor; and Priscilla, Queen of the Desert, seemed to be particular favorites.

The mood was festive and everyone seemed to be enjoying themselves. People walked casually up and down the boulevard—observing or being observed. Music blared at almost every street corner—from Cher clones doing a karaoke-aided tune of "I Got You Babe," to a Brazilian marching band composed entirely of drums. Food vendors sold their wares, and because it was before the election, Democrats tried to convince the citizenry that their candidates were worth the vote.

I cannot say with certainty who was gay or who was straight that night, although I suspect that most individuals were gay, lesbian or bisexual. At one street corner, however, a man and woman who seemed to be in their fifties stood and watched the festivities; they appeared almost as stereotypes of suburban heterosexual America. The man had on gray polyester pants and a checkered short-sleeve shirt, and the woman wore a plain blue dress and white tennis sneakers. She held a camera and as someone walked by, her husband tapped her shoulder and said, "Look at that one over there. Get a load of him," and she snapped a photo. Every now and then she said, "I got a good one, I did!" and he shook his head back and forth and said, "Incredible. Just incredible."

The pirate costumes Barry and I wore were not worthy of their photos evidently, but we watched them for a while before we rejoined the parade. As we moved on, Barry muttered, "Who invited them?" I suppose no group of people likes to be objectified—whether they be Native Americans who must endure Anglos mimicking their ceremonies, or Guatemalans who put up with norteamericanos videotaping their parades in Antigua during Semana Santa, or any individual putting up with tourists who think a particular lifestyle is exotic and have no compunctions about recording a particular aspect of that life.

This chapter is about invitations: Who gets invited? Who proffers the invitation? For what activities are invitations necessary? What makes for positive meaning in spectacle and what makes it turn into ridicule? One of the key arenas of investigation for proponents of cultural studies is popular culture, and in this chapter, I focus on how queers are defined in the late 20th century. I pay particular emphasis to what I will call the assimilationist perspective for lesbian and gay people. The assumption here is that if we simply fit in, then our problems will be solved. In order to be able to fit in, the straight majority needs to see that we are similar to themselves in all aspects but one—with whom we sleep.

Accordingly, I first discuss how queers might get invited and then consider how we should act once we have been invited. I conclude the chapter by reinscribing the notion of invitations so that we work from a more inclusive view of community that is less restrictive and invitational.

Assimilationism and Invitations

Bruce Bawer, a gay, cultural conservative, published *A Place at the Table* in 1993 among much fanfare; two years later Andrew Sullivan, another gay social conservative, published *Virtually Normal,* which attracted an equal degree of media attention. Both authors have made compelling cases for the assimilationist perspective. The underriding assumptions of this perspective are twofold. First, homosexuals are no different from heterosexuals. Second, the way to convince heterosexuals that we are similar is to minimize differences and accentuate similarities with the mainstream.

If homosexuals are able to turn these assumptions into political strategies, then our problems will be solved. Accordingly, Sullivan (1995, p. 171) suggests that all *public* discrimination be ended against homosexuals. He speaks quite clearly about his beliefs and works through various philosophical positions prior to arriving at a "politics of homosexuality" that calls for us to be treated in the same fashion as everyone else. Essentially, confrontation should be eschewed in favor of rational argument.

If Sullivan's text is addressed more to the straight majority, then Bawer's is more for the gay community. Bawer (1993) goes on at great length about how he desires gay men to present themselves and be presented:

> "The only time I ever feel ashamed of being gay," says a friend of mine, "is on Gay Pride Day." I know what he means, though my own emotions on that day are, at worst, closer to dismay than to shame. . . . There was more sashaying and queeny posing in a couple of hours than one could expect to see in a solid month of gay bar-hopping. Smart, talented people who held down respectable jobs in the corporate world or the fashion industry, on Wall Street or Publishers' Row, seemed to have done their best on this special day to look like tawdry bimbos, bar boys, and beach bums. Time and again, glimpsing this or that unconventionally attired or coiffed or made-up marcher, I found myself feeling momentarily as if I'd stumbled into a private costume party and seen something I wasn't supposed to see.

Unfortunately, however, this wasn't a private party; it was a public spectacle. (p. 155)

Actually, Bawer is not only dismayed on Gay Pride Day. He is angered about how "self-appointed spokespeople" present themselves on television and to the press (p. 26); how those spokespeople talked about sexual activity (p. 31); that we live in "gay ghettos" (p. 36); that we demonstrated in unconventional ways at the Republican convention (p. 39); that we confront the religious right (p. 57); that we protested our exclusion from the St. Patrick's Day parade (p. 63). And so forth. Those examples are merely from the first chapter of his book.

Although Bawer attacks his heterosexual confreres on the right, he reserves most of his venom for those of us who are gay, or as he says, "homosexual" (p. 13). *Queer* turns people off, and even gay, he feels, should be used sparingly because to many straight folks it "sounds like a political statement" (p. 13). He also uses "gay" to connote men. Throughout the book lesbians are overlooked—dismissed—with a quick comment that they are different so he cannot talk about them. When lesbians are mentioned, they are portrayed negatively (in Bawer's mind) such as "dykes on bikes." Sullivan, too, uses terminology that connotes the male, even going so far as to use the word *he* throughout his text. He does so, Sullivan (1995) tells the reader, because there are no other linguistic ways to discuss men and women that do not become cumbersome (e.g., he/she) but suggests that "for 'he' please read either male or female" (p. ix). Similarly, gay applies "to women as well as men" (p. ix).

In a curious way, the idea of difference is as central to assimilationist perspectives as it is to my own framework, albeit assimilationists offer the exact opposite proposition from myself. Sullivan works from the assumption that political change, rather than cultural change, is where we must focus our exclusive efforts. Queers, or as he calls us, "liberationists," do not have a viable political agenda and ultimately will not be successful.

Bawer took his title from a phrase by Bill Clinton that every American should "have a place at the table." Bawer ponders what it will take for us to get invited to the table and maintains that rowdy, "sashaying and queeny" types will only delay our acceptance into the American family. Rather than be different, we need to be like the mainstream. Indeed, Bawer argues that most of us are like the mainstream; in effect, we are a gay silent majority. Such an assumption is what drives Sullivan's work: If we are no different from everyone else, then we deserve the same public, legal rights as everyone else.

There are multiple levels on which one might respond. On a political level, I might comment that as someone who has been heavily involved in campus-based politics, individuals may shortchange themselves if they present their demands to a university board of trustees in drag. I am also not convinced that leather briefs and nipple rings are the appropriate attire for presenting a queer-friendly resolution to the faculty senate. On a personal level, I could add that I do not think of myself as a sashaying and queeny type, so I too am uncomfortable at times that somehow my identity is represented in that manner. On a cultural level, I may also note that there is much to be gained by thinking about the similarities that unite us rather than simply the differences that separate us. Finally, on a metaphorical level, I readily agree that it is important to consider who gets invited to the table and how we can be sure to secure invitations. (Far be it for any gay man to be left out of the festivities!)

At the same time that I offer comments that seem to be in agreement with the assimilationist perspective, it is also easy to offer counterarguments. Although presenting a demand in drag to the board of trustees may be questionable, where is the empirical evidence demonstrating that when gay and lesbian people have played by the rules, our demands have been met? For that matter, is there any evidence that groups who are discriminated against have a better chance to lessen their stigma and attain their rights if they try to act as the mainstream does? Where does the problem lie—with the sashaying and queeny individual, with the media, or with myself—when I am uncomfortable with my persona being subsumed by a representation that is dramatically different from how I construct my identity? If similarities are to be accepted as a cultural good, does it mean that I ought to strive to erase from myself any differences from the norm? And again, rather than simply desiring to finagle an invitation to the table, should we not be more concerned about who's handing out the invitations and what we have to do to get invited?

The assimilationists' complaint always has existed in oppressed groups. A Jewish friend noted how Bawer's *A Place at the Table* reminded him of discussions about the "good Jew" before the Holocaust who was admonished to fit in, to get along, and not be so different from others. The African American author Shelby Steele (1990) has written in a similar vein about African Americans. The history of immigration in the United States is one of debate and argument about the need for different groups to assimilate into the mainstream. Bilingualism and legislation that seeks to make English the official language of a state or the country is another variant of encouraging individuals and groups to become more like the norm. The first Americans in this country—Native Americans—have long been encouraged to drop their tribal ways and become more like their European visitors.

Yet Bawer also discusses how he worked for a rabidly homophobic magazine, *The American Spectator,* and tried to overlook the homophobia because he agreed with most of their political stances. How far must we go to fit into the mainstream? Should native people be forced to cut their braids so they will appear more like Anglos? Should Hispanic parents avoid teaching their children Spanish so they will only speak English? Should Hasidic Jews try to appear more mainstream? There is no simple generalizable rule for every situation for every group, but I do offer a rule of thumb: The definition of cultural democracy that I work from begins with the assumption that cultural difference and integrity are a strength rather than an impediment to securing the kind of nation we want to become. I am suggesting that in the long run, oppressed groups in general have not benefited when they have been forced to endure the subjugation of their ethnic and cultural identity in order to attain benefits that the mainstream holds out to them. And yet there will always be individuals who honestly believe that the correct tactic to take in the struggle for human rights is that of dignity and logic. We must always appear dignified. We must always beat the racist's hate, or the homophobe's taunts, with the cool logic of reason.

I want to be clear here. I agree with part of what Bawer espouses and Sullivan's logic is especially appealing. Bawer would probably not belittle my own personal actions, because I wear my Armani suit when I meet the university president and know how to act to meet the approval of the board; Sullivan may well agree with many of the suggestions I develop in Part II of the text. I am well aware of the cultural and political capital necessary to advance a particular cause; I spend it judiciously and with purpose. Assimilationist and queer proponents also often have many of the same requests and demands. I want a domestic partnership agreement that guarantees Barry and me the same rights that straight people have. I want equal housing agreements that ensure that someone cannot be evicted from their apartment simply because they are gay. Barry and I also lead lives that are not unlike the lives of our heterosexual neighbors: We work too hard, we enjoy one another's company, we go to the theater and symphony performances, we eat out at yuppie restaurants every once in a while and try to figure out how we can remodel the bathroom without going bankrupt.

I also agree that behavior and actions need to be evaluated. That is, we should not simplemindedly accept all actions as equal. Some acts are reprehensible and should not be condoned. I am thinking here, for example, of the ongoing controversy that surrounds the pedophile movement, NAMBLA. I suppose it is theoretically possible that someone over the age of 18 could have a meaningful sexual relationship with someone under the age of 18. The age of 18 as the age of consent is also problematic. Why not 17 or 19? We also know that adult and child relationships have occurred in other cultures and other centuries without harm to the child. However, we do not live in other cultures and other centuries, and we know that terrific physical and emotional pain has been done to children who have been molested by adults. Consent is central to a fulfilling relationship, and I do not believe that in general children can provide meaningful consent for a sexual relationship with an adult. I have little difficulty in condemning groups such as NAMBLA and not wanting to have anything to do with them.

I also bemoan any individual or group's self-absorption, so that they are unaware that their actions may have unintended consequences. Awareness of how others perceive us is crucial in any number of instances. A candidate who applies for a faculty position with a resume that holds numerous typographical errors will not get very far. A group that freely uses swear words in its announcements will invite rejection from groups that find obscenity objectionable and vulgar. If the group's intent is to shock and confront, then placards laden with street language may be appropriate. What concerns me is when individuals have not thought about the consequence of their actions. In our actions, we need to consider the possible consequences of what we intend to do and be aware that a message not only involves the sender, but also the receiver. The point is not that we should subsume our differences in order to be like the mainstream, but that we should be aware of how the mainstream will perceive our differences and go on from there.

A community implies membership, rights, and responsibilities. We cannot claim a place at the table simply because we are alive. Actually, we are assured a place at the table, but our actions can remove us, and therein lies the philosophical disagreement between what I have advanced here and what assimilationists offer. We should be assured a place at the table, whereas assimilationists focus on what we must do to get invited to the table. Those who hold the invitations are the powerful, who in this case are the heterosexuals—and in other instances are those who hold economic, racial, gender privileges. Rather than ask how we should conform to get a seat at the table, we need to consider the parameters of community, who is excluded and included, and what we all must do to advance a notion of community based on difference rather than similarity.

Thus, the assimilationists' argument is flawed on moral grounds if we accept the notions advanced in Chapters 1 and 2. A cultural studies derived from postmodernism rejects assimilation and metanarratives, and that is precisely what individuals such as Bawer would have us accept. The reason we reject one singular version of community is that, as Shane Phelan (1989) writes, "Metanarratives are those discourses that establish the rules of truth and legitimacy for narratives, the stories we tell ourselves about the world" (p. 140). As noted in Chapter 1, the work of cultural studies is to investigate the mediating aspects of culture, to interrogate its grammar and decenter its norms. The metanarrative of heterosexuality is manifested by our need to present our queer selves in a particular manner and by the way popular culture presents us. The result is that we face discrimination and silencing. Again, Phelan is helpful. She writes, "The struggles for a positive self-understanding and a sense of historical community have been conducted as a struggle to redefine and redescribe lesbians and lesbianism" (p. 135). Such a suggestion is the exact opposite of what assimilationists would have us do. By definition, assimilationists want us to fit in—to assimilate—and in doing so, presumably our queer identities will vanish. "Gays exist as a group," Bawer writes, "because there is anti-gay prejudice" (p. 86). If we behave ourselves, the vast heterosexual majority will welcome us to the table and the homophobes will be beaten. We will gain political rights. Thus, rather than try to decenter norms and investigate the language that is used to silence us, the assimilationists' hope is that we understand those norms and try to work within them.

The philosophical assumption that we can develop a world where we are all alike is at worst intellectually flawed and at best, boring. If we return to the four levels of response that I initially raised about the assimilationists' perspective, it becomes clearer why they are on the wrong track. On a political level, anyone who has been involved in change efforts knows that there are times when breaking the rules, or even the law, is morally justified. One need look no further than the civil rights marches led by Martin Luther King, Jr. to witness moments when another oppressed group demonstrated in ways that were not always appropriate to Bawer's decorum. Gandhi is another example. Ida B. Wells offers another challenge. If King, Gandhi and Wells had followed the assimilationists' logic, they would have tried to fit in hoping that acting more like the White, or the British, or the male, would propel their movements forward to equity. They chose another viable route.

On a personal level, I am hard-pressed to understand why the actions of others must be my own concerns. I fully understand that someone may slow a movement toward a particular goal by using a route that I would not use, but when we concentrate strictly on cultural artifacts such as clothes or street theater, we overlook the structure in which the event itself occurs. Again, assimilationists use culture in a way I do not. For example, I have two brothers who went to Notre Dame; I first taught at Penn State University and I now teach at the University of Southern California. Each university has a culture framed by football. On any fall weekend, I will turn on the television and see at least one of these schools enmeshed in a fierce football game with another major team. When the camera pans on the student body, invariably there are half-clad men and women who have painted their bodies blue and white, or green and gold, or cardinal and gold. As the months proceed and the temperature plunges, the students continue their antics. I have never heard people suggest that they are ashamed of being a Nittany Lion, a Fighting Irishman, or a Trojan simply because members of their community are dressed absurdly or, in the case of frigid weather, stupidly. The norm is that we laugh and applaud their school spirit. Penn Staters or the Fighting Irish or the Trojans are not summarily defined as half-naked and often drunken schoolboys who have painted their bodies; if that is the case, then we need to investigate why one popular icon gets interpreted one way and a similar icon—drag queens at a Gay Pride march—gets interpreted in an entirely different manner.

On a cultural level, I want us to concentrate not simply on similarities, but also differences. To say that I would have nothing in common with another queer if there were no prejudice is to conjure up an impossible world; it denies community to those of us who are different. Such a view also reinforces notions of a stable identity where the onus lies on the individual to conform to the power of the norm in the quest for civil rights and civil liberties. As I will explain in the next chapter, the point is not to argue that my differences from yours are so great that dialogue is impossible, but rather to consider how we might engage in dialogues of respect that honor difference. Instead of assuming that identity is fixed and determined, I work from the assumption that we are constantly in the process of redefinition and discovery about ourselves as well as each other. I get to the table not because I have proven my similarity to you, but because you cannot do without me in a world that is based on mutual respect and understanding—agape. Thus, where I find the political framework of assimilationists such as Sullivan flawed is that they fail to interrogate the philosophical basis for their politics which in turn feeds back on the cultural logic of the state. In effect, Sullivan infuses a rationality into his perspective that does not exist, otherwise we would not have been as mistreated and silenced as we have.

I am advancing a notion of community in keeping with what Audre Lorde (1985) described when she wrote, "We do not have to become each other's unique experiences and insights in order to share what we have learned through our particular battles for survival" (p. 8). The assumption of Lorde's comment is in keeping with the ideas discussed in Chapters 1 and 2. We do not have to renounce our identity in our engagement with one another, and indeed, if we must do so, then our idea of community is fundamentally flawed and true community will never be achieved. Previously, I have written that the organizing concept that we need to develop for community is not that of individuals who are invited to a table party or a legal forum but, rather, the idea of agape:

> An organization that works from the ideal of agape operates in a fundamentally different manner from other organizations. The underlying tenet here is that all life is interrelated. We are so connected with one another that if you are in pain, so am I. It is impossible to have a healthy institution when different individuals and constituencies are in pain. . . . The essence of this idea is that we are commanded to create community and to resist injustice. (Tierney, 1993, p. 23)

Martin Luther King, Jr. (1958) used agape as his organizing centerpiece. "I came to feel," he wrote, "that this was the only morally and practically sound method open to oppressed people in their struggle for freedom" (p. 79). Agape suggests that we accept one another's differences and work from those differences to build solidarity. Such an idea is fundamentally different from the assimilationists' notion that we must fit in. My assumption is that marginalization is perpetuated even when new voices are added to a group, but the core beliefs of the group do not change. The point then becomes that community cannot exist if all groups are not at the table, rather than considering what queers must do to be asked to the table.

Finally, on a metaphorical level, we obviously move the idea away from invitations and toward acceptance. Community implies inclusion, not exclusion. And yet community also implies responsibilities. How might we act if we use Bawer's notion of the need to get invited to the party, and how might we act if we take our acceptance at the table as a given? The answers to these questions imply two quite different strategies for action.

Table Manners

As I will explain in the following chapter, unlike any other oppressed group, one key factor for queers is that we actually may be able to dine at the table of the norm without the hosts and other guests being aware of our presence. We can hide our sexuality, or the others assembled at the table may choose to overlook who we are, or more likely, their heterosexism makes them oblivious to any sexual orientation other than heterosexuality. Barry and I went to a university function recently where wealthy donors were in attendance. I had to give a talk, and afterward, there was informal conversation. At one point, an elderly woman came up to us and we told her how busy we were, given that we had just moved to Los Angeles from Pennsylvania. She said, "You fellahs need wives. That's what you need. Then you won't be so busy." When I told her we were gay she responded, "That's nice. I'm glad you're happy to be here. California is fun! I'm sure you'll enjoy it." Proust could not have concocted a better situation for wordplay, misunderstanding and melancholia.

The situation was ironic and, in its own right, mildly humorous. The woman was approaching 80 and she was trying to be nice. I am never sure how far one must go to impress on a listener that I am queer. I suppose I could have said, "We're queer," but it may well have been just as likely that she would have responded as my mother did about my erstwhile college chum. And yet, amidst the canapés and champagne, once again heterosexism had reared its head. The problem of invisibility is an issue that confronts us every day.

How many of us are there? In the past decade there has been a great deal of discussion about whether we account for ten percent of the population as has long been reported, or if we are substantially less in number. Three mistaken ideas drive the desire to downsize the queer population. First, virtually all of the comprehensive studies that have been done about sexual attitudes and mores are based on face-to-face interviews. I know individuals who will not tell their best friends that they are lesbian or gay; why would they tell a stranger? Indeed, I wonder what percentage of the population is queer but is unable to acknowledge this fact even to themselves. Second, when the number of queer people is downsized to two, three, or four percent, the straight population readily accepts the number in large part because it makes common sense to them. Most people do not know anyone who is lesbian or gay, the thinking goes, and now we know why: There are only two in one hundred. Perhaps if everyone were open about their sexuality, the straight population would recognize the absurdity of the low reporting. Third, this obsession with knowing how many of us there are and discovering that we are less than originally reported is trumpeted as somehow making the cause of human rights less important. Of course, this goes against the ideal of agape. That queer people account for ten percent, five percent or fifty percent of the population is irrelevant. The cause of human rights and social justice is not a numbers game. Simply because Native Americans account for only one percent of the U.S. population or Jews are only five percent of the nation does not imply, therefore, that they can be discriminated against; in a democracy, everyone is accorded a place at the table of human rights, not only those who are statistically significant.

The implications of the underreporting and invisibility of lesbian and gay people are manifold. We of course should demand greater methodological rigor when sexual surveys are done. Funding agencies might also show more concern about how research is done that is obviously flawed methodologically and has important policy implications. The case should also continue to be made that statistical significance is irrelevant with regard to human rights. But most important, for those of us who are queer, we need, so to speak, to think about our table manners.

Even cultural conservatives acknowledge the need for individuals to come out and let others know that we are lesbian, gay or bisexual. The challenge, however, is not simply to come out, but the form our coming out takes. There are those who advocate an "in your face" action where we zap shopping malls and have a kiss-in, and others who believe a bit more decorum, to put it mildly, is in order. I am uncertain why we so often back ourselves into a corner of accepting either one approach or the other. In political struggles, tactics are all-important. As there is little evidence to support the conservative approach, it is equally fallacious to assume that confrontation is necessary at every turn. Even Michelangelo Signorile

(1993), the inventor, so to speak, of outing, said, "The only way to have a chance to change the minds of people who don't agree with you—after you get their attention—is by presenting the arguments rationally and respectfully" (p. 397). We need to understand what counts for good etiquette at a table; and when following the etiquette either succeeds in silencing or marginalizing us, then we need to discard that approach. I suspect that French-kissing Barry in front of an 80-year-old donor would not have advanced our cause very much, but I also know that a die-in for AIDS on the steps of Old Main when the board of trustees is meeting can be an effective strategy to press a particular issue.

The assumption that logic and good behavior always will advance our cause can only be made by individuals who have not sufficiently involved themselves in minority issues and do not adequately understand the opposition. Who are those people with whom we sit down at the table? Many individuals are sincere, ignorant people who do not know anything about queers. To a certain extent we can educate them about the injustices we face by using a passionate logic that enables people to see that we are similar to their sons, daughters, brothers, sisters, husbands and wives. But the structure of the system is not devised for people to learn about the Other—be they queers, African Americans, or immigrants who speak a language other than English. Of consequence, such work is most often done on an individual level where we move ahead step-by-step. I honor such work and see it as a vital component to what needs to be done.

We must also realize, however, that structures exist to protect the status quo; individuals of ill will, or individuals who have no interest in learning, are often in positions of power. Logic and honest dialogue are not sufficient for such people. Some years ago, for example, the queer communities at Penn State wanted to amend the statement on nondiscrimination to include sexual orientation as a category. We received support from the student body, the faculty senate, many members of faculty, and various schools at the university. However, the university has a very conservative board of trustees and the president at the time could not have cared less about the issue. At an acrimonious meeting, he acknowledged that he knew some individuals who were "homosexual" and had even had them to his house for dinner, but he had never discussed their sexual orientation with them. It was a private matter, he believed. Not surprisingly, what he proposed for the institution was that the statement of nondiscrimination be changed to say that the university was against all forms of discrimination, without mentioning sexual orientation. Here was an example, then, of how an individual could not get beyond his heterosexism. He was against blatant prejudice, but he was unable to see how the invisibility of a group reinforces prejudice. A suggestion to say merely that discrimination was wrong and not to name that discrimination was insufficient to us, so we were at a standoff with the administration.

The leader of the university, then, was an individual who at least was not overtly bigoted, but his refusal to engage individuals about their personal lives exhibited to many of us the worst form of paternalism, power and privilege. In effect, we could be invited to dinner but we had to render a significant part of ourselves invisible. In such circumstances, it would have been inappropriate for Barry and me to discuss our vacation plans, speak about our mutual activities with one another's families, or to engage in the familiar repartee that couples who know one another intimately so often display. We would not have been intimate companions but merely acquaintances. Institutionalized censorship of this kind reinscribes the power of the norm when overt acts of discrimination do not occur—being dismissed from the dinner table—because the oppressed deny themselves the same rights as those who are in the norm possess (Tierney, 1992). Self-censorship is not always bad. There is no point in needlessly offending someone. However, if I am to offend someone by merely making my sexual orientation known to them, then so be it.

We proposed a demonstration at Penn State where we were going to encircle Old Main with the hope of creating a media uproar. When the administration got wind of the demonstration, a vice president arranged a secret meeting offcampus with two student leaders and me. We agreed to call off the demonstration if they agreed to move the issue forward and lobby the board of trustees. We also let them know that we would not give up and would continue to create disturbances until the board put the phrase "sexual orientation" in their statement of nondiscrimination. The proposal eventually passed the board of trustees not because it was morally right, or our dispassionate rhetoric had convinced them, but because the administration finally realized that they would not be able to deal with other issues until they had resolved this one. It is unfortunate that oppressed and disempowered groups have to resort to confrontational styles in order to achieve our goals, but it would be even more disappointing if we simply accepted the status quo and its history of injustices.

Assimilationists would have us believe that ACT-UP, Queer Nation and other such groups have not advanced our cause and, if anything, have retarded the onset of gay rights. "It is necessary," writes Sullivan (1995), "to conform to certain disciplines in order to reform them" (p. 92). From this perspective, radical action is always wrong. I disagree. As the example above shows, there are times when individuals need to speak up, act up and demand that those who hold the power change. Some people are wicked. Other individuals in powerful positions are not malevolent, but they have no concern for people other than themselves. As we should not demonize everyone, so we should also not make the assumption that everyone just needs to learn about us for discrimination to change. We must employ multiple strategies to foment change because all the goodwill in the world will not alter an unjust structure that is manipulated by individuals who have an interest in preserving that structure.

Bawer (1993) notes that "self-respecting homosexuals who live openly among accepting people have no more problems or different problems than anyone else" (p. 97). Such commentary is lamentable. Who gets to decide whether Barry and I are self-respecting, what it means to live openly, and how accepting people act? The desire here is to make our lives "indistinguishable from the lives of heterosexuals" (p. 97). I hope for the opposite. I would like people to be able to live their lives on their own terms and not have to be indistinguishable in order for them to have the same rights and responsibilities accorded to those in the norm. The assimilationists' inability to see that we live in interpretive communities where one person's self-respect is another person's sashaying and queeny posing, precludes acknowledging the diversity that ultimately lies at the heart of the idea of agape. We are told to make ourselves over in the image of those who hold power. Rather than place the onus of change on those who perpetuate the structure of heterosexism, the assimilationists scold us that we are not acting appropriately enough to be invited for dinner.

Toward the close of his book, Bawer paints a melancholy portrait of his return to New York City from the march on Washington. The march brought up everything that Bawer detests: confrontation, questionable tactics, effeminate types, dykes on bikes. But on the train back to New York, he noticed that most of the individuals were gay couples whose "heads rested casually on their partners' shoulders as they dozed" (p. 222). Again, such a scene is what Bawer, Sullivan, Signorile, I, and countless others would like simply to be part of a normal day. Barry and I hold hands in public quite often; I would like to do so without the fear of imminent attack, or to have to think of such a small act of affection as a political act. However, the tactics which will enable us to do so will not come about by subsuming our queer identities, or merely learning good table manners. As

Guillory (1993) has noted, "Exclusion should be defined not as exclusion from representation but from access to the *means of cultural production*" (p. 18). That is, we cannot simply wish to be included at the table; we must desire—demand—that we are equal partners at the table where we honor one another's differences. In effect, we not only get to the table, but we also have a say in what's on the menu. Cultural capital, then, does not mean that we understand what good table manners are, but that we have the ability to produce meaning.

The Social Geography of Sexual Orientation

What are the implications for academe if we demand access to the means of cultural production? I believe there are many. Indeed, implications exist for academe in general and for queer studies in particular. And again, many of these implications have direct linkages to cultural studies. Only a generation ago, the study of homosexuality was almost exclusively in the domain of traditional departments such as psychology and sociology, and the perspective from which it was studied was exclusively that which was based on theories of deviance. The norm of the table or how individuals were to act at the table went unquestioned. The more liberal philosophies were those that sought to help the homosexual adapt rather than those that condemned. Foucault's (1979) work on the criminal justice system is helpful insofar as we can see constant disciplinary movements defining the homosexual as sick and in need of help, as a criminal in need of punishment, or as beyond help.

A queer studies of the kind I am suggesting works from different assumptions and investigates entirely different topics and issues. We move away from analyses, for example, that operate from an assumption that ultimately the object under study needs some form of treatment and toward an understanding of how the queer identity has been constructed by the social, cultural and historical parameters of a particular investigation. What does this specifically imply for someone interested in studying queers? Rather than focus on the individual and work from a deficit model of how he or she has come to deviate from the norm, we look at the broader range of social issues from a number of perspectives in order to come to terms with how the queer identity has been shaped and formed. I do not intend to offer a doctrinaire analysis here that suggests that when one studies queers, one must work from a particular perspective. Indeed, if cultural studies suggests anything, it is that multiple perspectives are helpful and necessary. As Best and Kellner (1991) have commented, "A multidimensional critical theory is dialectical and non-reductive. It conceptualizes the connections between the political, economic, social and cultural dimensions of society and refuses to reduce social phenomena to any one dimension" (p. 263). For example, one may construct a life history of one individual (Tierney, 1994), undertake a historical analysis of gay lives at a particular location over a period of time (Chauncey, 1994), or determine how a specific culture has defined the meaning of gay (Williams, 1992). All of these and many other approaches are viable. From the perspective advanced here, what frames queer investigations are two central points:

1. Studies that are decontextualized, ahistorical, and based on strictly essentialistic psychological models of the individual are dropped in favor of work that is constructionist and informed by a sociocultural understanding of the world.
2. The purpose of queer studies is more than simply the production of queer theory. Queer theorists advocate change and become involved in change processes.

By offering these two points, I am arguing for a distinctly different formation of study than many proponents of gay studies would accept. As there are feminists who are positivists, there undoubtedly will be lesbian, gay and bisexual scholars who desire the professionalization of knowledge in quite standard ways. I in no way mean to denigrate a particular venue for investigation, but it is important to point out that simply because a group of people study a queer theme does not mean that they are philosophically and intellectually bound together. Advocacy is also a topic of heated debate in academic circles. There are gay and straight intellectuals who want nothing to do with anything they determine is political. Their focus is to advance one or another theory. As noted earlier, cultural studies works from the assumption that all work is political and what needs to be done is the unmasking of the ideological parameters in all investigative work. By adopting an approach that seeks to reconfigure what social investigation might look like, I am suggesting that queer studies place itself at the heart of discussions about how the academy might change.

The assimilationist hopes for a day when whether a writer is gay or straight is irrelevant. Conservative proponents of gay studies see a day when a departmental configuration exists in which scholars who study different aspects of lesbian and gay lives come together. They would like to see structural changes occur in tenure line appointments, professional journals and conferences. They also assume that as traditional departments such as economics may have a Marxist, capitalist, and structuralist on their staff, so should a gay and lesbian studies department. I am suggesting an alternative configuration. In the text's final chapters, I return to this discussion with structural possibilities, but for now, I offer four points that pertain to how a cultural studies of queer theory might be attempted:

Denorming

As suggested throughout this chapter, conservative and liberal notions of the table are dropped. We do not unproblematically assume that invitations should be proffered to all individuals without first considering how it is that some individuals are invited and others are not. Researchers work to understand how norms came into existence, how they have been maintained, and how strategies have been employed to silence different groups.

Textual Production

If the object under investigation is seen as a text, we then extend the idea of denorming one step further. We look at the forces of cultural production that surround a particular investigation and try to come to terms with taken-for-granted meanings, how they have been constructed, by whom, and how they might change. What is the relation of power to the marginalizing of individuals?

Empowerment

If we consider how taken-for-granted assumptions have been constructed and how they might change, we then concern ourselves with how disempowered groups might develop access to the means of cultural production—cultural capital. As Guillory noted above, the point of cultural capital is not simply that we are able to place a queer or two in a canon of readings, but rather that we are able to empower lesbian, gay and bisexual people to attain the forces of production so that they are, in effect, not invited to the table, but participate mutually in the construction of the table.

Progress

History is not a linear narrative but rather a series of ruptures and displacements. We are ever vigilant as to how queer identities are shaped, how the forms of cultural production can incorporate images without significant structural change, and how historical constructions do not merely define how things were, but instead provide clues for how current society defines a particular area of inquiry.

These four points underscore why popular culture is so often an object of investigation for cultural studies. How have queer identities been portrayed? We know, for example, that the writers of *Melrose Place,* a popular television show, have had trouble with how to deal with the gay character in the show. Whereas every other central character has multiple lovers and steamy love scenes, the gay character, Matt, has most often been seen alone, or with a straight-acting former soldier, or a misguided bisexual doctor. For a few weeks, Matt played loving uncle to a little girl whose mother went off to Russia. During another few weeks, he came to the aid of one of the characters of the cast. When they finally got Matt into a relationship, they were unable to portray him kissing his lover on screen. Eventually, the viewer learns that Matt's lover is HIV positive; at another time the viewer learns Matt's latest flame is mentally disturbed. At a minimum, what the writers have been able to do is to move Matt's character along a particular plot line without having to show Matt kissing a man. The portrait of Matt, however loving and sensitive he may be, is of an individual who presumably did unspeakable things in bed, because he is the only one whom the viewer does not see there. Paradoxically, by the absence of any sexual contact with another man, Matt's sexuality becomes his defining characteristic.

Gay themes on television consistently follow similar plot lines. One possibility is that a straight character is mistaken for a gay man and is propositioned. More than ten years ago, this happened to Tony Danza in *Taxi,* and more recently it has occurred to Hayden in *Coach,* Miles in *Murphy Brown,* Jerry Seinfeld in *Seinfeld,* and Frasier Crane in *Frasier.* The joke, of course, is that these characters could not possibly be gay. Another possibility is to have a gay character who primarily exists in order to make a funny retort that highlights the rapier wit of, in general, gay men. (Lesbians are most often overlooked.) AIDS has provided a convenient vehicle as well to highlight how men may love one another without having to show men physically loving one another. There are, of course, vampires and serial killers who turn out to have homosexual tendencies, but in general, a casual viewing of popular culture might suggest that much progress has been made. Whereas a generation ago we never saw an explicitly gay character on television, we are now able to see them with increasing frequency, and they are often viewed in a positive light. The gay men who pursued Miles and Frasier, for example, were witty, intelligent and handsome men—not swishy, queeny acting. And although we still have more than a fair share of serial killers—*The Silence of the Lambs* comes to mind—we also have individuals who are made out to be heroes (Tom Hanks, in *Philadelphia*), albeit asexual heroes.

I do not intend to go into an exegesis of queer portrayals in popular culture over the past decade, but rather to highlight the importance cultural studies has for understanding queer theory. Rather than simply accept that progress has been made, for example, we need to come to terms with the manner in which queer people are constructed in relation to the norm. That is, although it is true queers are seen in a more positive light, they are still seen in two structural venues: (a) Gays lead gay lives, and (b) they exist by invitation. Lesbian and gay people always come out, so to speak, with queer portrayals. We are not merely the neighbor next door; now we are the gay neighbor next door. The idea that someone's sexual orientation is at the same time incidental and fundamental goes to the heart of denorming and textual production. If the viewer is unable simultaneously to see a queer as both similar and different from him or herself, then is it not fair to ask how much progress has been made? We are still seen as fundamentally different from the norm. In many respects, our actions on television are often in keeping with how minstrel shows portrayed African Americans two and three generations ago—comic, harmless creatures.

The gay man who is to be pitied is not someone who we think is empowered; rather, he is someone who exists by the goodwill of his heterosexual friends and family. The man who has AIDS goes home to find that his folks can accept him. The good-looking fellow who has a crush on Tony Danza finds that Tony will still be a friend, if not a lover. Matt lives with a good bunch of friends who accept him for who he is, even if he cannot be shown on television kissing his lover. The problem here, of course, is that all of these queer lives are seen in relation to the norm. This is progress?

The ironic—and critical—point about gay portrayals in popular culture is that although we bemoan such constructions, we also need to come to terms with the positive aspects that have taken place. Movement has occurred when positive queer characters are in a show. The challenges that two gay men have when one of them is HIV positive is a worthwhile plot line. I know of men who had AIDS and found love and support from their families. The show *Friends* had a lesbian wedding that was for the most part an affirming and positive portrayal. The point, then, is not to deride every portrayal that occurs in the mainstream media, but to use a cultural studies approach for how textual production occurs, how it has changed, and what yet needs to occur. In doing so, the researcher's role in academe is inevitably different from that of the disengaged intellectual safely lodged in an academic department.

I began this chapter by asking who invited the presumably heterosexual couple to the Halloween festivities in West Hollywood. I likened their observations to the uninvited tourist or researcher who is culturally different from a people but wants to obtain good data or good photos to take back home. I also questioned why queers must accept invitations to get a place at the table. On one level, there is a contradiction here. The implication is that someone needs an invitation to observe Halloween or Semana Santa, but queers should not have to be invited to the table. If I am advocating that queer folks should crash the party, so to speak, why can researchers and academics not crash parties too? The difference again brings into focus the four points I mentioned above: (a) denorming, (b) textual production, (c) empowerment, and (d) progress. From the perspective of cultural studies, the researcher needs to take into account his or her position of power and the role their texts play in the construction of norms. Crossing cultural borders may not need explicit invitations, but they need more sensitivity than simply that of the observer who has come to photograph an odd species or an exotic event. Empowerment begins with honest engagement between the observer and the observed.

On the other hand, the demand for acceptance at humanity's table is based on a view of community that accepts the fundamental interrelatedness of individuals and groups. We should not simplemindedly open up a process so everyone gets included, but the structure does not in essence change, for ultimately little changes. Instead, the idea of agape includes thinking about how we are able to change structures so that we enter into communion with one another. Marginalization is maintained if queers get to the table but the structure of the organization remains unchanged. This is why it is so important for us to look at lesbian and gay characters on television and in the popular media not as inevitable points of progress but as additions to a structure that maintains the norms of heterosexism. As Patrick Hill (1991) has observed, "Were a college or university truly committed to democratic pluralism, it would proceed to create conditions under which the representatives of different cultures need to have conversations of respect with each other in order to do their everyday teaching and research" (p. 44). Thus, when we use cultural studies, when we struggle to enact agape, we think of invitations in precisely the manner I have used them here. We accept and honor difference and struggle to come to terms with how we can understand better those who are different, and we also challenge a system that holds out invitations to some only if they will regress to the norm.

Thanksgiving at Our Table

I suppose most individuals, couples, and families have particular days that they mark as their own and that are more special than others. My brother Peter, for example, has made St. Patrick's Day a big day at his house because it highlights the Tierney family's Irish lineage. Barry and I have friends who always celebrate Easter with a magnificent meal. Thanksgiving has been a particular marker for Barry and me. We always have invited a houseful of people for dinner. Our first year in Los Angeles was no different, even though we only had recently moved to the area. The phone rang on and off throughout the day as friends and family called to wish us well. A baker's dozen of friends arrived in the early afternoon, and after drinking an eggnog that was almost too potent, we sat down at our table and ate a meal that could not have been better.

Toward the end of Bruce Bawer's (1993) book, he offers what he claims is a valuable message for gays in the 1990s: "Don't ask for a medal; don't feel sorry for yourself. Being gay is an inconvenience; so are a lot of things; get on with it" (p. 201). This chapter, indeed this text, stands in contradistinction to such comments. To be sure, we do not need medals and should not feel an all-consuming sadness. However, the assimilationist belief that my sexual orientation is inconvenient is in keeping with the assumption that individuals and groups who differ from the norm somehow need to conform so that they can get on with it.

A traffic jam on the Hollywood Freeway is inconvenient. A phone call when Barry and I have gone to bed is inconvenient. The realization that we are out of balsamic vinegar when I am making the salad for Thanksgiving is definitely inconvenient. My sexual orientation is not. Being gay is a gift for it has brought me particular ways of seeing and experiencing the world. I have made remarkable friendships with individuals—queer and straight—who I might not have known had I not been who I am. And most important, I have met Barry.

Yet I know what Bawer means. It is inconvenient when I am rushing somewhere and someone asks me a heterosexist question that presupposes I am married. I need to stop and pause and wonder whether it is worth the time to tell the person I may have only just met and may never meet again about my sexual orientation. But assimilationists fail to see the strength we have found, the ability to help change the world, because we are queer. As I discuss in the next chapter, a queer sexuality has also allowed me to create the possibility of alliances with a rich diversity of people whom I otherwise may not have met. Our queer lives have created much joy and communion with others. And this was what we gave thanks for at our queer table.

Chapter 4

A World of Five-Second Comments

Five Seconds of Bigotry

My brother Peter was the first person in my family to learn from me that I was gay. Every coming-out story has its own specific ingredients of irony and poignancy, but what unites almost all stories is the fear we feel as we embark on telling someone about our sexual orientation. My brother and I enjoy hiking, so I suggested we go for a hike as a way to tell him my news. On a sunny summer day, Peter and I climbed two 14,000-foot mountains near his home in Boulder, Colorado. His wife, Carol, and my nephew and niece stayed home, as did my "roommate," Barry. On the scale of mountain climbing, Grays and Torreys Peaks are simple. A clear trail takes hikers to one peak, and then another trail works across the saddle, finally reaching the second peak. As with virtually all 14,000-foot mountains in Colorado, the view from the top is incomparable, although on this specific day, I really did not notice the view. I had decided that I would tell Peter about Barry and myself, and I had resolved that I would tell him in the car so that we would have a nice climb together. Somehow the car trip did not seem to be the right time to tell him, so in the car I told myself that the walk up to the first mountaintop would be better. When we reached Grays Peak, I realized that actually the walk to the second mountaintop would be more appropriate; then as we walked along the saddle, I hesitated again and thought perhaps it would actually be best if I told him when we reached the second vista.

As we relaxed in the sunshine at the second peak, I still had not told Peter and wondered if today was the best time after all. Maybe on the way home?

The discussion on the hike home turned to our family, as often happens with my brother. Peter recalled how difficult it had been for him when he returned from the Peace Corps and moved back in with my folks and me. We were a devout Irish Catholic family and my older brother had decided that he no longer believed in the Catholic Church. I can count on one hand the number of times I saw my father get visibly angry, and Peter's proclamation that he would not attend Sunday mass any longer was one of those times. My father tried to throw my brother out of the house, but it was not in my father's nature to do such a thing, and he relented. Nevertheless, Peter was angry at my father's threat and ready to leave; what kept him in the house was a note I had written him telling him to stay. As he recounted this story, he pulled the note out of his pocket and I saw my child's handwriting and a letter I had long since forgotten, but he had kept in his wallet for more than twenty years. We leaned back and looked out at the "purple mountain's majesty" and Peter said, "I can't ever imagine Dad getting more angry than he was that day." We continued to gaze out over America and I asked, "What if I told him I was gay and that Barry and I were lovers?" A pause. He nodded and said, "Yeah, that might do it." And then we laughed.

In the ensuing months, my brother served as intermediary and negotiator between my parents and me. Eventually my mom and dad came to accept and love Barry as a member of the family. Peter and my oldest brother, Paul, and their families have always made Barry and me feel as welcome in their homes as is humanly possible.

Some years later, when I turned 40, Peter uncharacteristically sent me a long letter. He said that reaching 40 years of age was an event in a person's life that should not go unmentioned, and he wanted to pass along some memories he had of me. The letter was a beautiful cascade of an older brother's remembering what his newborn kid brother was like when I had been brought home from the hospital and he had wanted to hold me, what it had been like growing up in a family in the 1950s, and how I had visited him when he was in the Peace Corps. He also mentioned that he was glad I had been able to tell him that I was gay, but he was disappointed that it had taken me so long. "I wish you had trusted me more," he wrote.

In turn, I sent a long letter to him recounting my own memories and how close I felt to him. I also told him of a Christmas visit I made to his house when I had entered college. A gay friend of theirs had stayed with them a week before my visit and Peter recalled in wry terms how the gay man had decorated the Christmas tree. He told me that day that he actually felt that there was nothing wrong with homosexuality but that the idea of it "disgusted" him. His comments were made in the flash of a moment in the early 1970s. At that time I was so closeted that I could not come out to myself, much less anyone else. But I wrote in my letter to Peter that "those five seconds were all I needed to hear from you, because gay people live in a world of five-second comments." I surely did not want to be an object of ridicule, or disgust anyone, especially my brother, so I bracketed off that part of myself.

My queer self has changed so that today I would undoubtedly challenge someone—especially someone close to me—if they made an ignorant comment, but I often flash on my interchanges with Peter at unexpected moments. Some weeks ago an African American professor called me and told me how she had been appointed to an admissions committee and the previous chair had given her instructions. "Get this," she told me, "Sally said not to accept any international students, to just send their files upstairs!" She laughed, "I wonder if it hadn't been me whether she'd have said not to accept any Negroes either!" I laughed along with her and thought of a candidate who had visited Penn State when I was there. She was lesbian, but no one at the institution except for me knew it. She told me of her interview with her prospective department chair: "He made a joke about 'our Polish dean.' Saying that about being Polish threw me off. I wonder how the department chair would react if he knew I was lesbian." Eventually she withdrew from consideration.

Oppressed people endure countless, daily comments that force us to realize we are different and that, in many instances, those who make the comments have power over us. When my colleague noted how the ex-committee chair did not want international students and then thought about herself, I recalled my interaction with my brother. And yet oppression should not simply be accepted as a statement of fact as if all oppressed people are interchangeable. The challenges that straight Latinos and Latinas face, for example, are different from those of queers. In this chapter, I concentrate on those differences and similarities and then outline what we might do to create solidarity across groups.

Dueling Oppression

Oppression has gained a certain cachet in academic communities over the past few years that has made me uncomfortable. I have heard different individuals claim that they are oppressed because of their identification with one group or another. A young gay white male said to me at a conference that he felt oppressed by the heterosexist language used by many speakers; a senior Latina professor told me that she found her school's climate oppressive. An assistant professor in a school of business at a research university said tenure created oppression for him. A staff member who was bisexual said he felt oppressed because he was often overlooked by both straight and gay colleagues. A male administrator said anyone who wanted to know what oppression was like should try walking in his African American shoes for a day at his rural institution.

I also have lived and worked in areas where more traditional definitions of economic oppression might apply. The small Berber village in Morocco where I worked in the Peace Corps was a town without a doctor, running water, or electricity. Most of my students had no shoes, and one of them died from an illness that would have been easily preventable in the United States. As an undergraduate student, I worked in a homeless shelter in Boston and encountered men and women on a daily basis who owned nothing other than the clothes they wore. More recently, when Barry and I spent a year in Central America, I spent time in Guatemala where economists estimate that more than 60% of the population live in conditions of dire poverty. In an infamous area on the outskirts of the capital, thousands of people live in a garbage dump.

What, then, is oppression? Do we have any basis for saying that we are oppressed in academe when an alternative picture of oppression is a child eating refuse from a dump? I certainly do not mean to imply that any of the initial examples are false statements about oppression. Heterosexist language that renders me invisible can be oppressive, just as a tenure system can disempower assistant professors. Even if I have the power and privilege of being a full professor, I may still be oppressed, just as administrators of color might feel silenced and marginalized. Because identity is fluid and dependent on multiple interpretations, we have the potential to feel oppressed because of different actions on the part of others and our own internal makeup. And yet I am uncomfortable when the word falls off our lips too easily so that we appear neither to have processed what oppression means for me and just as importantly, what it means for someone else.

Oppression, in part, pertains to silencing, to being voiceless and invisible. In *Ain't I a Woman: Black Women and Feminism,* bell hooks (1981) writes, "No other group in America has so had their identity socialized out of existence as have black women" (p. 7). Later in the text, she points out her conviction "that the struggle to end racism and the struggle to end sexism were naturally intertwined" (p. 13). Throughout her texts, hooks offers powerful critiques of silencing. She is not only critical of those who overtly seek to repress and silence but also those individuals and groups with whom there should be alliances. She writes, for example, of her estrangement "from the huge group of white women who were celebrating the power of 'sisterhood.' I could not understand why they did not notice 'absences' or care" (hooks, 1989, p. 149). However much I resonate to her writing, as a queer reader I am troubled by our absence from her texts and those of others who also deal with multiculturalism, oppression and difference.

I ought not to create a self-defeating argument that purports to show that queers more than another group have had our identities "socialized out of existence." Such a strategy will only succeed in separating people who desperately need one another. I also need to be ever aware that gay white men in particular have specific economic privileges that other oppressed groups often do not have. However, I want us to honor one another as equals. Most often, lesbian and gay people are relegated to footnotes in texts about diversity. In Omi and Winant's (1994) book on racial formation, for example, we read, "Thus race, class, and gender (as well as sexual orientation) constitute 'regions' of hegemony, areas in which certain political projects can take shape" (p. 68). Why are we only noted within the parentheses? Some individuals and groups are ashamed that we claim solidarity with them, and others believe we are tangential to their argument. I hold the opposite belief: We have nothing to be ashamed of, and in discussions about oppression, we are central to understanding how marginalization functions.

I am not suggesting that all texts must offer a queer analysis. We need more, not fewer, studies that offer analyses based on race or gender or class or physical disability. However, far too often queers are relegated to commentaries within the parentheses, if at all, so that we are doubly silenced—by the mainstream and by those out of the mainstream who would rather not have to consider the messy topic of queer lives. Consider, for example, the usually insightful commentary of bell hooks.

At one point in a text, bell hooks (1989) argues for solidarity across groups. In particular, she notes how in Black communities "It must be continually stressed that our struggle against racism . . . is inextricably linked to all struggles to resist domination—including gay liberation" (p. 24). Unfortunately, whereas in one breath she calls for solidarity, in the next breath she demonstrates her ignorance of what it means to be queer:

> While we can acknowledge that gay people of all colors are harassed and suffer exploitation and domination, we also recognize that there is a significant difference that arises because of the visibility of dark skin.
>
> Often homophobic attacks on gay people occur in situations where knowledge of sexual preference is indicated or established—outside of gay bars, for example. While it in no way lessens the severity of such suffering for gay people, or the fear that is causes, it does not mean that in a given situation the apparatus of protection and survival may be simply not identifying as gay. In contrast, most people of color have no choice. No one can hide, change or mask dark skin color. White people, gay and straight, could show greater understanding of the impact of racial oppression on people of color by not attempting to make these oppressions synonymous but, rather, by showing the ways they are linked and yet differ. (p. 125)

Though sounding tolerant of difference, in one fell swoop, hooks seeks to erase my identity. Oppression gets defined as a violent act against someone, and all I have to do to deflect an attack is "simply not identify as gay." Such comments are always lamentable, but they are especially so in a writer as intelligent and sensitive as hooks. How is it possible for someone who concerns herself so much with the erasure of identity to advise us to obliterate our own? Once again, I hear a five-second slur, and I hear a voice telling me to hide, to suppress, to erase, to conceal who I am.

My point here is that oppression comes in various forms and ways. My obligation is not only to process what it means for me to be oppressed but also what oppression means for individuals who are different from me. A straight Black man undoubtedly faces obstacles and hurdles remarkably different from those challenges I face. The struggle for both of us, if we are to use the idea of agape, is to attempt to understand those differences and seek solidarity across them, rather than lessen, ignore, or try to obliterate, difference.

Some years ago, for example, I was a finalist for a dean's position at a major university. As the search committee winnowed the process they sent me the perfunctory information and told me that the provost would be calling to invite me to campus. Ironically, this was a campus that was interested in me because of my work with Native Americans, and some in the American Indian community were lobbying for me to be hired. Coincidentally, at the same time that my resume went into the provost's office, I published an article in a major magazine about gay and lesbian rights on college campuses. The provost read the article, did some additional checking, and found out that I was indeed homosexual. I received a polite letter saying that I would not be invited to campus because I would not be the right fit for what they wanted. I suppose if I had followed hooks's advice, I could have survived by simply not identifying as gay and erasing that part of myself. To be sure, an African American has no such choice, but to deflate the oppression queer people face to those moments when we walk out of a bar is to denigrate and misinterpret what it means to be queer in late 20th century America.

By saying that we face oppression in places other than bars is not to say that somehow my oppression is worse than yours, so that we create dueling oppression where there is a winner and loser. Indeed, hooks is correct when she calls for analyses that demonstrate how oppressions are linked and differ. A Black gay man, for example, who leaves that gay bar may not only face bigotry similar to that faced by his white counterpart, but he also may be unable to catch a cab home late at night—simply because he is Black. The oppressed person who is starving cannot even get into the bar. Thus, we need a better understanding of what we mean by oppression. In what follows, I outline five similarities and differences between queers and other groups that relate to the theoretical scaffolding previously outlined.

Similarities

Subjects/Objects. Oppressed groups are those that exist in relation to dominant norms. Blacks exist in relation to Whites; the physically challenged function in relation to the physically able, and queers exist in relation to heterosexuals. As subjects, groups define their own reality; as objects, those in the norm define reality for us. As Patricia Hill Collins (1991) notes, "Domination always involves attempts to objectify the subordinate group" (p. 69). Societies are sliced into dichotomies: black/white, queer/straight, and so on.

One key challenge is to realize that multiple dichotomies intersect with one another and often have competing demands. Community groups may call for a homeless shelter to feed the poor, and queer AIDS activists may demand greater public funding for AIDS prevention. Those in the norm are then capable of playing us off against one another, pointing out, for instance, that less funding goes to women's health than AIDS, or that not enough money exists for AIDS prevention because public money goes to low-income housing. What such an analysis highlights is that the norm should account for broad areas of civic understanding and definition. Individuals may simultaneously exist as object and subject in the public arena. A Chinese American may lobby for bilingualism in the schools and maintain that a queer-positive curriculum has no place in the classroom. Even issues of race break down according to specific ethnic or racial groups, so that during California's last election campaign, a solid majority of African Americans voted to deny public health and education to undocumented workers and their families, a majority of whom were Hispanic. Numerous public forums had a Latino or Latina arguing that Proposition 187 was a racist measure and an African American speaker suggesting that illegal aliens were taking jobs that should be held by members of the African American community.

Whenever there are discussions about removing Reserve Officers' Trainging Corps (ROTC) from a college campus because the armed services discriminate against queers, the administration invariably makes the point that low-income students will be hurt. There are even upscale homosexual Republicans who argue that they feel more at home in the Republican party in large part due to the economic policies of the party that reward the class to which they belong. Indeed, the economic power of many gay white men quite often places them in positions of oppressor and oppressed simultaneously.

There are too many divisions in the queer community that divide men from women, black from white, rich from poor. I would like to think that our community is more inclusive, but I have little other than anecdotal evidence to make such a comment. To be sure, on a dance floor on a given night it is entirely possible that greater racial, class and ethnic mixes exist than at a yuppie bar populated by my heterosexual friends. However, the gay male community has more than its fair share of members who are content to make casual sexist comments, to deny entry to a party to a particular racial group, or to look down on an individual who does not live in an similar economic class. Gay men seem particularly ageist and incapable of including our own senior citizens in our groups.

One similarity of oppressed groups, then, is that we exist in relation to dominant norms, and at the same time, we also often reside within a dominant norm. Exploiting such dichotomies is one way those in power are able to maintain norms. Individuals in groups recognize that other groups have interests quite different from theirs, so that alliances are not built and divisions remain on the border. We oppressed groups thus remain unable to articulate our own realities and instead have our identities and histories defined for us. "Objectification," writes Hill Collins (1991), "can be so severe that the Other simply disappears" (p. 69). What better description exists of queers? Throughout the 20th century, we did not exist—or if we did it was as deviants—if one is to read the histories done by those in the norm. Again, what unites oppressed groups is a mutual understanding that one way to change the relations between subject/object is to take control of naming so that we come into focus and exist for others and ourselves.

Standpoints. The ability to investigate how culture mediates life and how culture gets produced speaks to the need for oppressed groups to develop a specific standpoint from which they articulate who they are, where they have come from, and where they might go. As I will elaborate, naming who we are involves multiple acts—reclaiming our past, resisting hegemonic definitions of what is normal, developing unique cultural acts, and the like. But naming who we are begins with an understanding of what the consequences of being silenced have been for me as an individual and for all of us as a group. "Without a way to name our pain," writes bell hooks (1992), "we are also without the words to articulate our pleasure" (p. 2). To overlook our pain is to avoid a sadness and ultimate anger that foments change. An understanding that we have been erased from history and that there are numerous groups and individuals today who seek to maintain our silence begins a healing process that enables us to move in several directions. I realize that I am part of a "we." Because schools are places where we gain literacy, education becomes a central cultural component for change.

For queer people, the recognition that we are part of a group has meant virtually the rewriting of any histories about us. Our pain, from a heterosexist perspective, is simply that we are lesbian or gay. When the norm is defined as heterosexuality and any other orientation is seen as deviant and wrong, then those of us on the margins have no alternative than to be seen as deviant from a conservative perspective, or in need of help, from a liberal one. Our real pain has been that we were forced to believe that because we were lesbian or gay, we had an individual character flaw for which we were damned or pitied. The pain of carrying such a secret throughout one's life has forced individuals into wells of loneliness and isolation where any ability to speak of pleasure came at the risk of losing one's job or family or life.

In effect, as with other oppressed groups, queer people have subjugated their identities as a means of getting on with the daily act of living. Audre Lorde (1984) has written,

> In order to survive, those of us for whom oppression is as American as apple pie have always had to be watchers. . . . [Black women] became familiar with the language and manners of the oppressor, even sometimes adopting them for some illusion of protection. (p. 114)

Again, we see a similarity between Black women and queer people. We hide our own standpoint and act straight or act White or act male so that we may not be torn down. I noted in the previous section my concern about the lack of intragroup solidarity; the problem here is the inability of those within a group to express and articulate their own solidarity. We hide our own standpoint—sometimes even from one another—so that the dominant group cannot define us and limit us. Paradoxically, of course, the dominant group succeeds because we limit our public and sometimes even our private lives.

Indeed, we have had to live two lives. Our public lives seek to fit within the norm. Our private lives enable us to act naturally with one another, if we are able to come out to ourselves. As I noted earlier, like countless others, I hid my sexual orientation even from myself for years. When I finally accepted my queerness, it was many more years until I told someone else. Our internalized homophobia can be so great that we may actually be willing to die rather than admit that we are queer. In effect, as Lorde noted, lesbian and gay people become so familiar with the language of the oppressor that we internalize such language and hide our lives even from ourselves.

Even when we are out and open about our sexual orientation, we still regulate our public behavior. Many years ago, a very good heterosexual friend commented to me, for example, that she had never seen Barry and me express any physical affection for one another. I revealed to her how lesbian and gay people find it necessary to conceal their feelings even to the smallest degree so that they do not have to face hostility or derision. Once again, I explained to her about the five seconds of bigotry that control our lives.

When I lived and worked on the Fort Berthold Indian reservation, I learned how Indian people have had to live with this dualism as well. To be sure, American Indians will be recognizable to someone on the street in a way that straight-acting queers may not be, but they also have to control their public lives in ways that those in the norm do not have to. A Native American friend, for example, told me how he never had more than one beer with white people because he knew they always watched him to see if he would fit their stereotype of the drunk Indian. He did not have a drinking problem, and when we were alone, he might have more than one beer or glass of wine, but in public he sought to live a different life. If we do not fit the norm, then we are watched to see if we fit the center's portraits of us. On a microscopic scale, a white person watches what a Native American drinks to confirm a preexisting impression. On a larger scale, the heterosexual television viewer watches leather-jacketed men walk down the street arm in arm on Gay Pride Day to reinforce the notion that they are weird.

I am saying more here than simply that an individual acts differently in public than in private. All individuals have different public and private personae. However, as I noted in the Introduction with regard to dedications, individuals who come from a disempowered group seek to control their public actions for fear of being discriminated against or defined as aberrant members of a group. What those in the norm fail to realize is that such masquerading requires enormous energy and takes away from the critical work of developing our own standpoint.

The development of our history as gays and lesbians requires the construction of an articulated standpoint. In doing so, we are not simply involved in the development of an archive about our past. Archives are repositories of public records, and, in that light, the development of archives is important. But I am not simply suggesting that Japanese Americans, or Mexican Americans or queers develop an artifact or two for a museum but that we document how we have lived so that we might change how we live (McLaughlin & Tierney, 1993). The telling of our history is not a static act; it is an active commentary on our lives today.

Essentialism and Power. The inability of oppressed groups to articulate a standpoint and the duality that exists for us as subjects and objects of our own existence obviously speak to essentialism and power. However, what I highlight here is the manner in which the category of a group gets defined. What makes someone racist or heterosexist? Other than the most virulent members of right wing militias, I know few people from the mainstream who think of themselves as racist or heterosexist. Omi and Winant (1994) have noted that "Whites tend to locate racism in color consciousness and find its absence in color blindness. They see the affirmation of difference and racial identity among racially defined minority students as racist" (p. 70). From this perspective, a just society is one in which the color of one's skin is irrelevant.

We hear precisely the same critique about queers who are out. "I don't talk about my heterosexuality," the commentary goes. "Why do you have to talk about your homosexuality?" Homosexuals are always shoving it in straight people's faces. The liberal complaint is that what someone does in his or her bedroom is fine, but homosexuals should not be given special rights. We shouldn't flaunt our lifestyle. Everyone's equal. A just society is one where someone's sexual orientation is irrelevant. So the platitudes of the mainstream go.

If we return to the concepts developed in Chapter 2, however, we see that trying to make people raceless, or sexless, or overlooking their sexual orientation, is an essentialist trap that does little to change the inherent power relations that structure the relationships between groups. To the extent that policies, actions and structures reproduce structures of domination based on essentialist categories, they can be claimed to be racist, or sexist, or heterosexist. The unfortunate similarity that oppressed groups share here is twofold. First, those within the norm fail to see their actions in relation to maintaining and reproducing structural arenas of power and discrimination against an oppressed group—be they queer, African American, poor, or physically challenged. Second, the manner in which one overcomes discrimination is not by accepting essentialist categories that define us but by resisting them and developing our own particular standpoints. The Native American who cuts his hair or rejects the traditions of his culture, or the Latina who Anglicizes her name is not unlike the lesbian or gay person who struggles to pass in a straight world.

Resistance and Definition. Beginning the development of a collective standpoint occurs on multiple levels: We reclaim our history, we speak up for equal rights, we seek solidarity and meaning with one another. The elaboration of a consciously distinct culture also may serve as a catalyst for concrete political action. I never thought of potlucks as political acts, and I have thought of myself as a social person even less so. Nevertheless, when Barry and I moved to Penn State, we seemed to have a potluck in our house at least once a month for between half a dozen and fifty people. In a conservative and rural area such as State College ("Straight College") where the vast majority of the gay and lesbian community is closeted, the opportunity for men and women to come together once a month to share nothing more than a few hours with one another (and good food, of course) helped foster a movement that resulted in various political actions on campus. I am obviously not suggesting that potlucks are the only route to a just society; however, cultural events and artifacts that bring groups together and encourage solidarity can be cohesive agents for change.

What is remarkable is that quite often the creation of distinctly subcultural activities eventually gets absorbed into the mainstream. As bell hooks (1992) notes, "When young black people mouth 1960s black nationalist rhetoric, don Kente cloth, gold medallions, dread their hair, and diss the white folks they hang out with, they expose the way meaningless commodification strips these signs of political integrity and meaning" (p. 33). Perhaps even more troublesome is when the people who dread their hair, or get into rap or hip hop, or wear particular clothes, are white folks who have no appreciation for what they have appropriated.

We see similar appropriation of queer cultural artifacts. If a man wore an earring a decade ago he was a faggot; today he is probably a heterosexual football player. Whereas a straight actor would once never think of taking a gay role, today it is de rigueur for a famous actor to take on a gay role. The only actors who refuse to take lesbian or gay roles today are either virulent homophobes or closeted individuals. In New York or Los Angeles or other metropolitan areas, some of the most fashionable places to attend are gay discos.

One might think that we—queer, African American, Hispanic—should welcome the mainstream's interest in our cultural mores. And on one level, I do. When someone demonstrates an honest commitment to under-standing what it means to be different, I find hope and community. However, the mindless appropriation of things queer is the opposite of the idea of agape. When border groups' cultural artifacts are commodified so that we think being Mexican only means eating Mexican food that is sold in Taco Bell, we retard the opportunities for structural change. In effect, the power of the norm has absorbed and overwhelmed resistance.

Group Representation. One final similarity we share as oppressed groups is that we ourselves constitute a group. To be sure, definitions of race and class and gender change over generations and a lifetime. I do not vote myself in or out of a group. An African American can do little about his or her race. As a group, we are marked not simply as individuals but for our group status. My Native American friend who was self-conscious about drinking two beers in front of people was anxious not because of himself or his family but because he belonged to a group whose public persona was defined in a particularly stigmatized way. Queers, obviously, also have stereotypes. Gay men act one way; lesbians act another way. We all know the portraits. I enjoy reading the sports pages of a newspaper not only because I grew up in a family that emphasized sports but also because I know that many of my straight colleagues do not expect a gay man to know anything about sports. In effect, I am trying to explode their image of what it means to be gay. Similarly, I enjoy telling people that Barry and I belong to a gay group in the Sierra Club that does strenuous hikes every weekend because their stereotype is that they do not expect gay men to enjoy rigorous outdoor activities. Parenthetically, I might add we like to hike; we do not hike simply to alter people's beliefs, or to fit into a societal image of what it means to be a man. Indeed, hiking is one of the activities that initially brought the two of us together.

The similarity, then, is that individuals in an oppressed group share struggles, joys and pains with one another. What I have tried to point out, however, is that although the specific action may differ, oppressed groups also share similar experiences. At a metalevel, we face similar challenges. We struggle to develop our own standpoint. We are defined by dominant norms in which we partially exist as subjects and objects. Discrimination against us occurs through essentialist definitions and categories; the mainstream appropriation of cultural activities and artifacts stymies the development of group solidarity. The recovery of our history, the acknowledgment that we have much to share with one another, and the realization that group resistance and struggle are the first step toward change, lay the foundations for group definition and meaning.

Differences

Group Representation. Obviously, the nature of group affiliation also has dramatic variations. To be born as an American Indian has implications that are different from those of someone acknowledging in adolescence that he or she is lesbian or gay. The comment of bell hooks that I disagreed with at the outset of this chapter also has a degree of factual truth to it—two African American individuals who enter a meeting room at least know that someone else like themselves is in the room, whereas I have gone to countless academic meetings at which I am the only queer person who is out. Thus, the other meeting participants may think I am the only gay person in the room, and I at times have felt that way as well.

The secrecy of being gay is a double-edged sword. We may indeed hide our group affiliation when gaybashers come down the street to beat up queers. We also have a harder time finding ingroup affiliation. The result is a reinforcement of our loneliness and isolation. African Americans have no such choice. When members of the Ku Klux Klan want to "kill a nigger," there is no way that a black person may hide his or her skin color. Straight African Americans also will never face the degree of loneliness that queer people face—White, Black, or any person of color—when they think that no one else is like themselves.

Acceptance of one's sexual orientation and identification with the group also may imperil one's relationship with family, friends, and colleagues in a way that would never occur for someone who is Hispanic, for instance. Obviously, someone who is born into a Latino family does not risk being ostracized if he or she acknowledges a Latino/Latina identity in high school or college. When that person makes friends, for the most part the friends know that the individual is Hispanic. When an individual is hired into a business, the business has some degree of understanding that the person comes from a particular racial and ethnic background. To be sure, there are sons and daughters who have imperiled a relationship with their parents, friends or workers because they may have adopted a particular stance—militant, accommodating, or otherwise—with regard to their race or identity, but such an example is a matter of degree or style rather than basic acknowledgment.

A queer of any race, however, faces different challenges. We all know individuals who were disowned by their families when the families found out about their queer identity. Friends may no longer be friends. Individuals risk being fired when someone discovers their sexual orientation. The pathetic debate about gays in the military is perhaps the most obvious example of the risks faced by queers who are open about their sexuality. If the individual stays closeted, then he or she may remain in the military. The problem occurs when someone speaks up and announces that he or she is a sexually active gay or lesbian member of the military.

Again, the secrecy that group membership based on sexual orientation often suggests has multiple effects that highlight how group oppression differs. Some employers will not hire certain people simply because they are Black. Some parents will not want their sons or daughters rooming with an African American in college. Some individuals will not befriend someone else if he or she is of a particular race, from a particular class, or physically challenged. The gay or lesbian person does not face such overt acts of discrimination—*as long as they lie about their sexual orientation.* We will find employment, friendship, roommates, even marriage, if we deny explicit membership in our group.

Equality. Admittedly, Jesse Helms is an outlier in the U.S. Senate. At the same time, he has been elected to the Senate for a generation and he vocalizes what others often will say privately. When he has used the word "faggots" on the Senate floor, he has never faced the censure of his colleagues. If he, or anyone else, were to talk about "spics" or "chinks" or "niggers," it is not far-fetched to think that they would face immediate censure. When a congressman from Texas called a colleague a fag, there was much debate about whether there was even any reason to apologize. When Roseanne decided to have a scene in her television show where another woman kissed her, she set off an uproar. If she had had a Black man kiss her instead, the murmurs may well have been minimal, if at all. Baseball players from all racial and ethnic backgrounds take the field every day (when they are not on strike); any player who let the other players or the press know that he was gay would not last the season.

As Omi and Winant (1994) have noted, "Since 1965, it has been impossible to argue *for* racial segregation or *against* racial equality. Any 'legitimate' politics must claim to favor racial equality *in the abstract*" (p. 140). The challenge for queers is not segregation but ostracism. At the close of the 20th century, few individuals openly advocate that homosexuals should be put in concentration camps; however, an equally small number say that fair housing, nondiscrimination employment policies, or laws about adoption or marriage should be provided for lesbian and gay individuals. The legitimate politics in the straight world allows the discourse of discrimination to continue, if not expand.

As mentioned before, the differences between groups here do not suggest that one road is easier than another. Overt discrimination such as what we face denies us the means to policies and laws for equal protection that should be extended to any citizen. At the same time, we know our enemies. The easy acknowledgment that racism is wrong takes the rough edge off racism and lulls individuals into thinking that everyone wants a just society. But as I noted in the previous section, an essentialist notion of race or sexual orientation does little to change the inherent structure that drives racism. To be sure, I will see it as a major accomplishment if Senator Helms is no longer applauded or condoned for his vitriolic attacks on queers, but we should not be fooled into thinking that simply because one's discourse has changed the structure has changed or that someone's thinking about the subject has changed. Again, the appropriation by the mainstream of a particular activity or discourse does not necessarily signal fundamental change.

Speaking for/Speaking With. A colleague and I once planned to edit a book on lesbian and gay studies. I called someone who was straight and a legal scholar; I asked him if he would be interested in writing a chapter for the proposed book. The person forthrightly declined, informing me that the area was not one with which he was familiar. I wrote a proposal to a major foundation a few years ago that outlined a project for lessening homophobia in academe; the proposal got nowhere. Two colleagues asked me to write a chapter about lesbian and gay faculty members in an edited book about faculty diversity. When the project was completed, the editors informed me that another author had dropped out when he discovered that there would be a chapter in the book about queers. The leaders of a national association of higher education asked me to help form a caucus on lesbian and gay issues similar to other minority caucuses. When they announced the formation of the group, they received several letters from individuals who canceled their memberships because they did not want to have anything to do with an organization that "condoned the gay lifestyle."

Each example makes no sense in the 1990s if we substitute race or physical disability for sexual orientation. And again, the substitution does not lessen one group's oppression, but it underscores a difference. Few white scholars have any hesitation in studying a topic that focuses on race. Countless white authors now welcome the opportunity to write a chapter in a proposed book about race. Foundation proposals that are penned by Anglos who outline a project to study a particular racial topic number in the thousands each year. Many of them are funded. That an author would drop out of an edited book because someone else was going to write a chapter on the physically challenged is unthinkable, as is the idea that the creation of a Black caucus would force individuals to cancel their membership in a national organization. Again, it is possible that certain racial parameters might concern some individuals, but then we are dealing with a matter of perceived degree rather than the basic topic itself. That is, if the Black caucus were to be chaired by Louis Farrakhan, we might expect that some Anglos would vociferously object, but that is voicing a concern over the format rather than the basic idea. Thus, the center still defines the parameters of what is acceptable for an African American group on the margins, but the definition is quite different from what queers face.

As with the comments made above, I suppose I welcome more support from the straight community. I find it alternately lamentable and laughable that someone had trouble with a mild-mannered chapter about lesbian and gay faculty in an edited book; I also find it admirable that the editors never questioned whether to include the chapter. But it is troublesome when a member of a dominant group unhesitatingly assumes the mantle of an oppressed group. I am not suggesting that only queers can write about queers, or only Black women should write about Black women. However, when individuals are unable to question their own subject position and unproblematically assume that they understand the concerns of groups on the border, then a whole different set of problems and issues arises. The easy acceptance that we should start a special interest group for the physically challenged or Native Americans means that as an able individual or an Anglo I do not have to do anything. In effect, we have voted for membership at the table once again, but we have not questioned how that membership gets defined. With queers, the issue is more open and confrontational. We may win a vote here and there, but others will resign their membership from the club if we do.

Dominant Comparisons. When Japanese immigrants came to this country, they did well in school. Why don't Chicanos? The Irish and Italians have assimilated into the mainstream, so why have the Blacks been unable to do so? Why can't girls learn math and science as well as boys? Such questions imply answers based on dominant norms and directly relate to the discussion of the relationship between subject and object in Chapter 1. Each question implies that the objects (Japanese Americans, Chicanos, Blacks, girls) need to act like the subjects (white/men). At face value, the change is simple. In one way or another the individual in a group needs to alter a particular personal characteristic so that he or she will also be successful. Develop a work ethic. Create a stronger family structure. Learn to be more aggressive. Alternatively, we might conclude that individuals in particular groups are unable to compete. Girls cannot be more aggressive, for example, and they need to learn their place.

Queer comparisons with the mainstream are built on an entirely different discourse. In effect, there are no comparisons. The point is not to be more masculine or feminine, because regardless of the character trait, the result remains the same—the individual is still queer. In order for the objects (queers) to act more like the subjects (heterosexuals), it is apparent what they have to do—obliterate their personalities. They do not simply need to work harder or grow up in a traditional family. The consequence is that either queers remain deviant, or they do not simply assimilate but have to go through a fundamental character change as well.

Thus, the manner in which oppressed groups must work with dominant norms is quite different. Racial groups must struggle with the idea of incorporation. Assimilation is benign. The assumption is that an individual does not have to do very much to succeed—get up earlier, work harder, be more disciplined. The consequences are that when such change does not take place, the burden of failure falls on the individual and group. It is not the mainstream that has failed to honor cultural difference; it is the subculture's inability to adapt. Structural sexism is not what creates a girl's inability to advance in math and science; it is that girls are just not interested in those areas of inquiry or don't have the minds for math.

The queer community has no hope of incorporation. We might try to act like Ozzie and Harriet, but it is apparent to everyone that we will never be Ozzie and Harriet. In some respects, this awareness is more threatening and more fundamental. White people might believe that to succeed, all a Black person has to do is act White. But we know that a queer can act straight—we do so all the time—but will never be straight. The oppressive challenge with regard to race, then, is dramatically different from what queers face.

Identity and Community. Lesbian and gay people grow up for the most part without any sense of an internalized history. That is, not only are we ignored by the mainstream, but until recently, we have had no past on which to draw and therefore no cultural pride or heritage. Patricia Hill Collins (1991) has written how White definitions of community revolve around competition and domination, whereas "Afrocentric models of community stress connections, caring, and personal accountability" (p. 223). I could never make such a comment about the queer community. Have we historically "stressed connections?" I have no idea. The women's community might have given the same response a generation ago insofar as little work had been done about women's lives in the past.

On a personal level, we also grow in families and communities when we learn what it means to be an African American male or a Native American woman. Perhaps there are African Americans or Native Americans who want to alter what those definitions mean, but they at least have something to change. Gay or lesbian youth have little, if anything, to go on as they struggle to define their identity. I did not meet anyone who said "I'm gay" until I was in college. I had no awareness of what it meant to be gay, for example, when I was in high school, and I grew up in a suburb of New York City. What kind of isolation exists for lesbian and gay youth in rural Texas?

Again, my point has not been that one oppressed group's struggles are worse than another's but that there are fundamental differences in how we see the world and how the world sees us. Whereas a gay or lesbian adolescent may grow up without any role model, a black youth may grow up with a positive or negative self-image that is based on what he or she sees in daily life, on television, and at school. Our history for the most part has been absent both internally and externally, whereas the history of people of color is often mangled but is nevertheless there. Which is worse: obliteration or misinterpretation? Such a question is absurd. What we need now instead is to consider what we might do as oppressed groups to deal with the problems that I have outlined.

Coalitions

"What I really feel is radical," writes Barbara Smith, "is trying to make coalitions with people who are different from you" (Smith & Smith, 1981, p. 126). Accepting that coalitions are necessary and possible is a first step toward the creation of a movement that seeks to build voice for those of us on the borders in order to overcome oppression. Rather than think of someone else's oppression as strictly someone else's concern, we enact the idea of agape and realize that fundamental connections exist between groups and individuals.

If we accept that dialogues across groups are possible, we do not necessarily have to assume that our positions are similar. However, we make the commitment to try and understand difference. The implication here is twofold. As I noted in Chapter 1, academics and community scholars have a vital role to play as local public intellectuals in creating the histories of our past lives. Works such as Chauncey's (1994) study of gay New York, Kennedy and Davis's (1993) oral history of a lesbian community, and Newton's (1993) study of Cherry Grove are examples of works that play a critical role in the lesbian and gay communities, enabling us to understand how group representation functions. In effect, we are not alone.

On the other hand, as members of an oppressed group, we have an obligation to learn about the Other and not simply confine our concerns and analyses to our own specific background. In particular, white gay men who hold economically powerful positions in society have an obligation to understand how the economy functions to provide privileges to some and deny other individuals basic economic justice. I am suggesting that individuals such as me ought not to participate in a march for queer rights while stepping unthinkingly over the homeless en route to our destination. Oppression is linked; until we understand these linkages and form coalitions, we will continue to deny ourselves the critical support that we all need from one another.

When we accept that we have an obligation to try to understand oppressed groups other than ourselves, we run unique risks. Our standpoints are not always similar, and we ought not to make automatic, lazy claims to solidarity. Coalition building is hard work. At the same time, because my background differs from that of people in other groups, I have an obligation to try and understand difference, rather than dismissing people because they are different from me.

The clearest example of groups' claiming that they will not speak for the other is gay men (such as myself) who write that because they are not lesbian, they will not concern themselves with lesbian lives. I appreciate the concern. Those men who have processed the idea of difference are simply saying that lesbians should speak for themselves. And yet, often implicit in such words is the feeling that the author is now off the hook. "I've done the politically correct thing," goes the feeling. "Now I can get on with the text." Dialogue across difference means that there will be conversations, and I will struggle to understand and write about groups other than my own. Paul Monette (1994) wrote,

> One of the great breakthroughs I made as a writer in the last ten years was to be able to write about lesbians. Ten years ago I silenced myself because I was so afraid I would get it wrong and come out with a stupid stereotype that wouldn't help anybody. It was my friend Katherine Forrest who said to me, "We have to populate our books with one another." (p. 126)

Such sentiments stand in contrast to those who claim to study difference by studying themselves. The identity politics that has brought about many insightful breakthroughs over the past generation runs the risk of denying the possibility of coalitions. We must resist this suggestion. I am not saying that every text should be populated by all oppressed groups, for there are certainly times when an author needs to concentrate forthrightly on a particular area of inquiry. Ultimately, in order for us to understand ourselves, we must understand others. In order for us to end discrimination against ourselves, we must seek to end discrimination against others.

PART

ACADEMIC PORTRAITS AND
STRATEGIES FOR CHANGE

America I'm putting my queer shoulder to the wheel.
—Allen Ginsberg
Collected Poems 1947-1980 *(1984)*

Chapter 5

Counterfeiting
The Academic Closet

A few years ago, a subcommittee of the Pennsylvania legislature held open hearings throughout the state about proposed changes in the public school curriculum. The head of the Lesbian and Gay Task Force in Pennsylvania asked if I would testify about the importance of a gay-inclusive curriculum. As I prepared my testimony, I spoke about what I should expect with a friend who had appeared in front of other legislative bodies. He presented a picture that was both calming and boring: empty chamber rooms with a handful of state legislators lazily grinding their way through testimony from the citizenry. I told myself that although I would not make the five o'clock news, I also had nothing to get nervous about if what I was about to do was simply a rote experience. I would speak about the importance of a gay-friendly curriculum and be home in time to prepare dinner for Barry.

They held the hearings in a neighboring town's high school. As I approached the parking lot, I was surprised to find it filled with cars. School parking lots are not usually full in the summer; I thought perhaps a softball game was taking place, but the playing fields seemed empty. I asked a janitor which classroom I needed to go to for the legislative hearings. "It's in the auditorium," he drawled. "Standing room only." I got nervous. The auditorium held five hundred people.

A friend saw me when I entered and immediately began to laugh. He had guessed why I was there and as I slid into a position next to him he teased, "They'll love you! The Moral Majority or some sort of group is here in force and they are testifying about how we need a back-to-basics curriculum. I'm sure they'll enjoy what you have to say." Sure enough, the speaker on the auditorium stage was recounting her experiences about providing education at home for her children because of the liberal values of the public schools. When she finished, the chair called out my name, and I approached the stage.

Even without the overhead lights of the television cameras, I would have been sweating. The only other time I had appeared on television was when I testified at a hearing of the faculty senate at Penn State in support of the sexual orientation clause and told the committee that I was gay. Before I sat down, I handed out my prepared testimony and spoke to the state senators about the need for a curriculum that was affirmative for all children. When I prepared the testimony, I had made a decision to put it on Penn State letterhead. I finished my commentary, and the chair asked if anyone had a question. Immediately one legislator asked me if my use of the Penn State letterhead implied that my comments had the official endorsement of the university. I told him I was responding as a faculty member and as a citizen. My area of inquiry was education, and I was speaking about multiculturalism as an expert in the field. At the same time, I also told him that my background as a gay man had prepared me to speak on the issue. The auditorium was absolutely silent. There were no further questions, and I exited the stage, my footsteps making the only sounds.

As I noted in Chapter 4, somewhere in my past I realized that I could not continue hiding my sexual orientation. The problem, of course, is that coming out is a never-ending experience. Even though everyone in my department or college may know that I am gay, state legislators do not. A dean may know, and the provost may not. I constantly need to retell my story, and, in doing so, I re-create for people who I am in ways that straight people usually do not have to resort to. I no longer fear or resent having to tell people who I am, but I am aware that it is a task and responsibility for which I have to prepare. I never unconsciously or casually say to an acquaintance, "Oh by the way. I'm gay." I am always aware of my words and my audience. Being openly gay is being in a constant state of preparation. I have no alternative.

In Part I, I offered theoretical analyses of how I construct what I call a "cultural identity" and what its implications are for the creation and maintenance of community. Referencing postmodernism, I discussed cultural studies and queer theory and argued that we need to think of how to engage in a cultural politics that enables norms to be decoded and silenced groups to engage in cultural production. I have also used the idea of agape as a way to create a dialogue across difference, and I pointed out the necessity of basing our analyses on contextual and situational frameworks.

In the next two chapters, I turn to a discussion of those contexts and situations that are specific to academe. Increasingly, colleges and universities have done studies of lesbian and gay life on campus. I do not intend to write yet another chapter outlining the parameters of homophobia on campus, but I should offer a summary of what we know.

Over the past decade, several campus studies have investigated the climate for lesbian, gay, and bisexual people at their institutions. The institutional surveys are remarkably redundant: Seventy-six percent of all gay, lesbian and bisexual respondents in a Rutgers University survey, for example, knew individuals who had been victimized. Fifty-seven percent of the respondents in a similar survey at Yale reported fears for their safety. Forty-five percent of lesbian, gay and bisexual respondents at the University of Massachusetts-Amherst had experienced verbal abuse. Sixty-four percent of Penn State's lesbian and gay community reported fearing for their personal safety. Ninety-four percent said they expected harassment at the university in the future (D'Augelli, 1991, p. 225). In what follows, I provide contexts for such numbing statistics.

I should note that as I have developed this text, a handful of gay, lesbian and queer readers have commented on the data from this chapter. "When I entered university life 20 years ago," wrote one reader, "I experienced a number of the situations described. Yet during the past 10 or 15 years, my own experiences have been so largely positive that I don't know why all of his interviewees seem so downtrodden." Another wrote, "For some 20-plus years, I have openly acknowledged my sexual orientation as a gay male faculty member. Never over the course of this time have I experienced the discrimination or negative encounters that dominate Tierney's analysis." A third suggested that the portraits of the past might have been true to what he initially experienced in the 1940s but that he found a "pervasive unreality" to the descriptions that follow about academe today.

I offer three responses for readers to consider as they develop their own interpretations of what closeted academics have to say. First, the qualitative data that I use dovetail with the surveys cited above about homophobia in academe and other studies about business organizations (Woods & Lucas, 1994). In effect, I provide qualitative depth to what the breadth of the quantitative surveys has documented. Second, all of the readers in academe whom I just quoted have come out. To be sure, individuals in the past and even more today are open about their sexuality; they do not face the fear or harassment that the following interviewees highlight. Nonetheless, such individuals are the exception, rather than the norm. Third, I have purposefully collapsed the data so that they appear as a tapestry of collective interviews of closeted individuals rather than as a composite case study of one institution. Obviously, a gay academic in an English Department at Vassar, for example, may have had an experience different from that of a counterpart in a math department at Oral Roberts University. My point, then, is to concentrate here on the closet and how individuals have related to it; to be sure, case studies that seek to highlight the specific contextual experiences of the broad array of lesbian and gay people at one institution can only help enrich our understanding of the parameters and contours of queer lives in academe. They await further investigation.

My purpose here, however, is to consider what it means to be gay or lesbian on campus from the perspective of those who are gay or lesbian— with one hitch. I offer portraits and analysis of what some individuals have chosen as an alternative to being out; in other words, I focus on closeted academics. Because I am concerned with individuals who live hidden lives, it is impossible to provide the exact percentage of how many people are out of the closet and in the closet in academe. And again, percentages also vary from campus to campus, depending on a number of variables: location, size, institutional affiliation, support networks. However, anyone who has an understanding of lesbian and gay life in academe most likely will not quarrel with me if I suggest that three quarters of lesbian and gay individuals on college campuses are closeted. Thus, in this chapter, I write about those who I believe make up the vast majority of lesbians and gay men in academe.

The data from this text are drawn from work I have done over the last decade that at times was explicitly geared toward sexual orientation and at other times not. For example, in a study of promotion and tenure (Tierney & Bensimon, 1996), I did not exclusively seek lesbian or gay voices, but some of the statements made here are from individuals who came out in their interviews with me. I also conducted life history interviews (Tierney, 1994), with individuals whom I quote here, although the purpose was not initially on the focus taken in this present work. I also chaired a commission at Pennsylvania State University when, among other activities, we interviewed 20 gay men and lesbians about their experiences at the university (Tierney, 1992; Tierney et al., 1992). Most of these individuals were closeted men and women who had a great deal to say about the parameters of invisibility. Finally, specifically for *Academic Outlaws,* I interviewed 15 individuals over a four-year period. I interviewed some individuals once for about an hour and have spoken with other individuals multiple times in different locales (e.g., conferences, their campuses, or homes). All of these interviews help account for the data of this chapter. Again, I want to stress that I am not saying the closet is the pervasive way of life for all gay and lesbian academics today, nor perhaps even yesterday. At the same time, to ignore the experiences of closeted individuals does an injustice to what numerous people encounter and have encountered while they live their lives on campus.

I first outline what the closeted academic world is like today by discussing four key aspects of academic life—(a) the hiring process, (b) socialization, (c) settling in, and (d) promotion and tenure. I then present snapshots of what it was like to be gay and closeted in academe a generation ago. The chapter concludes by considering what the consequences of the closet are as we approach the 21st century. In large part, I argue that fundamental shifts have occurred, so that what I will call a "queer sensibility" points toward a greater need for us to come out and speak up. We explore the parameters of the academic closet, then, in order to understand its etiology, context and history.

The Current Context

The Job Market

A fact of life for aspiring academics at the close of the 20th century is that proportionally fewer tenure-track positions are available today than at any time since World War II; at the same time, graduate schools continue to turn out a huge supply of doctoral students. Whereas a generation ago if a tenure-level appointment came open in a department or school, the faculty expected to advertise the position, today constant fears exist about whether the dean or provost will convert the job to a nontenure-track position, or simply abolish it. Similarly, a generation ago, a graduate student in physics or philosophy had multiple opportunities. The newly minted physicist might have turned to postdoctoral work, a faculty position, or a research opportunity in a laboratory; the philosopher had a more constricted spectrum of choices, but academic jobs were still plentiful. Today, 200 applicants may apply for a position in physics at a mediocre institution; an applicant may apply for 100 jobs, receiving only form letters in return, and then take several part-time positions for a number of years with the hope that teaching experience might enhance his or her vita.

I am neither bemoaning nor explaining the causes for academe's current fiscal and hiring dilemmas; rather, my purpose is to consider the consequences of such a market for academics who happen to be lesbian or gay. "I went for my job interview," said one individual, "and was constantly on the lookout not to slip up, not to appear gay, not to give them any reason for excluding me." A second person who was in a relationship added, "A friend advised me what to do, down to every detail. Our answering machine had this innocuous message that said, 'John and Jim can't come to the phone right now. Leave a message and we'll give you a call back.' He told me to change the message because if I got a phone call from members of a search committee, they might figure it out and I'd be dead." Another person agreed: "I have worn an earring for years. I finally got an interview, and my adviser asked me if I was going to wear it to the interview. I took it off." One individual wore a lapel pin with a red ribbon: "That was my big statement. I really thought and thought, talked to other grad students. Can you believe that I worried about such things? It's surreal."

Surreal or not, the vast majority of lesbian and gay people have to consider such issues en route to the job market. The struggle in any job interview, but especially one in a tight market, is not to offer a search committee any reason for rejection. For many closeted lesbian and gay academics, their sexual orientation is one such reason. One individual had this comment:

> I can't separate my feelings of insecurity from my feelings of being a gay man. I think most junior professors have a tough time; your sexual orien-

tation only amplifies it. I see my colleagues making decisions about hiring and I see how irrational most decisions are. Somebody last week said we shouldn't hire someone because she didn't "feel good" about the person—and that was it!

Multiple interpretations exist for such comments. As with the liberal reader I considered in the Introduction who accepts lesbians and gays but does not change his or her mental imagery, the heterosexual liberal may find it hard to believe that a closeted academic might actually give any thought to deciding whether or not he or she should wear a pink triangle on a suit coat. Job decisions, after all, are made on criteria based solely on a candidate's qualifications, the thinking goes, so the firmness of an individual's handshake is irrelevant, if not absurd. From a different angle, an outspoken queer activist might deride closeted actions as immensely hypocritical. Many other observers might claim that such counterfeiting verges on paranoia. And yet we define paranoia as a disorder marked by irrational suspicion.

But is this behavior really irrational? The pervasiveness of societal prejudice against lesbians and gay men makes it easy to understand why they remain in the closet. People have lost jobs and have had their careers destroyed when an employer has discovered that they are gay or lesbian. Not every individual in this situation has been fired from a job, and not everyone who knows someone is lesbian or gay will seek that person's dismissal. However, some have lost their jobs and some do wish us harm. "The problem is not in your department where probably everyone knows you," related one individual. "It's the anonymous committees that make decisions. . . . It's easier to use your prejudices if you don't know the person." Another person added, "I went for an interview and one person really pressed me whether I had children and would I want to put my kids in the public school here. I really felt he was snooping. I didn't like it, but what could I do?" An interviewee who has served on search committees said, "It can be a very difficult process. We create a gauntlet and have people run through a battery of interviews. It's not that if someone is gay, they'll be automatically rejected; it's just that in a series of twenty interviews, there's bound to be one person who will have personal beliefs at odds with homosexuality. If that person presses his case, the candidate is in trouble." Another person offered a comparison: "We know that women have a hard time, that minorities have a hard time; why wouldn't gays? Anyone who thinks the search process is blind and neutral is living in fantasy land." Such comments relate to the discussion in Chapter 4 about similarities and differences for subjugated groups. The prejudice of an individual can deny someone employment merely because the individual is Black, lesbian, or physically challenged. The similarity is the prejudice; the difference is the coping mechanisms that individuals employ.

The lesson that these interviewees have learned is that they had best keep their sexual orientation private. Some of them assumed that such action was warranted for any professor, and others felt that it was a pity. The overwhelming response, however, was that in job interviews, they should not give anyone an opportunity to see them as vulnerable. Vulnerability, weakness, got defined as being lesbian or gay. Once again, we find the definition of being lesbian or gay is an inconvenience, if not a downright hindrance.

Socialization in Academe

We become socialized about how we should lead our public lives by the myriad of experiences that lead up to our present working lives. Graduate school teaches students that research is more important than teaching, so we should not be surprised when new faculty members concentrate on research. By and large, colleges and universities do not have campuswide discussions about what defines good teaching, so new faculty members usually follow the example of teachers they admired. When new faculty members arrive on campus, they usually do not find any structured orientations in place and therefore are on the lookout for how senior colleagues act. At many institutions, for example, senior professors stay at home and have minimal interaction, or they may opt out of teaching freshmen, so new faculty become socialized to the mores of the workplace without benefit of their advice. Similarly, the socialization of lesbian and gay faculty members occurs in three primary ways: (a) personal background, (b) experiences in graduate school, and (c) role modeling by senior gay faculty members.

Personal Background. "Being gay has always been a struggle for me," said one individual. "I was raised in a conservative family and it's something you never talk about. I think my family knows, but we never mention it. So I certainly don't talk about it here." A second person concurred, "I have always been in the closet. It's just something you learn to live with, to accept." A third young professor added, "I once told a friend of mine in high school that I thought I was gay, and it turned out to be a mess. He told others, my family found out about it. I'm a quick learner: Don't tell anybody or you'll be hurt." A fourth person was not entirely closeted: "My parents know and my sister is a real support. They're all okay with it, but my parents are worried about what others think. So my partner and I never visit. I don't mingle here. It's just not an issue."

Other individuals argue that being private about their private lives is entirely acceptable. One person, for example, said, "I believe the line about what I do in my home is my own business and no one else's. Work is work and it should stay that way." Another person commented how he thought it was inappropriate to mix social affairs with business; whether he was straight or gay should not affect how he performed his work. "I have always kept to myself," claimed another, "I'm a real loner. I guess that's partly what attracted me to being a professor. I could keep to myself." His life consisted of keeping a Spartan office and avoiding social contacts with colleagues. "I know individuals who I assume are straight and they act just like I do," he concluded. "So it's not any different." A final person pointed out that it was possible to separate the private from the public persona: "Yes, it's schizophrenic, sure. But what's the alternative? I grew up this way. I am this way, and I'm happy. Why should I change?"

Experiences in Graduate School. Graduate school often reinforced for individuals the importance of staying closeted. Obviously, a graduate student at the City University of New York will have a different experience from someone at Notre Dame, but most people had tales closer to the following individual:

> I was at a new student reception when I first got there, and two professors made a joke when they walked in the room together; they sort of minced around in a real queeny way. As if "God forbid, don't think we're a couple!" People laughed. It was over immediately and clued me in for the rest of my time there. They weren't even professors in my department, but I just knew that it wasn't okay. I wanted to get through with a minimum of hassle, and being gay would only raise the ante.

Another individual was openly gay and said he learned his lesson: "This will sound strange, but I never really thought about it very much. I don't, as they say, flaunt it, but I brought my partner to a party. After that, this one professor who had been nice, was quite cold and distant." The student went on to describe how his experiences in graduate school had taught him that he had best not let others know that he was gay once he was on the job market. Some individuals related how they were active in gay circles and closeted in the graduate school: "My university is not that different from any place. There was nothing gay anywhere in the school, so I just shut up about it. I knew another gay man in the school, and I had some friends who knew I was gay, but there's this huge social divide between faculty and students anyway, so I just kept it up."

Other individuals thought it ludicrous to even consider letting people know about their sexual identity. As one person commented, "My professors were totally unavailable for that kind of thing. They worked on my papers, on projects, on the dissertation. They helped me find this job. They were not my counselors." "I just never thought of faculty in that way," said another. "Graduate school was a continuation of the divide between my gay life and the rest. And I don't mean that negatively." "You know how intense grad school is," summarized one person. "Work, work, work. You're never good enough and they're always looking to shoot you down. I wasn't going to give them the opportunity." Thus, from this individual's point of view, her sexual orientation was a negative factor in her doing her work successfully.

Role Modeling by Senior Gay Faculty. We heard the comment above from the graduate student whose professor had counseled him to take his earring off for the job interview. Other academics interviewed mentioned that they could have used advice but did not find any: "The gay students union was where I spent most of my time. Occasionally you'd see an article in the student newspaper about something gay and a gay professor might be quoted, but I didn't know any. It could have helped." "I was at a bar once," said another, "and I bumped into an older professor. We were both totally embarrassed and we sort of avoided one another." A third person commented, "If your 'gaydar' is any good you can sniff out who's gay and who's not. But you'd never know it. I don't even know what I wanted them to do, but they were no support." "The most formal and distant professors were the ones I suspected of being gay, like they had something to hide. 'Is that going to be me?' I often asked myself. The answer turns out to be yes."

Once junior gay professors set foot on a campus, they often find other lesbian or gay faculty members. "There are potlucks, and they're nice," said one professor, "That's the extent of my interaction. I don't want to be out. Too risky." A second person concurred, "There are a few activists on campus, but that's not me. I've never even talked to them." A third commented, "There's a woman in liberal arts, and we go out together, but

I just don't really get involved here." A fourth summarized: "I get up to speed real fast. There are lots of closet cases here, and if senior faculty are like that, I just can't risk it."

What I take from such comments is the Foucaultian notion of how those who are not in the majority are constantly kept off base. People remain closeted because of the dynamic strategies at work in the culture. Without opportunities for solidarity or agape, and, given the economic constraints of the market, gay individuals will not risk revealing who they are. Risk in the 1990s is defined as claiming a lesbian or gay identity; as we shall see in the discussion about the past context later in this chapter, risk received another definition fifty years ago.

Settling In

"It is a very oppressive atmosphere. I am unable to be who I am," concluded one lesbian academic about life at her university. A second person added, "Visibility for gay men and lesbians does not exist—there is no indication on this campus that we exist." A third person concurred, "The people I work with would be antagonistic if they found out I was gay." A fourth person said, "I'm concerned with the way that people view me. I'm worried—sensitive—to what people will think, worried that they will say, 'God, this person's a faggot.'" And a fifth: "I don't want to be rejected at the human level; I don't want negative relationships with the people I work so closely with on a daily basis. I don't want them to have reasons to dislike me."

The result is that individuals learn how to cope. They may seem overly formal or distant, but they keep a sharp delineation between their gay selves and their academic selves. A tenured faculty member, for example, never goes into the gay bar in his town "because it's just too public." Another person is actively conscious that he should never touch a male student, that as a faculty member, he should use his office desk as a barrier between himself and his students, and that the office door always should remain open when he meets with male students.

Another professor commented how he was especially careful in the classroom, "Right now, I'm applying for jobs and people ask for my course evaluations. All I need is a vocal minority talking about my moral stability." As a consequence, he feared discussing issues of sexual identity in his class, even though on occasion it might have been appropriate in an undergraduate course in psychology. One person acknowledged that "I'd be scared to be an adviser to the lesbian and gay student association because that is being too obvious. I am close to tenure, and I don't want them to find a reason not to give it to me." One assistant professor went so far as to say, "I wouldn't say in class that I'm gay. I have a unit in my class on it and that's enough. I might tell my students that I agree with the pain that gay people face or something like that, but I wouldn't come right out and say that I am gay." Even a unit in one class would be too much for some people: "No way. Nothing gay in my class. Guilt by association." Another young professor said, "Here's a contradiction, a hypocrisy on my part. I tell students to be vocal, not to accept being pushed around, but I won't always speak up." Finally, a summary from another gay professor:

> I really struggle in every class I teach whether to come out to the students. I know that some students say, "I don't know anyone who's gay." They only know gays as sick psychopaths in the movies—sad, pathetic creatures. I feel it incumbent on me to be a role model. I don't know if I want it to be an issue—but it is an issue. I go back and forth like this all the time. So I decided that I'll tell the graduate students but not the undergraduates—as if I need to protect the undergraduates.

A double bind exists on a daily basis, according to another gay academic: "My colleagues talk about their day-to-day lives, relationships, problems, but I can't. I can't share in their experiences because I choose not to share mine." Thus, he needs to listen to the stories of his colleagues but does not feel permitted to offer his own.

Another person commented that he was especially careful about letting people know about his partner: "We've been together five years, but I would never think of taking him to a party or putting his picture on my desk. 'Who's that?' someone would say, and then I'd have to explain." Another explained how to survive: "You have to talk about life in safely nongay terms: 'I went to Cape Cod' (not Provincetown—a dead give-away)." Another person summed it up: "Enforced lying is a form of discrimination." At the same time, this person did not feel there was any recourse other than to lie.

Given the framework developed in Part I, I find such comments unsettling. These faculty members fear the normalizing relations at work in the academy. Although some are able to decode the grammar of their cultures, they do not have the means available to them to decenter or mediate the discursive codes and acts that frame their lives. Ironically, then, in an educational institution that ostensibly is about the development of voice and the enablement of individuals to define the means of cultural production, we find faculty members who are silenced and powerless.

Promotion and Tenure

Arguably, no institutional structure in higher education is more important than that pertaining to decisions about promotion and tenure. As anyone who has gone through the process well knows, the manner in which someone gains tenure is remarkably convoluted and abstruse. No one really knows how many journal articles he or she must publish to satisfy the tenure committee. How teaching gets evaluated or what is an adequate amount of time to spend on service-related activities is also a mystery. A tenure-track candidate is likely to hear one year that a chapter in a book will not count at all in the review process and the next year discover that the new dean has changed the rules, and chapters in books do count. One person will say that coauthored articles are as good as single-authored articles, and another person will point out that presentations at conferences are important. Someone else will say the opposite. A candidate in a professional area such as business will hear that it is better if he or she publishes in disciplinary journals and then hear that only publications in the professional journals are worthwhile (Tierney & Bensimon, 1996).

Making the whole process even more confusing for the closeted lesbian or gay faculty member is the belief that one's sexual orientation needs to be hidden. "As soon as I got here," said one gay academic, "a senior faculty member sat me down and told me that I needed to go to the conferences and establish a working relationship with people who might be able to review my work. It was all social. Go to the receptions, hobnob, that kind of thing. I hate to do that, and I basically hate it because it's when I am most uneasy about being gay." A second person said, "I feel the same [about hobnobbing]. My alternative is to [be] only with gay/lesbian scholars at a conference. But must we ghettoize ourselves as scholars, too?" Another person offered a vignette about when he felt vulnerable: "I ended up going to dinner with a group of people I barely knew, but I felt that I had to do it because that's what you do to make contacts. Everybody ended up pulling pictures out of their wallets talking about their kids and I just sat there sweating bullets, hoping no one guessed my secret. It was terrible." A third person commented, "People don't realize that the most innocent question raises my blood pressure. 'Are you married?' evokes not only a quick 'No' but some immediate follow-up comment to redirect the question away from my personal life." "I took my lover to a conference," said someone else, "and I totally screwed up. I never should have done it. I was literally afraid of being seen with him." Another individual commented, "What you learn is that an awful lot of work gets done informally, casually, and if you're not good at that, you're at a disadvantage."

Similarly, working with senior colleagues is one way to get one's name out into the academic world. A senior professor can be of tremendous help in navigating the often confusing world of how to get published and how to garner grants. Yet again, such close collaboration often necessitates an informality that a closeted professor gravitates against. "One guy in another department, but in my area," said one person, "seemed to honestly want to help me. I enjoyed working with him and I also had something to contribute to his work. He felt that I must be lonely because I was so private about my life. He started to invite me to his house for dinner with his wife and kids. He even tried to set me up with someone once, so I withdrew." "When you're totally work oriented, or people think you are," suggested another person, "people give you all sorts of additional work. 'Here, let Greg do it. He's got nothing to do this weekend.' That kind of thing." "I find that I have to set boundaries in ways that I suspect straight faculty do not. Personal boundaries. As if I have some big secret. Well, I do," said another. "Tenure would make anyone neurotic," concluded someone else, "and if you're gay, then you begin the whole process that way. You're always on the lookout."

In a helpful text about the corporate closet, James Woods (1994) has pointed out in his survey of closeted businessmen: "Rather than fabricate a sexual identity, they try to elude one altogether. They provide their coworkers with as little evidence of their sexuality as possible" (p. 141). The same point can certainly be made for closeted academics, but in some respects, the manner in which they present their public personae differs from that of the business person in two ways. First, the public persona of the academic is generally related in some way to that of a role model. As a teacher, the academic inhabits the role of a person to whom young people may look for guidance and even an understanding of how to live. Second, the academic works in a schizophrenic universe that is intensely private and at the same time quite public. That is, the faculty member may spend more time at home in front of a computer screen composing a text than his or her counterpart in the business world who goes to work every day at 8:00 a.m. At the same time, the academic works in an environment that is remarkably protean, informal, and visible when compared to the business world. College and university life is full of commentary, observation and critique in ways that are foreign to the structured world of business. As one person noted, "I was not prepared [for] how gossipy everything is. Who eats with whom in the faculty club, who's doing what, that kind of thing. It's exactly the opposite of what I wanted. I don't want people to know me, because if they do, they'll find out, and then I could be in trouble."

I am not saying the academic world is better (or worse) than the world of business. I will also be the first to admit that as role models, academics—gay or straight—often are miserable failures. Nevertheless, the roles that we inhabit do come with the implicit assumption that we have something of worth to impart to students. However much the business world may want us to, we do not deal in markets and commodities; the work of academe is in some way related to intellectual, moral and ethical development. Indeed, as one of the people interviewed noted above, the gay academic often feels it necessary to be a role model for gay students as well as for straight students who may never have been able to shape an opinion about gay people other than what they have seen in the movies— "sad, pathetic characters."

Again, the sad irony is that the intellectual and existential challenges that we face exist within a culture that has been remarkably successful at silencing lesbian and gay academics. Or rather, lesbian and gay individuals may understand how hidden norms operate—as I said in Chapter 2—but without a strategy to overthrow those norms, our knowledge changes nothing. We may understand what cultural capital we need to survive, but such capital obliterates our personality as we strive to hide by "passing." The challenge, then, is not merely to understand our situation as individuals but to strive for commonalities and action by building communities of difference.

To be a queer academic in an environment that looks at homosexuality as deviant is yet one more stressful condition to be faced by the closeted person. Woods (1994) has noted that 62% of gay respondents to a survey said that their sexual orientation creates "stressful situations" at work (p. 10). The same can certainly be said for academe. One individual, for example, went so far as to say that the choices of research method and department depended in part on his sexual orientation: "I have felt safer in data-based research than in qualitative or ethnographic research," he explained, "because I don't have to reveal myself." This individual also had a choice of entering a college of education or a college of social science. "The reason I chose a social science department instead of something like a college of education is that I thought social science would be less homophobic than a college of education. That was a conscious choice. I thought about it."

The point here is that any workplace will have norms that have been built over time and will be rebuilt by the current constituents. An organization's culture is loaded with discursive symbols that tell the constituents and other audiences what is important and valued in the organization. Organizations may advertise, for example, their history—"a century's worth of New England pride"—a special aspect—"the best humanities program in the nation"—or atmosphere—"where faculty work with students on individualized projects." If such examples highlight major aspects of the organization, countless other symbols also inhabit the workplace that teach individuals about the culture. Pictures on office desks of husbands, wives and children, family potlucks, or married student housing tell gay and straight individuals what is valued and what is not. A single joke at an office party clues people in to beliefs and accepted behavior. All too often in academe the closeted academic looks hither and yon and discovers affirmation about why he or she should stay in the closet. As Sedgwick (1990) has noted, "Closetedness is a performance initiated as such by the speech act of a silence—not a particular silence, but a silence that accrues particularity by fits and starts, in relation to the discourse that surrounds and differentially constitutes it" (p. 3). The discourses that surround closeted gay and lesbian people marginalize them and reinforce silent norms. Heterosexism requires everyone to assume that individuals are sexually alike, so that a culture of silence builds for those who are different. Silence comes in various ways. Individuals hide some aspects of their lives and absent themselves from other community activities.

However, as important as it is to understand the tension between public and private lives of gay academics and the different experiences of being closeted in one organization as opposed to another, we also need to be aware that the context of the closet is ever-changing and redefinable. What it means to be a gay academic today is invariably different from what it meant a generation ago. A liberal interpretation of the foregoing data would proffer suggestions based on a real world that is entirely understandable. From the point of view of queer theory and cultural studies, however, we must also come to terms with what *gay* means throughout time so that we might better understand the structural implications and contours of the closet. Accordingly, I now turn to a discussion of the academic closet prior to the present era.

The Past Context

"It's important to remember," recalled one older interviewee, "that being gay back then didn't mean you decided to be out or not out. No one was out." "Today people are more open. Back then no one was," agreed another. A third person explained, "If you want to get involved today, there are student groups, faculty groups, staff groups. When I got my first job, there was not even a hint of anything like that. If someone had said let's start a homosexual club, people would have thought he was crazy." "The first time I remember anything like a gay culture on campus," remembered one person, "was in the 60s. Prior to that it just wasn't talked about. People went about their business."

"A lot of the gay men I knew were married," said one interviewee, and another added, "Nothing was said. It was all done off campus." Some disagreed: "Things were quiet, yes, there was no choice but to be secretive. Like now, there were places to go. In a basement of one building, behind the drama building, that kind of thing." "I think it had to do with the kind of place you taught at," recalled another. "I started out at a large urban university and there was a bathroom there that was very well-known in the city. Later on, I went to a small liberal arts college and there was nothing. I would never have thought of doing anything on campus at that place. It was too small, too easy for disclosure." "Back then," said another, "I knew a lot of gay men who were married, and I also knew straight men who were single, so it wasn't as clear as it is today." "The war (WW II) played a role," said one professor, a veteran. "Some of our first experiences were in the army." Another recalled:

> When I got out, I went to the VA office and I happened into a bathroom. There was something scrawled on the wall of the bathroom—looking for a good time—and there was an address. I went there and it was my introduction to the Everard Baths. I loved the baths. I had no guilt at all. I also never disclosed it to anyone, especially my wife. There was always a sharp separation between my gay life and everything else.

Such a separation, however, was distinctly different from the separations that closeted gay men and lesbians face today in the workplace. Whereas today we might think of the workplace closet as having a door one could ostensibly open and step through, a generation ago, the closet seemed to have no door at all. I also need to stress that I am discussing the academic closet. In Chauncey's 1994 text about gay New York in the early 20th century, he provides many helpful descriptions of gay men successfully navigating the waters of split identity—being gay in some locales and not in others. I am suggesting, however, that gay academics had no such choice in the workplace. They may well have populated the bars, theaters and dance halls that Chauncey discusses, but they did so as private citizens. In their public worklives they were not gay.

People neither chose to take an earring off or put a lapel pin on at work, nor did they ever consider taking a partner or friend to a cocktail party at the faculty club. "The bars were a great place to socialize, to get it out of the system. I went there almost every weekend," said one retired professor. Another said, "I don't drink, so I didn't go to the bars. I went to the baths. In one town, it was like what we have now, and somewhere else, I remember it as a rooming house sort of thing. They were very social, very relaxing." "Today there are potlucks, bridge clubs, coffee houses, film festivals, discussion groups, even bowling leagues, for God's sake! When I entered the profession, we had two choices—the bars or the bathhouses."

Several individuals recounted how they occasionally met colleagues and students in their local and far-flung haunts. These meetings, however, did not bring about a sense of community on campus; rather, they were opportunities for shared experiences in one's private life. "Over the years, I became used to occasionally meeting a student in the bathhouse," said one person. "I made a point of not having a relationship with any students. That's a good rule for anyone—gay or straight. But I'd see them there and they'd see me. We didn't speak about it, and we didn't get together afterward. It just didn't happen." Another individual said, "The first time I saw a student in a bar, I was very nervous. Then I realized he was just as nervous as I was, so over time I just got used to it." A third person said, "Sometimes I created something of a friendship; I suppose you could call it that. This one guy and I shared a car sometimes on the weekends when we went into the city. We were friends. But it wasn't like today. Heterosexual men had male friends then, too, so no one thought much about it." "Since there were so few places to go to, it was inevitable that you'd meet people you knew," explained another person. "I had met a professor in a bathhouse when I was in graduate school, so I knew what to expect."

"Sometimes you might meet someone on campus and guess that they were gay. But I never hunted them out and I never approached them in any way," said one person. Another said, "I was in the humanities, so I'd meet students on occasion and raise my eyebrows about them. You know, sort of, 'I bet he's gay.' I didn't say anything to them, of course." A third commented, "A student once approached me and seemed to want to speak to me, I remember, but I turned the conversation and made it clear that I wasn't a therapist. It was just too dangerous." And a fourth noted, "I knew a guy who I suspected was gay who was in the administration, but we never talked and I never saw him wherever I went. Then one day he was gone. Another faculty member told me he'd been fired because he had been arrested for something. He was just gone in the dead of night."

Socialization occurs whether an institution's participants plan it or not. The socialization of a gay faculty member in the 30s and 40s and through the 1960s primarily meant that the idea of homosexuality was a singular phenomenon related to a sexual act and not discussed, observed or addressed within the confines of campus. Thus, unlike the categories that I was able to develop in the previous section—role models, graduate school—no categories are apparent from the interviews with older faculty members. No such frameworks existed then.

"I don't think people—straight people—thought about it very much," one older academic suggested. "It's different from now when sex seems to be on everyone's brain." "People got in trouble for being homosexual, sure," agreed another person, "but there was a clear definition of what being homosexual meant—sex with a man by a man, or two women. Today I think the sensibility is different." "Coming out in the 1950s would have been a disaster," said another, "because back then, almost everyone—and I mean everyone—saw gay life as deviant, a Sodom and Gomorrah sort of thing." "People didn't think about it," countered one person. "I don't think people thought it was deviant. They just didn't think about it."

Such comments also highlight a clear distinction between the present and past. People were not out in the way that some are today; a comment, then, that "I am portraying older faculty who were closeted" would be meaningless. All faculty, with rare exceptions, led hidden lives.

One point that ought to be stressed is the distinction the individuals made between their acceptance that what they did was wrong—"an aberration," one person said—and the relatively guiltless lifestyles they led. "Sometimes I think younger people have this picture of lonely men in rooming houses then and how today it is so much better. I was never lonely; I never lived in a rooming house, and I am not convinced today is better," suggested one individual. "People use 90s eyeglasses to think about the past for us," said another. "What you need to remember is that straight people lived a different life then, too. There was a completely different take on things back then." Others disagreed: "Sometimes it got me down. The holidays. Being the bachelor and going home. People always trying to fix me up. But I wasn't racked with constant pain." And another: "My life was never boring. I was always on the run to Europe and various glorious haunts. But sometimes I think I was on the run so much because I didn't want to have to settle down and think about the life I could not have. I don't regret it though."

Thus, individuals often were able to hold onto the idea that they were simply different from others but that it was also somehow wrong. "It's just something you learned how to live with. Sometimes I ignored it, other times not. It was an instinct, and I acted on it. I never really figured out the right or wrong part," explained one person. A second commented, "I grew up in a Catholic family, so part of me was really bothered. But I also met a priest in a bathhouse. It's hard to explain. There's this part of your brain that just acts. You don't feel terrible. You just feel." Another individual said, "I lived outside of the mainstream, so I just shut it out. There was this odd split that made us realize we were doing something that was not acceptable, but that wasn't wrong." And finally: "The main thing is that it wasn't talked about. Heterosexual masturbation was wrong, too, you know, and in the army, guys did it all the time but never verbalized it, so it stayed secret. When it became verbal, it became wrong."

One individual talked about the divide that existed between his early years as an academic immediately after World War II and today, saying, "We've crossed the place where that kind of Victorian silence is possible any more." I find such an observation helpful in thinking through the parameters of the academic closet. My point here is not so much to define why there has been a shift in what it means to be gay in general but, rather, to suggest that a shift has taken place in academe in particular. A shift in what it means to be gay or lesbian is not merely a transformation from the lonely individual in a boarding house to the liberated and content academic of the 1990s. Rather, what it means to be lesbian or gay is distinctly different now, and such a transformation suggests alternative ways of constructing sexual orientation in the academy. The idea of a continuum, then, from closeted to liberated, is probably mistaken. Instead, we see different interpretations of words like gay, closet and out.

I discussed earlier the tension that exists between those who propose an essentialist definition of sexual orientation and those who are social constructionists. What these interviews have helped me to sort out is how, for at least this century, a dynamic tension has existed between both theoretical notions. Gay academics have taught in U.S. colleges and universities throughout the century—an essentialist notion. What it has meant to be a gay academic, however, has dramatically changed. In one sense, in the early 20th century, being gay meant very little with regard to how one conducted one's academic life. Choice did not exist. The compartmentalization of one's life placed sexuality outside academe. Unlike women or people of color, who could be excluded from the campus solely because they were women or people of color, the ability of gay and lesbian people to counterfeit their sexual orientation enabled them to survive on campus. Many gay academics also lived with a dualism that enabled them to act on their sexual desires and at the same time perceive such wants as aberrant. Furthermore, with regard to one's professional life, how one defined being gay in large part had to do with the sexual act.

As noted, authors such as Chauncey (1994) and Kennedy and Davis (1993) have made compelling cases that a gay and lesbian culture existed in the early part of this century in locales as divergent as New York City and rural America, and those cultures were often celebratory. As Chauncey notes, "Many gay men celebrated their difference from the norm, and some of them organized to resist antigay policing" (p. 4). From the interviews of senior academics, we might also partially accept such an argument. Bathhouses, bars, and rooming houses seemed to exist where men and women were able to claim a lesbian or gay identity and were comfortable with themselves.

However, let us focus again on those in academe. We are at a point in our social history where being gay is something more than the sum and difference of sexual acts. If we accept that organizations exist as cultures, then how was homosexuality defined within that academic culture at a specific time? What did it mean to be a gay academic in 1940 and in 1990? What are the consequences for how we think about the future? Obviously, one's personal life invades one's professional life at various points. What I am suggesting, however, is that the idea of identity as an all-embracing concept that we carry through all our multiple roles is in need of reconsideration and redefinition. What it meant to be a gay academic in 1940 is that one had same-sex attractions. The notion of lesbian and gay studies as an area of inquiry for the most part was nonexistent. In the earlier part of this century, for example, faculty members were not fired for studying lesbian and gay issues but often lost their jobs as economists, sociologists, and philosophers, for studying socialist or radical phenomena. An optimistic interpretation is that queer studies was a legitimate area of inquiry. The more logical conclusion, however, is that those in the academy could not conceive of such an area of study. If gay meant what I did sexually with another man, then it did not affect my work life. If gay is a socially circumscribed term fraught with multiple meanings and interpretations, then the potential for how it affects my work and the workings of the academy is vast.

Eve Sedgwick (1990) has pointed out how contemporary sexual identities are consistently blurred so that everyone, especially those in the minority, is in a perpetual state of anxiety. Following Foucault, Sedgwick believes that the power of the norm achieves its goal—conformity—by constantly manipulating these identities so that one is forever kept off balance and out of control. As Best and Kellner (1991) note, "Power operates not through repression of sex, but through the discursive production of sexuality and subjects who have a 'sexual nature' " (p. 47). The stable homosexual identity of the early part of this century, then, where individuals knew who they were and how to behave, was a function of power, just as the unstable academic gay identity is today. The difference is manifested in how power functions, and how groups and individuals respond and resist.

From this perspective, the stability of identity is not developed tabula rasa, person by person but, rather, is conferred on individuals by disciplinary regimes as a way to control them. Foucault (1980) notes, "There is no binary division to be made between what one says and what one does not say; we must try to determine the different ways of not saying such things. . . . There is not one but many silences, and they are an integral part of the strategies that underlie and permeate discourses" (p. 27). What Foucault means is best highlighted by the divergent voices we heard from the closeted gay academics of today and yesterday. How they have defined their gay identities is by no means uniform. Their silence exists in a variety of discursive notions about how their public roles get circumscribed by their private gay lives. What we mean by the closet today is meaningless if we apply it to similar situations a century ago.

Institutions, individuals and the society in which they are embedded help create the meanings of terms like gay. The discourses that have surrounded gay and lesbian individuals act in concert with the ideological formulations of the institution. These formulations act to marginalize people by the dualism inherent in their private and public personae. Because we assume that everyone is similar, differences act to disturb the norm, which in turn, reinforces a culture of silence for those who are different. In the 40s, silence was all-encompassing so that choice did not really exist; in the 90s, silence gets chosen more consciously.

A cultural politics surrounds how knowledge gets defined, studied, and enacted, which in turn structures how we have thought about what it means to be gay in academe. Accordingly, concepts like knowledge are inevitably related to power and ideology; to speak of knowledge as if it were a reified object is to overlook the theoretical scaffolding on which it rests. Thus, we learn how a traditional definition of an academic area such as English or history did not merely represent a reified idea but also reflected the interests, for example, of men or the upper class. We have arrived at a time when what it means to be gay in academe is radically different from what it meant a generation ago. Being gay in academe does not only mean a same-sex attraction but also how I organize knowledge, how I think about my intellectual work, and how the academy rewards or sanctions books of this sort.

Again, outside the portals of academe, writers such as Proust, E. M. Forster and Genet engaged in philosophical and literary inquiry about what it meant to be homosexual, and such works went well beyond a confining definition of homosexuality as same-sex attraction. However, within academe, the gay professor did not alter his or her work plan or how he or she thought about knowledge. Today alternatives exist. Such a reconfiguration of knowledge is not merely a continuation or extension of being gay but also offers a dramatically different way of conceiving of sexual identity. Such a point plays directly into the idea developed in Chapter 1 about understanding knowledge and location. From this perspective, sexual identity is a mixture of essentialism and constructionism that not only is reconfigured over time and context but also occurs within the multiple and often conflicting contexts in which our lives are played out. An individual could share a gay culture in dance halls and bars as a private person but that did not get transferred to campus. Today, the culture enables individuals and groups to come together, to make decisions about whether they should form groups, and to decide whether to be closeted or out.

The implications of such a view are manifold. Chauncey (1994) has argued that the baths and bars of the early part of this century may well have been examples of closeted behavior, but at the same time gay men "opened and closed [them] at strategic moments. In such closets, a gay world was built" (p. 225). The point is well-taken. Perhaps the decision of whether to wear a red ribbon to a job interview could not have taken place without the initial construction of the closet or some variation of it. What seems clear from these interviews, however, is that the academic closet has not been constructed in concert with those larger societal closets of bars and baths. In effect, there was no academic closet.

As we approach the 21st century, then, we now have alternative ways of thinking about academe and of acting on them. Rather than adducing simple facts and figures for who's gay and who's not, we need to consider disciplinary regimes and how we gay people function not merely as sexual identities or by way of sexual acts but how our queer academic identity gets framed and shaped. We concentrate on the cultural and structural contours of the organization instead of the easy acceptance of the world as it is. Rather than assume, for example, that gay and lesbian studies is but one more traditional department in a static structure, we should focus on how we might disrupt the structure. Instead of thinking how we might be able to make the gay or lesbian individual fit into the culture of the organization, we should struggle to come to terms with how the organization needs to change its culture, symbols and discursive systems. And as gay and lesbian people, we acknowledge that with choice comes a responsibility that previously did not exist.

In the next chapter, I offer an alternative portrait of lesbian and gay life in academe. By way of a piece of ethnographic fiction, I attempt to highlight the multiple tensions that exist for us daily on campus. The purpose here is to point out not merely the external tensions caused by homophobia and heterosexism but also to consider the internal problems we encounter as we struggle honestly to communicate with one another.

Chapter **6**

Ashes
A Short Story

The early mornings of the weekend were when Harry was most at home in his adopted city but also when he most longed for the prairie. He had grown up in a farm town of 1,600 people in North Dakota and, like most boys there, loved sledding on Sanish Hill in the winter and swimming in Fisher's Pond in the summer. He liked the firm crunch of boots on leaden snow on a crystal clear night in the dead of winter and treasured that first gulp of ice tea after working in the fields of summer.

His daughter teased him that he was a romantic, and she could not understand how he ever survived on the prairie. "It's so boring there, daddy," she'd said more than once, and he never was sure how to express to her his love for a life that she would never experience. After his mother died a decade ago, there really had been no reason to go back. His brother and he had sold the farm when their father died and they had had to move their mother into a nursing home. He had faithfully visited her as often as he could when crisscrossing the country, but he also knew in his heart that he enjoyed going home. He liked to sit in Stan's Cafe and order pancakes for breakfast and drink coffee with the regulars. After a steak dinner at the Elks Club, he loved to drive up to Sanish Hill at night and look out on the stars that stretched all the way to Canada. His wife and his daughter did not have much interest in stargazing or in flapjacks.

Ellen and he had a relationship that was not overly demonstrative—he was not that kind of man—but it was civil and warm. They were best friends and she always looked out for his interests. When they met in college, he had wanted a career in politics and chose a wife who could help him advance that career. She was pretty, not a dazzler like the woman his brother married, but then, he wasn't a dazzler either.

He tried to keep in shape, but he traveled so much that he seemed to be fighting a losing battle. His father, even in old age, was rock solid. Harry's frame was large like his father's, but portly. "It's this job," he told himself when he looked at the balding figure in a mirror. "Too much airport food, not enough time outdoors."

What Harry viewed as a series of accidents, others saw as a clear trajectory of what he had wanted to be since graduating from college. He had given up the idea of politics when he was young and one thing had led to another; the political life transformed into academic administration until he had become president of Central University. Cardinal Richardson occasionally kidded Harry that he was such a clever politician he should run for state office, but Harry demurred. He liked his job and did not plan on starting a new career.

Central was his third presidency and probably his last; he had checked himself into the hospital a few years back for what he had thought might have been a mild heart attack. His doctor had given him advice that was good common sense—eat better, take long walks, reduce stress. Unfortunately, common sense, as he often pointed out to Ellen, did not come with the job of being a college president.

He had returned from Vietnam as a decorated soldier; like many who went there, he had become disillusioned after seeing so many of his friends die. He wanted nothing to do with politics and entered graduate school to study engineering. Soon after joining the faculty ranks, he realized that the quiet and reflection of the professorate would not appeal to him forever. He liked setting goals and figuring how to get there. He decided he wanted to be a college president and figured out how to do it. He rose rapidly through the administrative ranks and by the age of 45 had accepted the presidency of a medium-sized private college. After five years and a very successful capital campaign, he was nominated for the presidency of a large public university where his talents in fund-raising were actively sought. He stayed at Lexington six years and discovered yet again that the political life was not for him. Battling with state legislators over appropriations was drudgery and he wanted out. He waited until his daughter graduated from college and then he and Ellen looked around, "for a good challenge—and a good climate" he had jokingly told his friends.

He had arrived at Central five years ago. Ellen loved the place. She had never lived in a major city before and, as the president's wife, found her life a constant round of social gatherings that fitted her personality. Harry liked the job, but not the city. Central was the oldest university in the region and the largest employer in the largest city in the state. In some respects, he felt he had the best of both worlds; he could be involved in the political life without having to be a politician. He knew the governor by first name, and the senate candidates from both parties had sought his endorsement in the campaign last year. The mayor was a friend. He had breakfast with the cardinal on a monthly basis and, for good measure, attended an ecumenical lunch that was hosted by the Reverend Shilling of First Lutheran. He just needed to watch his heart and Ellen's lungs. She had given up smoking as soon as the doctor detected a spot on the lung, but he continued to worry.

Harry didn't really mind fund-raising either. He had learned as a teenager that he had a knack for selling things. "Selling tickets for a high school raffle is not that different from selling the university to a donor," he liked to say. "Look the guy in the eye, have a firm handshake, always tell the truth, and have a smile on your face. People buy earnestness and they want an upbeat attitude."

But he never felt at home in the city. What bothered him most were the never-ending car alarms, the rat-a-tat of jackhammers building a new this or that, and the pollution common to any major city but especially this one.

On those early weekend mornings when he padded outside barefoot in his gray silk bathrobe to get the newspaper, he could briefly hear the chirping of the bluejays. The sound of birds was special, something he could not hear during the week, and he wondered how long he would have to endure the harshness of the city until he could convince Ellen to get out of the rat race and retire somewhere to go fishing and take proper care of themselves. "I could even get this hulk of a body back to where it's supposed to be," he'd told Ellen a week ago. She'd just laughed; she'd heard these complaints, she thought, for as long as they'd been together. If it wasn't the city, it was something else.

He gave himself three more years. He'd be 62, and their pension would be enough. Three more years.

Across town, Doug continued his vigil at Skip's bedside. Skip and he had been together long before they had both tested HIV positive. Then Skip had received his official designation as a PWA. "I joined a club," laughed Skip when Doug had come home one day a little over a year ago. "Doctor Lark told me that I now officially qualify as a Person With AIDS. Those pesky T cells dipped below 200. Membership entitles me to all sorts of prizes. I get free entrance into exclusive groups, the government will give me cash awards for disability, for health, for housing. I expect Ed McMahon to come knocking on the door any minute to fill me in on the details."

Doug was not small, but he was slender. Skip, who was 6 feet 2 and 200 pounds, once could enfold him in a way that made Doug feel uniquely special. Skip's embraces were strong, secure, energetic. Since being diagnosed, however, Skip had had trouble maintaining his weight. He was frequently tired and his body tone had gone flaccid. Arms that had once lifted weights with ease now got tired carrying a book from the bedroom to the study. A walk from his car to his office was now beyond him. A neuropathy on his right foot soon slowed him to a crawl so that now he spent most of his time on the back porch while Doug worked in the garden—Skip's garden.

"The potatoes will be up early. The spinach any day," said Doug one morning, "and we'll have tomatoes by midsummer, I'm sure. Can't wait to see them." He hurried into the house, "to wash my hands," he'd said, but they both knew the meaning of Doug's constant chatter. The garden was a marker. All winter, Doug had spoken excitedly about their getting out to plant in the spring. He'd ordered seed catalogues, and they would sit in their small art deco living room in front of the fire and choose which flowers to plant along the fence in the back and where to put the spinach.

Doug knew that what he was doing was silly. The health costs continued to climb and the costs of the drugs that Dr. Lark prescribed were outrageous. They soon learned that the cash prizes from the government mentioned by Skip amounted to almost nothing. Skip first complained bitterly about what he called their "amazing shrinking bank account," but he'd grown so tired that he left these matters entirely in Doug's hands now. And Doug didn't want Skip to worry, so he chattered on about the garden.

At night, after Skip had finally fallen asleep, Doug listened to his labored breathing. Recently, Skip had grown worse and rarely left his bed. There wasn't much time. Doug thought they'd take small steps and get through them—they'd order seeds and then plant early vegetables and then late ones and they'd get to fall and—

Skip's love of the outdoors carried over to his work at the university. A half-dozen years before, when the administration had tried to pave over a small park near Skip's building, he had rallied the students to preserve it. Once he had saved it, he set about creating a people's park. "People need green space. Kids need a place to space out. I need a space to space out. I want couples there, lovers, friends, workmen." Doug had heard it all before and simply smiled at one more madcap idea from Skip.

Because of his labors, the grounds and buildings crew came to respect Skip, "even if he is a fag." He worked with them in the park and over time, they no longer called him "Sir" but "Skip." Sometimes they even used his last name, as if he were one of them. When he put the rose garden in, they joked that it should be commemorated as the "Professor Skip Memorial Rose Garden," but privately they were impressed. They secretly appreciated his knowledge of plants and flowers as much as his willingness to sit there and have lunch with them, something no other faculty member would ever think of doing.

The fruits of Skip's efforts were always evident. The garden in the back of their house had abundant flowers, herbs and vegetables. The park by the office was filled with flowers in a riot of color. Joseph's Coat, a climbing rose, formed a border around the park. The rose garden had over a dozen different kinds of flowering rose bushes—yellow Grandifloras, brown Butterscotches and a remarkable scarlet Queen Anne's Lace had made the park a favorite stop for the tour guides around the campus. Skip was proud of his work, and, more often than not on a sunny day, students who had office hours with him found him on the stone bench in the park. He had even tried to hold a committee meeting there, but a colleague objected to sitting on the damp grass.

Following Dr. Lark's diagnosis, the change in Doug and Skip's relationship was as dramatic as the change in Skip's body. Before AIDS—that was the way Doug now thought about the world, life before and life after AIDS—Skip had been the one who had made the plans in their lives. Doug, a computer programmer at Central for fifteen years, had met Skip at the first gay and lesbian reception held at Central a dozen years before. Skip, a sociology professor, was a well-known activist.

Initially he had been closeted, but over time, most people just grew to know he was gay, and eventually those who did not know found out directly from Skip. He was instrumental in starting a gay and lesbian film series and smoothed the way for the drama department to stage its first gay play.

"I'm tenured," he'd often laugh. "I bet that makes people wonder if we should keep tenure." Central was also a liberal enough place that it could tolerate Skip's brand of activism.

Right from the start, Skip had provided the direction for their relationship. "We should move in together," Skip said to Doug after they had dated for a while. "It just makes sense. It will save us both money, you'll have the benefit of my cooking, and I like the thought of waking up to you for the rest of my life." Skip had a penchant for ending his sentences with a slight lilt in his voice. Doug also found his shy grin and intense blue eyes irresistible.

For his part, Doug was a kind man with a soft voice who was difficult not to like. He had been a rugby player in school and had kept in shape by bicycling virtually everywhere he went. "You'll also be able to get a ride to school when it rains," concluded Skip when they had agreed to live together, "so you won't be catching pneumonia on that damn bike of yours." They moved in together the next week. In the ensuing years, their friends spoke of them only as a unit—"DougandSkip."

As Skip grew ill, however, Doug found himself making the decisions. He began to do the cooking. Skip stopped being the faculty adviser to the gay and lesbian student association and Doug became active in the faculty/staff group. Doug learned everything there was to know about gardening, even though he'd never so much as weeded before. He tended to their backyard garden and brought weekly missives from Skip to the grounds and building crew about what should happen in the park.

At first, the changes in Skip's routine were harder for him than the illness. "You burned the goddamned pot roast," he yelled one night when Doug's dinner was slightly overdone. "How damn hard can it be to follow directions." Doug nodded and tried to overlook the comments, but that too, inevitably set Skip off: "Don't fucking patronize me. I have enough shit to deal with without you trying to act the part of Florence Nightingale. Goddamnit to hell."

Doug didn't have problems with the new role, even with the occasional outbursts, except during quiet moments when he realized why he was doing what he was doing. Skip was going to die. When Skip had proposed that they move in together so that they could wake up next to one another for the rest of their lives, Doug's romantic side had envisioned two men united in love forever.

And they did love one another. Passionately. Skip had no qualms about running up to Doug on campus and giving him a kiss if they hadn't seen one another all day. On occasion, Skip would take Doug's hand when they went out to dinner. "I don't give a damn who thinks what," Skip would say. Doug's secretary had grown used to the occasional delivery of flowers to the office and would frequently sigh, "I'm going to send my husband over to your house so you can teach him how to treat the person he loves."

They had a commitment ceremony in the park on their tenth anniversary. Doug's initial reticence about such public displays of affection changed over time to acquiescence and then comfort and pride. Cycling home at the end of the day, he knew that Skip would have something planned, or they would just work independently on their projects until it was time for sleep or the ferocious lovemaking that had yet to grow routine.

Doug's romantic fantasies had never included spending so much time fruitlessly trying to balance their checkbook in hospital waiting rooms. His life this last year had been filled with taking Skip to the hospital for one or another emergency. Skip had woken up one night unable to breathe. Another night, he had had an allergic reaction to a new drug. He fell and bruised himself one afternoon. The eczema covered all of his body one week so that he looked like a leper until they got the drugs back in balance, and another time, he suffered a prolonged bout of diarrhea.

Through all of these trips, Doug tried to figure out how they would pay for everything. Their families had no resources and they had survived comfortably on their dual incomes when they were healthy. But the savings were gone and Doug had taken out a second mortgage on the house to make ends meet. Alone in a hospital waiting room, Doug increasingly saw horrible choices and a horrible future—they were destitute in one future, and the other future was one without Skip.

Doug had never envisioned spending a Saturday morning drinking his café au lait at the side of a hospital bed in the center of their living room. The doctor had said the week before it was only a matter of days, and Skip was adamant that he did not want to die in the hospital. He was unconscious and his breathing was heavy. Occasionally he coughed but had rarely opened his eyes these last two days. Doug sat there and tried to recall life before AIDS.

Jason had tried all week to get hold of Mari Lee; they had ended up playing telephone tag. "If you knew how to use e-mail," teased his partner, Errol, "you could have reached ML five days ago. But you're such a nincompoop about it, that here you are spending your Saturday morning on the telephone rather than in bed with me. Who'd believe that you're a distinguished faculty member of Central University when you're barely removed from hunting and pecking on your Olivetti." Jason ignored Errol, dialed the phone number and hearing Mari Lee's voice, held his right palm outward in Errol's direction and mouthed the words, "Shut up." Errol wrinkled up his nose, picked up the newspaper, and shimmied past Jason into the living room. Jason grabbed the metro section as Errol vamped by him in his red cotton pajamas.

"Hi ML. Have you seen it? I've been trying to get hold of you to figure out how we should handle it."

"Seen what, Jason?" yawned Mari Lee. She respected Jason's desire to create change at Central but, like most of the others in the gay community, grew tired of Jason's constant requests. Jason talked the way he looked—tight, compact, full of energy, black jeans, five-and-dime T-shirts.

She didn't want to speak to him on a Saturday morning. Her friends talked about how people were "Jasonized" after a conversation with him, and she just wanted to finish her brioche in peace this morning. She had to get to the cleaners, grade the papers, and hoped to hook up with Jessica for dinner. She would keep the dialogue to a minimum.

"It's in the metro section, right here, on the first page." He began to read from the newspaper: "Central University is set to recommend to its board of trustees that homosexuals be able to register as domestic partners and receive the same health and personnel benefits currently accorded to married couples. If passed, the policy will be the most far-reaching of any university in the country. University spokesman Jason McCloud said, 'It's evidence of Central's commitment to advancing the cause of lesbian and gay rights. Under the leadership of Dean Sorcinelli, the benefits committee will recommend a comprehensive package of health and personnel benefits to the full board of trustees at their next meeting.' "

"That's great, Jason, I see it," said Mari Lee as she simultaneously thumbed through her newspaper, drank her daily concoction of carrot and guava juice, and moved a stack of laundry from the washer to the dryer. She wanted to cut him off before he read the whole article to her. She actually was impressed that Central might get a domestic partners' agreement, but Jason's grandstanding had grown tiresome even to Mari Lee. He was the loquacious version of Forrest Gump for the gay rights movement, a friend had said; whenever an important pronouncement was made, Jason's picture was sure to be printed.

"Great! It's better than great! Everything's going to change. I think we need to have a meeting. That's why I was calling. Recommending to the board doesn't mean we'll actually get it, and we need to strategize about our next step. Can you call the people on the list and tell them there's an emergency meeting on Thursday night? It won't take much time. I also told Sandy to make calls too. If you do the women and Sandy does the men, the work will be split. I think we need to plan our next steps. Brian Sorcinelli has been great. The president is a question mark, but he hasn't been a roadblock and that's a big improvement over five years ago. We're really on the right track. I'm going to talk to Doug since he's officially chairing the group. Skip is pretty sick, but maybe Doug can come; otherwise, we'll have to do it. So see you Thursday night. Let me know how it's going."

Jason hung up before Mari Lee agreed to make the phone calls. "Typical," she muttered as she put the phone down and started the dryer. As she retied her bathrobe and looked out the kitchen window she wondered how Skip was. How Doug was. Skip was her oldest friend—all the way since high school. She always had been overweight and, as the only minority in Horace High School, had had few friends. As she laughed years later, "A loudmouthed, fat Filipina who dressed in Mama Cass outfits did not exactly have to worry about being elected Most Popular Student." Skip was one of the few students—and the only boy—who befriended her. He constantly asked her what it was like to grow up in the Philippines and eventually they came out to one another. That she had ended up at Central was "a blessing from the ancestors," they'd agreed.

When Skip moved in with Doug, she became almost as close to him as she was to Skip. He was not funny like Skip, but he always listened to her in a way that most men did not. Mari Lee was a respected feminist on campus; her work on Wordsworth had earned her a Guggenheim a few years before and since that time, even the most conservative faculty members had kept quiet.

She had initially had a difficult time at Central. Her weight and diminutive size were matched by her equally powerful voice. Many of the faculty were put off by her willingness to engage in seemingly endless public debate about feminist issues. The women's health center. Women's athletics. A women in science program. Mari Lee's causes were legion.

Skip had been her constant ally and confidant. They supported one another professionally and personally. When Skip had staged a sit-in to protest an inadequate university response to antigay graffiti four years before, ML was the only other professor who participated in the sit-in with him. When she started a take-back-the-night march, Skip, at her request, was the only man in the front line of the march. When Skip and Doug almost broke up, ML played counselor. And when she had made tentative moves to update her wardrobe—"You're becoming a lipstick lesbian," Skip had shrieked—she turned to Skip and Doug for advice on what to buy. "I thought you'd never ask," said Skip and then planned a weekend outing of shopping that transformed ML from an academic spinster to looking like a woman in *Vogue*—albeit slightly overweight—and reading *Mirabella*. At Skip and Doug's commitment ceremony, ML agreed to be one of the two grooms and had shown up with Brian in matching blue velvet tuxedos and lavender sashes.

Unlike Skip, Jason was one of the bossiest men she knew and she had a good mind to just blow him off, except that she felt his heart was in the right place. He was so socially inept that she often felt bemused by what he wanted. Even Skip could barely tolerate him, and Skip liked everyone. "He wants to be the head homosexual on campus," he'd said, "and look at the way he dresses. He should come to me for fashion tips too, and then we can see who's the head queer here. I bet he can't even dance. What kind of queer is he?" Yet, ever loyal to the cause, she walked into her study and flipped through her address book, looking for the names she would call on and off through the weekend.

Brian Sorcinelli was painting his garage when his wife yelled out to him, "Harry's on the phone, Brian. He says he wants to talk with you." He considered telling Judy to say he'd call back later, but it was odd for the President to call him at home on the weekend, so he thought he had better take the call. Brian was a sloppy painter, and as he got down from the ladder, he shook his head back and forth, exclaiming at the mess he had made of the garage floor. "I knew I should have hired some college guys. There's gray everywhere," he said, as he walked past his wife and headed to the phone. "A blind man could do better. Look at the mess I made. You never should have gotten me into this."

"If you think the floor is a mess, you should see what you've done to yourself," Judy laughed as she checked on her almond macaroons in the oven. Ellen and she had to attend a Sunday afternoon tea for Central's Goldenleaf Club—"RWWRs" is what Brian called them (rich widows without relatives), and she had agreed to bring macaroons, one of her favorite recipes.

Brian looked at himself as he picked up the phone. His mop of black hair had streaks of gray paint. His tan face and eyeglasses were speckled with paint. His hands were more gray than white. He felt like a fool.

As soon as Brian took the phone, he knew something was wrong. Harry usually delighted in small talk, and they often joked with one another about being from the Dakotas—he from Rapid City and Harry from some small place up north. "I know I can trust you, Sorcinelli," Harry told him when he was hired. "A man who's been through the Dakota winters is someone you can count on."

Brian said, "Hi Harry. Sorry for the wait. I was out painting the garage, or actually painting the garage and everything else six feet near it." Harry ignored him and got straight to the point:

"Have you seen this morning's paper?"

"Some of it. Sports. The front page. I'm sure glad baseball's back in action. Did you see—"

"The metro section, Brian. Have you seen the metro section where Central is on the front page announcing that we've become a homosexual rights lobby. Did you see that?"

Brian in fact had not seen it, but a reporter had interviewed him over the phone the previous week. He had completely forgotten. "Oh yeah, I knew it would come out sometime. How does it look? One of my faculty sure has worked hard in getting them here. The personnel committee—"

"You wanna know how it looks? Let me tell you. It's 1:15 on a Saturday afternoon. Two trustees called me this morning and Sanford Carlisle. Ellen and I went to do some shopping, and when I got back, I had a message to call the Cardinal. What do you think he wants, Brian? I've been blindsided. Carlisle says he'll have to reconsider the addition to the library if that's what his alma mater is about. The trustees were livid."

Brian at first did not see the problem. "Things like this blow over. The older folks blow it out of proportion. The cardinal—"

"You don't get it, Brian," exploded Harry. "This is exactly the opposite kind of news we need right now. We need good news. Instead we have articles saying we're going to be the leading homosexual university in the country. That's just great. And that twerp Jason McCloud gets quoted as a 'university spokesman.' We're about to start on a capital campaign and I've got my board mad at me and the cardinal ready to cut my nuts off. The lead donor is reconsidering. This is a royal screwup. Listen Brian, never, ever, do something like this again. Always check with me first. If I ever have my Saturday or any other day destroyed like this again, you will have hell to pay. I don't need stress like this, Brian. I'm a reasonable man—I don't mind small changes, maybe—but this kind of publicity is simply unreasonable. Check with James on Monday and see how this can be taken care of. I don't want to have anything to do with it, and the board certainly will not approve it if it comes to them, but it won't. The provost can clear up your mess. It will be cleared up."

The president hung up. Maybe he's just homophobic, Brian thought. All his life, Brian had had friends who were gay; Judy's brother was gay. Their best friends at the university were Doug and Skip. Brian winced. He had called Doug last night and learned that Skip was close to death. All morning out in the garage, he couldn't stop thinking about Skip. Skip had chaired the search committee for Brian's job and they had become friends immediately upon his arrival. Brian had even helped Skip on occasion out at the park; Skip, along with ML, was who Brian relied on for advice—"my postmodern kitchen cabinet," Brian had joked with them.

Brian just didn't think that the policy they recommended was a big deal. "This is the 90s," he said to himself. "Lots of universities are planning the exact same thing." He'd check with the provost on Monday and work it out. He thought about calling Doug but didn't want to be a nuisance. He grabbed a handful of macaroons and headed back to the garage.

Harry called the provost over the weekend and made his position very clear. When Brian phoned him, the provost had been cordial but also quite firm. The provost felt Harry needed to be "more educated" about the topic, but there were so many other issues on the burner that this one had to be sacrificed while it still could be. "Get yourself out of this, Brian," he'd said. "I'm telling you as a friend and as the provost. Harry was quite icy with me. This is not something that you should spend time on and hurt your career with. I can't support you either. It's just not worth it. I know it's stupid, but that's the way it is. Stall or delay or something. It's almost summer, and we can hope it will blow over in the summer."

Before the meeting, Mari Lee contacted everyone on Jason's list. Most of them grumbled about the need for yet another meeting but said they would try to make it. Unaware of the president's anger, Jason spent the week calling everyone he knew and quite often repeated what they had just heard from Mari Lee or Sandy. Little matter. Jason felt that receiving two messages would let people know the importance of the meeting—he wanted to be sure they got it right. Jason's bull-in-a-china-shop attitude turned many people off. He suspected that he was unpopular, but he also knew that someone had to be a leader. "What more important thing could you be doing than going to this meeting?" he'd said to more than one person. "Get your priorities straight!"

He was, however, circumspect with Doug. When the phone rang, Doug let the answering machine respond and heard Jason's voice talk about the meeting and his hope that Doug could attend, "although I know it's tough right now with Skip. I'm thinking about you guys," he said and hung up. Doug had not been out of the house since the weekend. Although some people had come over, he felt very much alone. Mari Lee had spent much of Saturday with him. Brian had phoned. Skip had been so close to both of them, and Doug appreciated how much support they were for him now, too.

One of the volunteers from the Buddy program came every evening and stayed through the night, but even with someone in the house, Doug felt that he was there by himself and, in a way, that Skip had already left. Doug would go into their bedroom, undress and crawl into the queen-sized teak-framed bed that he and Skip had bought when they moved into their house a dozen years before. Doug was unable to sleep. He lay half between waking and sleeping.

Toward morning he felt a terrific chill and, opening his eyes, saw what he thought was the first glimmer of morning light, except that it was still dark outside. He put on his jeans, went upstairs, and quietly sat at Skip's bedside. The volunteer was asleep in the overstuffed easy chair from Skip's school office. The volunteer had curled himself into a tight ball whereas Skip always sat loosely in the chair, covering every inch, one leg draped over the arm, another tucked up in a corner of a cushion, arms thrown out behind his head as he talked to a never-ending stream of students. Now Doug knelt down over the bed, held Skip's hand, felt the faintest of grips, saw the briefest glimmer in what had once been remarkably blue eyes, heard the last exhalation of breath, and watched Skip die.

The volunteer stirred and immediately knew what had happened. He did not say anything and tried not to disturb the momentary peace that had settled in the small house. The living room was warm, even though the fire had long since died out; it was a warmth that Doug had known in childhood after he returned from ice-skating and his grandmother made cocoa for him, a warmth he also knew from falling asleep in Skip's arms and waking next to him on mornings such as this one. Doug sat there holding Skip's limp hand, and time, once again, was absent.

Brian and Harry met when the president came to the provost's weekly Tuesday lunch meeting with the deans to brief them about the upcoming capital campaign. Harry was outgoing and chummy toward Brian and acted as if nothing had happened. They walked into the room together and the older man joked with Brian about how he had seen him jogging earlier that day, "Pretty good pace, Sorcinelli, I must say. I bet I could give you a run for your money, though." Brian smiled and suggested they take a run sometime. "I'd like that. Ellen and Judy always seem to have things up their sleeves. One of these days when the girls go off together, you should sneak on over and we'll take a run, and afterward, I'll introduce you to some damn good beer. I've started a microbrewery in the basement. Very tasty stuff if I do say so myself." Brian said it was a deal and the meeting began. There was no mention of their weekend phone call, but at one point in his briefing, the president said, "We have to be very careful about the board's feelings. They are instrumental to our success, so think twice before you come up with any knuckleheaded ideas that might aggravate them." Brian knew what Harry meant by "knuckleheaded ideas."

Going back to his office after the meeting, Brian saw Mari Lee walking across the plaza dressed in a white long-sleeved shirt, dark tie, and jeans. Noontime at Central meant the plaza was awash in humanity. Brian sometimes went there just to feel the press of humanity. He loved the electricity there. On the plaza's makeshift stage was a band called A Pint of Guinness singing a version of Irish reggae. While he approached her, Brian thought that Mari Lee looked old; he wondered if he, too, was aging so visibly. He saw with some alarm, however, that she had been crying.

"Skip died. Doug called me and asked me to let you know, to let the others know too."

Brian shuddered even though the day was warm and the sun was out. He had never known anyone who had died from AIDS. Brian felt foolish, inappropriate, standing there amidst hordes of students on bicycles and skateboards, not knowing what to say. He had been a coward not to go over to see them last weekend, he told himself, keeping himself busy painting the garage, doing errands. He had just not wanted to say good-bye; now it was impossible.

So much of their lives was intertwined in that plaza. When Skip had organized that sit-in, Brian made sure that the police were told how to behave. On days when Brian felt betrayed by an administrator or a faculty attack, Skip had always cajoled him into getting an espresso at the Daily Grounds. They had sat in the park right there countless afternoons with Skip refusing to let him turn cynical, and they had ended up laughing away once pressing day-to-day concerns. What would he do now?

"I'm so . . ." He looked off. "Doug. How's Doug? Is there anything —"

"I don't know," ML said. "How do you feel after your partner has died? What can I do, Brian? I feel so helpless. I've prepared myself for this ever since . . . Skip was the first person I came out to in high school. He was so strong. He was a part of me. For years, he and Doug were the only two gay people here who were out. Skip always won you over with his laughter. Doug . . ."

Her voice trailed off, enveloped by the punk reggae group's offkey, offbeat noise. Harry and the provost walked by and they waved to Brian; he nodded to them in return. He draped his left arm over Mari Lee's shoulders and awkwardly bent down and hugged her. He felt momentarily safe being enveloped in her arms. Her tears soaked through his cotton shirt as he said, "I . . .I want to do something."

Eventually, Brian let go of Mari Lee and trudged back to his office. He thought it would be wrong to disturb Doug; he had no idea how to respond.

He called home, but Judy was across the city with Ellen at an afternoon concert. Off and on all afternoon, he returned in his mind's eye to his encounter with Mari Lee, remembering how he had wanted to be of comfort to her but had not known what to say, what to do. He only knew that his stomach ached as if he had eaten something bad or had drunk too much liquor.

Jason called to remind him of the meeting and sounded as if he didn't know about Skip's death. Brian wondered if he should say anything and decided against it, wanting to hold his words. As evening approached and the campus quieted down, he looked out his window onto the plaza and unconsciously rubbed his right thumb, trying to remove the remnants of the weekend's paint. A group of teenagers stood in a circle at one edge of the park and played Hacky Sack. A boy and girl sat on the bench and necked. A graduate student sat cross-legged and read from a book. Skip would have been pleased. The roses were in brilliant multicolored bloom, too. Brian shook his head, turned off the lights, picked up his briefcase and keys, and headed to his car.

By the next evening, most of the university had heard of Skip's death. The campus and city newspapers ran obituaries. They quoted Jason about Skip's importance to the gay and lesbian community and how they had lost a voice and a friend. Brian said how valued a colleague Skip had been to the university. He was survived by his "long-time companion, Doug Blaine," the notices said. By the time Brian arrived at the meeting, the room was packed and they needed to make space for him. He looked for Mari Lee and could not find her. Jason was at the front and spoke about the events leading up to the meeting and where he thought the group was.

Although Jason chaired the committee, Brian was an ex-officio member and actually held more sway than anyone else in the room. He was a straight white male who was dean; he should have been suspect to many of the committee members, but he had won the confidence of the group by his consistent, methodical support. That his best friends were Mari Lee, Skip and Doug also helped. His low-key manner, self-deprecating humor, and understanding of the issues helped win over even the most outspoken graduate students on the task force. He approached the current meeting in much the same way that he had approached the other meetings, and not until he sat down, did he realize that he was in a difficult position. He was well organized and had a terrific mind for detail. Usually if someone asked a question, he was able to provide a reasoned answer without hesitation. But this meeting was different.

He was surprised by his reaction to Skip's death. He had thought he was prepared. Until Skip had become too sick to speak, Brian had talked to him or seen him almost every day, and they had often spoken about death. "Doug's scared," Skip had whispered to him one night while Doug prepared dinner in the other room. "He doesn't want to see me die, but—"

Eventually Skip and Doug did talk about death, but for months, the conversation between Skip and Brian was mostly about death and dying. Brian again felt terrible that he had not gone over there last weekend.

And now that Skip was dead, Brian could not stop thinking about death. Perhaps if he had been less consumed, he would have thought more about the meeting. Unlike other times when he could sit back and listen, tonight he would have to stonewall and say that all the work that the task force had done was for nought. Or he'd have hell to pay. He actually didn't think Harry would remove him as dean, but he knew that he'd be frozen from any of the plans that were in the works. If Harry wanted to bury someone, he could do it without a trace, Dakota loyalty or not. How strange, thought Brian abstractedly while Jason talked about the newspaper article and a radio interview he had done, "What I say in the next hour can affect my career more than anything else I've ever done." A rustle in the back of the room brought him out of his reverie. He looked up and saw Mari Lee and Doug enter.

After her encounter with Brian in the plaza, Mari Lee had wandered around the campus and finally decided to check on Doug. She had perfected a playful knock so that when she went to her friends' front door, they immediately knew it was she. It seemed now out of place to knock that way on Doug and Skip's—Doug's—front door. Instead, she found herself momentarily standing at the door, unsure of what to do. She was about to ring the bell when Doug walked up behind her.

"Hi ML. I've just gone to the crematorium to arrange things. Skip wanted—well, you know all that stuff. He feared we'd wax him up and put him in a funeral home for all—" She embraced Doug and let out a huge gasp of air.

"Oh Doug. I feel so—" bursting into tears.

"It's right to feel empty, ML. I do. But I also feel, I don't know, relieved. He was in such pain these past months. He really never complained, except when the pain was terrible, but I knew he hated it. He'll always be with me, with us. I know that. I feel that. I felt him die. Like the spirit left the body. There was a peace that filled the room. I don't believe in spirits, but it was a good feeling. Like it was right, it was time."

He broke free from her, paused, and turned to open the door. "I miss him already," and he shook his head back and forth to keep the tears from falling uncontrollably. As they stepped into the house, Mari Lee grabbed onto him and held him.

The bed was still in the living room, but much of the paraphernalia of dying had been removed. The water bottle with a straw, the lotion for Skip's sores, the hospital diapers, the myriad pills and aspirins no longer sat lined up along the window's edge near the bed. He had collected all of the hospital and insurance forms and stuffed them in a tattered grocery bag. She heard a noise, and Doug pointed toward the kitchen. "Ken is helping me clean up."

The volunteer came out to greet her and stripped the bed of its sheets, saying, "I'm going downstairs to do a wash. If you need anything, just give a yell." They made small talk for a while, but the volunteer had done most of the chores, and there was nothing for ML to do. "I should leave you alone, Doug," said Mari Lee, "but give me a call if there's anything you want." He appreciated that she was giving him back his space. Ken was infinitely kind, too, but as soon as the laundry was done, Doug hoped he'd leave as well.

Over the next few days, Doug didn't speak very much. He talked to ML again and Brian came over, but Brian also realized that Doug wanted to be alone. Doug sat quietly out back on the patio. He noticed that the first burst of spinach had taken hold and that the wisteria was coming into its own.

One morning, he got up from the lawn chair after finishing his coffee and, while absentmindedly weeding the garden, saw that the cactus flower had opened. "Look at that!" he exclaimed, then caught himself and quickly shook his head so tears would not fall. "Who am I speaking to?" he thought. He didn't want to let himself start crying for he was afraid that if he started, he would never stop.

He wasn't really sure of his next step. He had to pay the bills in that grocery bag. He needed to return to work. Even though Skip and he weren't married, his boss was supportive and had given Doug a week off while Skip was dying.

Skip had been adamant that he did not want a funeral; although Doug had never said anything, they also couldn't afford one. Skip had said that after he was cremated, he wanted a service in the plaza park to celebrate life and his ashes scattered in the garden. Doug took ML to pick up Skip's ashes. They took the ashes from the mortuary in a silver pot—an heirloom in Skip's family for three generations.

Going home in the cobalt blue Miata, Mari Lee asked Doug to let her out at the university. "Jason's meeting is tonight so if you let me out here, I can go to it and just catch a ride home."

Doug pulled over to the curb and parked. "Maybe I should go too. Jason's expecting me."

"Jason should be the last of your worries. He should be the last of my worries too." They both laughed and Doug added, "It would be good for me to go. I need to get out sometime and I might as well start now. Let's sit in the back, and if I get tired, I can just slip out." Mari Lee was holding Skip's ashes. She motioned to the pot and said, "What should we do with, er, um—"

"Hmmm. Presents a problem, doesn't it? I don't think we should take him with us. Leave them in the car. It's his car anyway."

Mari Lee gingerly put the pot down on the passenger seat and just as carefully locked the door.

"Jesus, ML. It's not as if you need to be so quiet you won't wake him up. I'm fairly certain he's not going to come out of the bottle, some sort of queer genie."

She lightly hit him on the arm and scooped his hand in hers. "Let's go then. We're already late."

Not one seat was left by the time they entered. They grabbed a space by the wall next to the door as Jason droned on. "So the text of my interview will be on the Internet, and I really think it's a good talk, so check it out if you weren't listening. Maybe we should get started. Brian, why don't you bring us up to date on what the next step is. The board meets in a month, right?"

Brian cleared his voice as much to stall for time as for anything else. "I think," he began, "we need fallback positions. Are there alternatives other than going to the board with this kind of thing? I think, maybe, our next step"—he took a deep breath—"is to talk over the summer and let the report get disseminated around a bit."

A tattooed student with "Queer Nation" emblazoned on his right arm said, "You mean we just wait?"

Another said, "But we've done all this work. Wait? Just wait? Lame, man, really lame."

Jason said, "No, no, that's not what I said. I've told people this was going to the board. Why should we wait? I told people this was going to happen now."

Brian felt hemmed in. "I'm just thinking, just trying to make sense. . . ."

An odd silence descended on the group. The meeting had barely begun, and now there was nothing to say. Knowing Brian too well to accept this, Mari Lee spoke up. "You're not giving us the whole story, Brian. Someone told you something, the president or the provost or somebody and now you're thinking we have to back off. That's chickenshit."

Brian blanched; his mouth went dry. He studied the palm of his hand, and another silence fell on the group. No one was prepared for stopping; they were supposed to plan how to proceed. Brian had no idea what to say. Even Jason was silent.

Doug spoke for the first time. "Skip, Skip's ashes, are sitting in the car. I was able to take care of him at the end because my boss let me off. We're broke now—I mean, I'm broke now." He paused for a moment as if to let the message sink in.

"I was lucky at least that my boss let me take a week off. Some of us don't even have that. Luck is a weird thing. There's nothing lucky about death. I want the same rights that you have, Brian. We were together for such a goddamned long time. And you're telling me we should wait a bit longer, just a bit, until Skip and I have the same rights as you. I can't wait any more, Brian. I won't wait. Sorry."

Doug turned to ML, gave her a hug, and walked out of the room.

The meeting continued for a short while; Brian would remember it as one of the worst experiences of his life. People wanted answers that he could not give. One student called him a hypocrite, and no one objected, not even Mari Lee. She kept shaking her head and eventually disappeared. The meeting ended without closure except that Jason swore he would see the president in the morning. Brian had never felt so alone. People huddled in small groups and made way for him so that he exited by himself, a leper.

The cool of the late spring evening made Brian shiver as he left the room. His armpits were soaked; he had not brought a coat. He stuck his hands in his back pockets and started across the plaza, the place he so loved. It was the heartbeat of the campus. On football weekends, it was packed. During Christmas vacation, it was for solitary residents. And this night it was deserted and lonely and strangely beautiful, bathed in the incandescent glow of periodic street lamps. Fitting, he thought, that he was walking alone here. He had played the hypocrite and now had no idea how to extricate himself. If only Skip were here. He could call him for advice.

He reached the plaza park and saw a figure sitting on the stone bench. He put his head down and was about to walk past when a voice calmly called out, "Brian." He looked up and saw Doug holding what looked like an urn. He moved to the bench, sat down next to Doug and opened his mouth, but no words came. They sat there, saying nothing. Doug's hands were wrapped around a silver pot, and then Brian realized what it was. He turned his body sideways so that he too could touch the urn. To the touch, it was warm and comforting. They both looked down at it and heard footsteps from behind.

Mari Lee sat on the ground between them and reached out to place her hands on it as well. Slowly, imperceptibly, their hands all touched. Brian cried. Eventually they stood up and each took a handful of ash out of the pot. Even through his tears, Brian was surprised how gritty the ash was, more like rock shards and sand than ashes.

Mari Lee had already felt the ashes when she and Doug had scattered half of them in Skip's garden earlier that night. She wasn't sure why she had known to go back to the house, but Doug was sitting on the patio and appeared to be waiting for her when she entered. She hadn't knocked, had simply walked to the back of the house. After scattering Skip's ashes, they had returned to the plaza park. She had gone back to the car to get her pullover and, while she was gone, Brian had walked by and been called over by Doug.

All three now stepped into the park and moved toward the rose bed. They dropped their handfuls of ash and stood close together. A blue jay squawked overhead, disturbed in its sleep.

Queering the Academy
Structure and Change

Phone Calls and Testimonies

A few times during the academic year, usually in the late afternoon at home, the phone rings, I answer it, and a muffled voice asks to speak with Professor Tierney. I identify myself and the caller then apologizes for disturbing me at home. "I've read an article of yours," the voice says and pauses. I wait. "I was wondering, is it really that bad for members of faculty who are out," the voice may ask, or simply say, "I'm gay and closeted. I don't know what to do." The callers are frequently graduate students or new faculty members, although I have also received calls from senior professors and administrators. They usually do not identify themselves but locate a place of employment—"I'm in a small town in Louisiana and I could never come out here." Frequently, the social geography of the caller provides a rationale for being closeted or fearful, although I have also heard other reasons—a homophobic department chair, dean, or administration. When I attend a conference, I inevitably find other individuals—or they find me—in a quiet corner of some crowded hallway who ask questions about how I have survived.

I obviously do not wish to suggest that all queer people act in this way. A portrait of the anonymous caller who fears for his or her job is not the only picture I wish to paint on the canvas of gay academic life. Not everyone is silent. Many individuals are outspoken, content, and proud. Some of us are closeted, and others are out in varying degrees. The closeted person today becomes an activist tomorrow. Vocal advocates for change on campus may not have told their parents or families about their queerness. At the same time, I cannot wish away these phone calls and encounters. Many people are closeted and afraid.

As noted in Chapter 5, some activists might suggest tough love for anyone who is closeted and calls me. "Stop being a coward," the proponent of tough love might say, "and come out of the closet." I believe such a strategy is largely mistaken. It blames the victim rather than the oppressor; shaming a person is also usually counterproductive. We ought not to denigrate the pain and silence that people like the ones who call me inevitably go through on their route to gaining voice. All gay and lesbian individuals know the personal ramifications of what it means to come out, and the phone callers or e-mail writers are simply responding to what I have written about coming out in the academy. If the prospect of acknowledging one's identity is fraught with anxiety in the personal realm, then obviously the same will be true in the workplace. I try to suggest ways for the individuals to come out at their own speed and point out that I could never go back into the closet myself. We constantly need to reaffirm the importance of coming out. No action is more important than enabling others to see us as we are. Indeed, the path to writing this book has been cut by those lesbian and gay academics whom I may not know but who spoke out when no one else had the courage to do so. We learn by example, and when we find others who stand up and speak out, then we may not be so afraid; we learn that we are not alone.

I am also troubled when senior professors look to their younger colleagues to confront the administration on a particular issue but will not place themselves on the line. Coming out inevitably entails risks, but these risks vary from individual to individual. I may never become a college president because I am open about my sexual orientation, but I also cannot be arbitrarily fired because I have tenure. An untenured faculty member with a homophobic department chair faces challenges that are different from those of his or her senior colleagues. Consequently, as a community, we constantly need to speak honestly and openly with one another about our expectations and needs. Again, such a suggestion goes to the heart of what I mean by building a community based on agape. Sometimes the other person needs to hear that he or she is letting us down by silence. A letter of complaint to the college president, for example, is strengthened by having numerous signatories; when people have internalized their homophobia to such an extent that they refuse to offer any demonstrable support, then they at least need to be made aware of our disappointment. We should acknowledge the specific demons of everyone who is rendered voiceless, however, and we should also be made aware of our relationships and responsibilities to one another.

I invariably feel depressed after a muffled phone conversation or a secretive encounter in a conference hallway. However encouraging I have tried to be, I hear the loneliness in the person's voice and I begin to feel powerless myself. I worry also that those who approach me have taken from my writings a largely negative portrait of queer life in the academy. Rather than emboldening them, am I only confirming their worst fears? The postmodern irony is that in reading an article of mine deconstructing how academic discourse has framed queer lives and made our history invisible, closeted readers may conclude that the case study so precisely parallels their lives in academe that their decision to remain in the closet has been justified. My desire, of course, is to achieve the opposite effect. I hope that by explaining injustice, we will change what is immoral, rather than legitimate it.

Accordingly, in the remaining two chapters, I outline an agenda for change and propose strategies for achieving that change. My intent is twofold. First, I draw on the theoretical argument developed in Part I and consider the practical implications of admittedly abstruse ideas. Second, I use these ideas by drawing on the previous two chapters in Part II. Data are always open to interpretation, and short stories are even more so. Obviously, some people abhor homosexuality so much they assume all lesbian and gay academics should remain closeted. Indeed, some of the most homophobic characters in society would delight in our coming out because they could then take part in witch-hunts to destroy careers and lives.

These chapters, however, work from the assumption that ultimately the social and academic closet is a confining place in late 20th-century America and that we deserve equal protection and rights within the academy. This would make it unnecessary to be in the closet. To reconfigure the closet, we need action on multiple fronts within power's domains. Foucault has argued that power is relational; it does not simply involve a struggle between the haves and have-nots. Power is "exercised from innumerable points, highly indeterminate in character and never something acquired, seized or shared. There is no source or centre of power to contest" (quoted in Best & Kellner, 1991, p. 51). Such a comment provides an interpretation distinctly different from the idea that one individual or group holds power and another does not.

However, Foucault has been misinterpreted; individuals falsely assume that the Foucaultian notion of power makes it a version of Weber's iron cage where it is omnipresent and omniscient. From this view, struggle is impossible. Some of the more nihilistic versions of postmodernism also offer such arguments. Conversely, Foucault states, "As soon as there is a power relation, there is a possibility of resistance. We can never be ensnared by power: we can always modify its grip in determinate conditions and according to a precise strategy" (Kritzman, 1988, p. 123). These final two chapters are about the development of such strategies.

I previously pointed out that when we speak of *post*modernism, we should not fool ourselves into thinking that it has no relationship to modernism. In the final chapter, I highlight the distinctions by discussing the implications in the academy of cultural studies for queer studies, and I expand on Foucault's notion of power. In this chapter, I point out the similarities of modernism to postmodernism and how we might improve conditions for lesbian and gay lives in the academy. That is, the manner in which knowledge gets defined, structured and implemented in the academy will be vastly different if we work from a modern rather than a postmodern perspective. Our immediate rights on campus, however, will not be significantly different whichever one of the perspectives we subscribe to. Indeed, the goal of this chapter is to clarify those structural changes that need to occur if lesbian and gay people are to be treated as equal citizens in the academy.

An Academic Contract

When I visit college campuses or speak with colleagues about their agendas for change, we often end up in dialogues that are hard to assess and even harder to implement. "We want to lessen homophobia," I might hear, or "The university needs to be more accepting," or "The violence must stop." I obviously agree with each statement, but what are the implications? How should the university respond to such problems, and how should it be held accountable for these sweeping criticisms? When the institution wants to increase its funding, it creates a development office to oversee the acquisition of funds. When retention of staff became a problem, many institutions created roles and offices that focused on increasing retention. Most individuals have not considered the structural and policy-related implications for an institution seeking to honor diversity in general and queer lives in particular. I deal with curricula and educational issues in the final chapter. What I develop here are five points that any college or university ought to act on if it wants to make the university an institution based on equity and justice. I also offer these points because they are simple, clear, and straightforward. We need to develop and advance an agenda that is understandable to the numerous constituencies on campus. An infinite list of desires and hopes inevitably gets lost and buried as different individuals come and go. In what follows, I suggest a contract that might be developed, maintained, and implemented. It details what we require and, implicitly, what we will not demand. We require the following:

1. That the institution's statement of nondiscrimination have an explicit reference to sexual orientation
2. That the institution's housing contracts for undergraduates, graduates, and faculty not discriminate between straight and queer individuals and couples
3. That the institution have an approved domestic-partner policy that accords to queer couples the same rights and privileges as married couples
4. That the institution have an office specifically responsible for overseeing the implementation of such policies and ensuring equity
5. That the institution make explicit its nondiscriminatory policies to external constituencies

Nondiscrimination Statements. A first step for a postsecondary institution should be to implement a nondiscrimination clause that includes sexual orientation as a protected category. All colleges and universities have some sort of nondiscrimination statement, but they usually apply to groups of people who are protected by federal or state mandates. Thus, the statement is usually little more than a recitation of the obvious. Federal law does not allow federal dollars to be used for organizations that discriminate on the basis of race, for example, or a particular state will not fund institutions that allow gender discrimination. Even a private institution must abide by federal standards and policies or forego federal funding.

We should be aware of the legal distinction to be made regarding lesbian and gay people. Because we have no federal or state protection, a statement against sexual orientation does not have the same legal backing as a statement against racial discrimination. When people of color sue institutions over racial discrimination, they have the backing of federal and state law to support their claims. If we were to make a similar argument, we would have no grounds for a case. A nondiscrimination statement is a policy that may or may not have a basis in law. A college, for example, may also have a policy saying it will deliver a quality education even though there are no federal or state initiatives mandating quality. Thus, when we fight to include sexual orientation in a statement of nondiscrimination, we should be clear about our ultimate goal. We will still not have equal protection. We will still be denied the equal rights and benefits accorded straight people. If our inclusion in a statement of nondiscrimination had legal merit, for example, then any institution that had such a statement would have to amend its housing policy so that we would not be discriminated against. We have no such recourse.

Why, then, should we fight for such a clause? There are at least three reasons. First, including sexual orientation in a nondiscrimination statement will prepare us for the day, however distant, when a state, or the federal government, passes legal protection for queers.

More important, however, even though we will not have the force of law behind us, such a statement at least acknowledges our presence and explicitly states that a goal of the institution is equal protection. Goals are more than functional artifacts in an organizational plan. They highlight what an institution's participants consider to be important. In this light, the institution will have a policy that speaks against homophobia.

Finally, implementing such a clause on a college campus will involve a considerable battle between those who believe that such a clause is morally wrong and provides special protection for us, and those who believe it is right. We should welcome such a discussion in any organization but especially in academe.

Essentially, the fight over a clause is an educational argument. To be sure, there are bigoted individuals who have no desire to listen to what we have to say. But the vast majority of the populace in academe is similar to the broader society. They in general have not thought very much about homosexuality, and they do not think they know anyone who is queer because most of us remain closeted. The battle over nondiscrimination enables us to tell our stories. We have the opportunity to educate the academic community about what it means to be queer and why discrimination is wrong. Such a story is exactly the one that we want to tell. The argument is then based on our grounds and ultimately winnable if we are well organized. And yet, throughout this struggle, we need to be aware of the limitations of this approach and acknowledge that including sexual orientation in a statement of nondiscrimination is no more than a first step in a contract for equity.

Such a strategy is also in keeping with my argument in favor of decentering norms, mediating within the overriding culture, and inserting ourselves into a discussion about the grammar of culture. We accept the role of public intellectual, explain the importance of such a change for an educational enterprise, and provide ourselves with the pioneering tools for the creation of cultural production.

Including lesbian, gay and bisexual people in a statement about nondiscrimination will also signal to the academic community that we honor diversity. Those academics in Chapter 5 who spoke of the closet and their need to remain there will at least receive one signal that they do not have to stay there. Obviously, such work is the task that individuals like Skip, Doug, Mari Lee, and Jason set for themselves. But one symbol will not re-create the universe. Brian's struggle between doing what is right and what is necessary for his career applies to anyone engaged in such a battle. He's neither Pontius Pilate nor Judas; he's simply human.

Housing. Each institution is unique. A battle over nondiscrimination may take two years at one institution and be implemented immediately at another. But I have listed these issues in this sequence on purpose. Once we achieve a statement of nondiscrimination, the logical next step will pertain to housing. I offer this suggestion primarily because it is incremental, finite, and inexpensive. Access to married student/faculty housing is incremental—it is one specific policy that does not have excessive ramifications. It is finite because any institution will most likely not have more than a dozen couples who would apply for such housing. It is inexpensive because no additional funds will be needed to implement the policy. In effect, if couples have to apply for such housing through a lottery, all the policy would do is increase the competition. The argument that queer couples would apply in such great numbers that more buildings would be needed, would be negated as soon as the administration saw little change in the overall number of applications in the first year. A lottery, or a first-come-first-served approach, would also negate the fiscal concerns inevitably raised by some skeptics.

Unlike the nondiscrimination clause, such a policy will have a concrete impact on the lives of some lesbian and gay people. That is, after the passage of a nondiscrimination clause, no one's life will be demonstrably better. But the passage of a fair housing clause could provide inexpensive housing for queer couples. Implementing such a policy would most likely require three steps. First, work with the housing office to change the name from married student housing to something else. Second, if there is resistance to the change because of possible expansion costs, make the argument that no institution that has had such a policy has incurred any significant costs but that we are willing to see what kind of costs might occur at this particular institution. Argue in favor of making the change for five years and then reexamining it. Suggest a five-year time horizon because this will give the policy significant time to become widely known; obviously, if the policy is in effect for only one year, no significant change may occur. Five years also allows the university to see the effect of the change over time. Third, argue that the requirements for a lesbian or gay couple be parallel to what the institution requires of straight couples. That is, if the institution requires a statement from a heterosexual couple that they have lived together for a specific length of time, then the same requirement should be expected of lesbian and gay couples. If the institution requires a marriage certificate, then lesbian and gay couples should be asked to submit a document from a lawyer that attests to their relationship. Any lawyer can draw up such a document for a queer couple. Barry and I, for example, have a living will that outlines the endurance of our relationship. If the institution requires that straight couples do nothing more than check off a box on a piece of paper that says they are a couple, then that is what should be asked of us.

Two potential pitfalls come to mind. First, a change in housing policy should not necessitate broad discussion and debate; it is best if the policy change is implemented within the housing office. We cannot sustain queer issues on the front pages of institutional life in every case at every moment. Because our issues are not at the forefront of institutional life every day does not mean that progress cannot occur. Housing is one such example. It is to our benefit if we do not force multiple levels of decision making on every issue concerning lesbian and gay lives. It would be inappropriate, for example, for the president or the board of trustees to insinuate themselves into an issue as microscopic as a housing policy. If the issue unfortunately does move in such a direction, we should then be prepared to ask the academic community why decisions of this nature must involve everyone's time and consideration when similar issues for straights do not.

Second, the demand for some form of affidavit attesting to a relationship obviously will necessitate a degree of disclosure that some closeted couples might resist. Confidentiality cannot be assured. Couples will come and go from student and faculty housing at all hours; it will be obvious that they are lesbian or gay. Indeed, if they were not lesbian or gay they would be in violation of the housing agreement. Thus, there is no way around some degree of personal disclosure. There is little that we can do to overcome the fear of some couples that they will be outed if they apply for such housing. I also believe we should not institutionalize homophobia even more than it already is. At the same time, such couples still need to be protected from harassment if and when rumors begin. Hence a statement about nondiscrimination as a first step is essential.

Again, such a change addresses those cases in Chapter 5 when students and faculty spoke about the need to hide their partners rather than celebrate their union. Institutions that acknowledge committed queer relationships such as the one between Skip and Doug are dramatically different from those described by the interviewees in Chapter 5. By claiming the right to change the definition of *commitment,* we become directly engaged in developing cultural policies and college communities based on equity, social justice and human rights.

Domestic Partner Agreements. In the time that has passed from when I initially wrote the draft for this chapter to when I saw the galleys for the book, the issue of gay marriage has exploded on the U.S. scene. States have passed laws outlawing gay marriages. In a sadly ironic event, Representative Robert Barr (Republican of Georgia) introduced a bill in Congress preserving the sanctity of heterosexual marriage that has now been signed into law by President Clinton. During the time that Barry and I have lived together in a monogamous relationship, Representative Barr has been married a third time; reports of President Clinton's having philandered his way through Arkansas in the 1980s are still legion. I hardly think that either of these men could look all of us gays in the eye and speak about the sanctity of marriage with a straight face.

No institutional policy can enhance our lives more than the implementation of a domestic partners agreement. However, unlike a housing policy, a comprehensive, fully implemented domestic partnership policy for gays will be likely to cost the institution real dollars. For that reason, I suggest that the domestic partners issue be taken on only after fair housing has been achieved. In part, fair housing sets a precedent for equal treatment in other areas of the institution. Once the administration realizes that housing costs have not gone up and that comparable examples from other organizations can be useful indicators of what might happen at their own institution, then the administration will not be able to use the scare tactic of inordinate cost increases when a domestic partners agreement comes up for discussion.

We also need to be cognizant of the real issues that frame discussions about domestic partners. Harry's discussion with Brian in Chapter 6 about a domestic partnership clause had nothing to do with the cost. Individuals—trustees, mayors, religious leaders—will protest against such an agreement on moral grounds, and politically minded administrators will use fiscal issues to obfuscate their real concerns. As critical intellectuals, we must not allow the discourse to be captured by those who oppose communities of difference and promote hostility instead of agape. The story in Chapter 6 may be fictional, but we all know individuals like Skip who have had the courage to stand up and protest. Too often when we think of leadership, we conjure up images of a Gandhi or Martin Luther King, Jr. and know that we will never be able to achieve their greatness. Such a belief excuses us from action. The image of leadership I am suggesting here is more of individuals like Skip and Doug and Mari Lee, all cultural citizens of Central University engaged in the practice of agape.

Here are some obvious steps toward the broadscale implementation of domestic partners agreements. Certain privileges can be granted to domestic partners that cost the institution nothing. The use of the swimming pool, or a library card, is a benefit often granted to the spouse of an employee; they should be granted to domestic partners as well. Bereavement leave would also cost the institution nothing in real dollars and would signal equal treatment for people who find themselves in the same position as Doug in "Ashes." Educational benefits are a next step. Although providing courses for free or for a reduced amount would impose a financial burden on the institution, again, this would not be in real dollars. The university is not spending money that it already has; it is simply not taking in money that it might or might not garner.

The final step will cost real money—inclusion in a comprehensive health plan that parallels what straight couples have. We need to be quite clear about the nature of the argument. At no institution, organization or municipality that has implemented a domestic partners plan has there been a documented significant rise in costs (Tierney, 1996); at the same time, there is a great need for further research about implicit, explicit, and symbolic costs of implementing such a plan. Obviously, clear and honest documentation first needs to be gathered to convince those who have forthright questions and concerns about the costs of a particular policy. But we also need to be clear that most often, fiscal concerns mask the real issue, namely, that powerful, homophobic individuals do not want to grant lesbian and gay couples the same rights as straight couples.

If the discussion revolves around fiscal matters, then easy comparisons can be made. For example, the cost of implementing a domestic partners agreement at most institutions is usually equivalent to the cost of the benefits and retirement package for the college president. Such comparative data are compelling. If a concern is strictly based on finances and nothing else, then one must wonder why the organization is more willing to pay retirement funds for one individual than to provide benefits that would increase the satisfaction—and presumably the productivity—of its employees.

If a housing policy has already been implemented, then we would hope that the lessons learned from those changes could be applied in this case as well. Whatever policy exists for straight couples should also apply to lesbian and gay couples. If straight couples only need to check a box on a page that says they are married, then we should have a similar option, and so on. And finally, because administrators will continue to raise flags about cost, the strategy that the plan be instituted for an experimental phase of five years should again be applied.

One potential pitfall is that a domestic partners agreement is too substantial an issue to require merely the approval of an assistant in the housing office. At a minimum, a vice president for human resources will need to become involved, and, more than likely, the president will have to make the final decision. The main issue, however, is to ensure that the board of trustees does not become involved. The point should be procedural; it should not have anything to do with a gay or lesbian agenda. The board does not involve itself in finite areas such as minor changes in health policy. For a board to involve itself in this manner in the decision-making process of the institution is at odds with its explicit function. Just as boards of major companies do not concern themselves with administrative matters, so also there is a difference between governance and administration at colleges and universities.

With the issues of housing and domestic partners benefits, I have offered two suggestions that are both honest and strategic. First, in a decentralized institution such as a college or university, individuals who are responsible for a particular matter should make the decisions concerning that matter. If we follow this rule, we will in general have a greater likelihood of implementing a fair housing policy. At all costs, we want to keep these issues away from a board of trustees that is generally more conservative than the academic population. Second, suggesting that we implement an experiment in housing or health for five years will provide a sufficient time line to test the actual costs to the institution. At the same time, organizations have terrible memories. What is an experiment today becomes institutionalized tomorrow. Because the costs for either program will not be significant, the chances are great that the experiments will be accepted immediately.

Structural Responsibility. Someone within the organization should have a specific charge to work on issues of equity for the lesbian, gay and bisexual communities. The University of Massachusetts-Amherst, the University of Pennsylvania and Ohio State University, for example, all have officials whose jobs pertain to lesbian, gay and bisexual issues. These administrators coordinate workshops, seminars, and outreach programs for faculty, staff, administrators and students. Such officials will be advocates for changing and improving the climate by working with different stakeholders whose policies have an impact on the gay, lesbian and bisexual communities, as is presently done for women, people of color, and other underrepresented groups. In this connection, the concerns of other oppressed groups parallel our own, as do some of the solutions.

We are involved here with a simple matter of organizational change. One often hears that a particular issue should be the responsibility of everyone; although I agree, the follow-up comment often made is that no one is then accountable for advancing the issue. In the literature of organizational theory, we often see reference to someone who is an idea champion and someone who has structural authority for moving the idea forward. Without having a role cemented in the structure, the danger arises of relying on individuals alone. Thus, when a vocal advocate for a topic goes on sabbatical, grows tired of the battles and meetings, or leaves the institution, a void can come about that may not easily be filled. Furthermore, dealing with issues such as domestic partner agreements or housing policies is exhausting, time-consuming work. Although we surely want to involve a broad panoply of individuals, there should be someone who sees his or her task as centrally tied to such issues. Faculty members, other administrators, and students will be involved on a voluntary basis; they get no released time for such work, and, indeed, the work is often not seen as a viable service to the institution.

Creating an office with specific responsibility for queer issues will provide no immediate change or benefit, but it is still essential. An analogy is apt. If an institution's participants want to increase fund-raising or undertake a capital campaign, they undoubtedly will create an office for development with an individual who oversees the campaign. Simply creating an office will not increase the institution's coffers. However, without an office, there is little likelihood that change will occur, but with an office, there is great possibility for change. Creating an office, like having a nondiscrimination clause, becomes a potent symbol for the importance the institution places on a particular issue.

One final suggestion is that the individual and office should not be lodged within student affairs. Creating an enhanced campus climate for queers must involve the whole college community, not just the students. Indeed, domestic partner agreements in large part refer to full-time employees of the institution, and housing policies relate to faculty members as well as graduate and undergraduate students. Whom the official reports to is highly dependent on the size and nature of the institution. A community college may have such an official report to the president; a state university may have this area within the domain of an affirmative action office; a large public university may have a vice president or vice provost with specific responsibility for issues of diversity. The main point is for the organization's participants to recognize that queer concerns are worthy of the appointment of such an official and that the issues are broad ranging and cover the gamut of institutional life.

From the idea of cultural studies offered in Part I, we see how education becomes more than simply a curriculum. Educational issues span the life of the institution and they come up in administrative offices, dorms, secretarial offices and classrooms. The idea of what it means to be gay or lesbian or bisexual does not merely pertain to what is discussed in a psychology or sociology class but, rather, has meaning in multiple arenas.

External Communication. How an institution communicates to its external constituencies that it supports equity for lesbian, gay and bisexual individuals is perplexing and fraught with difficult dialogues. In general, such communication tends to be administrative and, frequently, through the president's office. Those individuals and groups with whom one communicates are frequently opposed to lesbian and gay rights. Wealthy donors, as seen in the short story (Chapter 6), are often conservative, and they will claim the power of the dollar to denounce gay rights. Alumni will announce their displeasure. Conservative state legislators will try to cut appropriations to a public institution. The U.S. Department of Defense will issue directives that may deny funding for an institution that does not allow recruiters on campus. Unlike other multicultural groups, queers often do not have numerous vocal advocates to counter such criticism. Wealthy, queer-supportive donors, as well as lesbians, gays or bisexuals, frequently do not speak up. Only a handful of organized lesbian and gay alumni organizations operate in the country. State legislators fear political suicide if they are too vocal for queers. And we all know the pathetic history of the Defense Department's "Don't ask, don't tell" policy. Heterosexual African Americans, on the other hand, at least have some state legislators who will speak up in their support, and there are many alumni organizations that support equity for straight people of color. Such an observation highlights one area of divergence for queers and other groups, so that our strategies of how we gain support and who will support us may vary.

This fifth and final point to the queer contract is the least clear, potentially the most explosive, and undoubtedly of the most strategic importance. There are three suggestions here. First, the institution needs to speak with a clear and consistent voice. If we reflect on the lamentable debacle over gays in the military, one point that stands out is President Clinton's waffling on the issue. Someone needs to coach a university or college administration about specifically what to say; what is essential is that although they do not need to be as outspoken as I may be, they do need to express clear, consistent support for advancing diversity that includes gay, lesbian and bisexual rights. In "Ashes," for example, it is unfortunate that the provost and Brian had not educated the president prior to the announcement in the newspaper. After that, homosexual issues became a problem rather than an intellectual issue. I recognize, for example, that it may be impossible for a president to utter the word queer, but it should be made known that it is unacceptable to use the word homosexual or to avoid mention of us in a broad comment in support of diversity. Similarly, the alumni office should actively encourage the creation of a gay, lesbian and bisexual network, just as there are other specific networks.

Second, the official position of the institution should be published and widely disseminated. Any organization with whom we work and that is at odds with the policy of nondiscrimination should be alerted that they are in violation of the institution's policy. Clearly, the most significant impact will be for those institutions that have defense contracts or a Reserve Officers' Training Corps (ROTC) on campus. I am not calling for the removal of ROTC from campus, however much I would like to see that occur. The removal of ROTC for some institutions potentially places in jeopardy millions of dollars in contracts and, more important, scholarships for low-income students. One consequence can be that those groups with whom we are in alliance will not support us. Instead, what we should advocate is that the institution communicate (a) its disapproval of the armed forces policy on gays, (b) that we intend to work with them to see how they can change the policy specifically as it relates to ROTC, and (c) that in the meantime, any queer student who applies to ROTC, comes out, and is dismissed, will have his or her scholarship assumed by the institution. The point here is that an abrupt dismissal of recruiters or programs from campus is not likely to happen and will promote more discord than I frankly feel it is worth. We need alliances across oppressed groups and this is an issue that will create division rather than unity.

Finally, in its external communications, the institution should explain that it does not support an affirmative action policy for queers that duplicates affirmative action for women and people of color. Our problem is not that there is an insufficient number of us on campus. The closeted academics of Chapter 5 are many; their problem was not representation but voice. Again, this highlights a difference among oppressed people. Heterosexual Hispanics face discrimination in a different manner from that faced by queers. The struggle for the institution with regard to lesbian, gay and bisexual rights is to create an environment where we feel free to come out. Affirmative action pertains to the creation of an organizational culture where individuals do not face discrimination and harassment in admissions and campus life. Because the discrimination differs from group to group, the strategies should differ as well.

I am fully aware that there are those in the queer community who will say that we must call for an immediate ban of ROTC on campus and that we should demand inclusion in the affirmative action hiring plan of the institution. For the reasons stated above, I believe such advocacy is in general mistaken. It creates divisions across oppressed groups. We call for something—the removal of ROTC—that is not likely to happen, and we misread the basic intent of affirmative action.

I have offered five points to a contract that promotes equity and speaks structurally to what needs to occur in the institution. The five points are simple, understandable and capable of being communicated to different constituencies. In what follows, I turn to a discussion of strategies to enact such an agenda.

Strategies for Action

Structures. As we often fall prey to goals that are unclear, so we also assume too often that solutions reside in the president's office. This assumption is faulty and misguided. A first step is to understand the significance of the difference between a public and private university, to understand the power of the board of trustees, and then to get to know some of the individuals on the board.

The worth of knowing the difference between private and public universities has to do with the amount of independence from the state legislature an institution may have. A public university is not automatically more conservative than its private counterpart. A state with a policy of nondiscrimination in sexual orientation for its government employees can be helpful when a public institution balks at implementing a nondiscrimination clause. A public university in California, for example, will probably be more open and liberal than a private institution in Texas. In general, however, state legislatures are often worrisome roadblocks to creating a better environment for college campuses. Vocal criticism from just a handful of state legislators can interfere with an institution's plans to offer a gay studies course, hire a coordinator, or try to develop an equitable housing policy. There is no simple solution for dealing with bigots. However, it is a mistake to ignore them. Instead, as we plot our course for enacting the contract, we need to understand the external environment surrounding the institution and lay the groundwork for dealing with different legislative constituencies. What one discovers quite often is that there is always a significant percentage of politicians and aides (like the fictional provost of Central University) who really do not care one way or another about a particular issue; what they do not want to see happen is that when something is attempted, it either fails or explodes into a politically costly issue. Politics is about winning and never appearing foolish.

We often approach organizational change not from the perspective of politics but from that of social justice. In the short story (Chapter 6), the students at the meeting and Jason, to a certain extent, believed that domestic partnership was morally right. I fully understand and agree with such beliefs. However, we should also understand that many people involved in this issue see it from a different perspective. Conservative opponents also think of queer issues in moral terms—albeit from a completely different vantage point. But many, if not most, individuals in political posts—legislatures, state offices, college administrations—are more concerned with managing the issue. When we acknowledge this point, our outlook can become different. We think not only that something should change because it is morally right but also because we have created an environment that makes such change politically manageable. We might bemoan the fact that politicians and leaders are not persuaded by moral argument, but it also behooves us to recognize that individuals like Gandhi and King were not only moral agents but superb politicians as well. They knew how to work their audiences and also where to find the Achilles heels of their opponents.

Good politicians study the environment of those with whom they have to work. One of the most powerful and least understood bodies on a college campus is the board of trustees. It may only meet a half-dozen times a year, but it has the power to hire and fire the president. An institution's president pays very close attention to what the board says and what it wants. Just one board member's expressing displeasure about a particular issue can rally the board in ways that will give the president terrific problems. Institutions also try to shield their board members from involvement with the college constituencies except in the most superficial of ways. The chair of the board may hand out diplomas at graduation, or another board member may be asked to give a speech on Founder's Day. If a queer group of students expresses its desire to meet with the board, most administrations would undoubtedly reject the request. In part, the administration's denial is standard procedure and a good idea. Board members should not get directly involved in the daily life of the campus. But when they do, it is our responsibility to understand the board and its members and figure out how to work with them. To simply overlook the board is a mistaken strategy.

Earlier, I suggested that we should try to prevent certain issues from coming to the board for a decision. The more levels of decision making, the less chance of implementation for any issue. However, change agents need to prepare themselves for multiple possibilities. Thus, an institution's constituents should be ready to educate the trustees. One strategy should not preclude the other. Indeed, I am suggesting that both actions are necessary.

Consequently, we need to think of ways to reach the board. Not every board member will be homophobic. A board of two dozen will undoubtedly have some members with family or friends who are queer. Some trustees will be closeted; we are, after all, everywhere. All of this information will be helpful to us. We should never be content when we are told that we cannot speak to the board. Instead, we should carefully initiate and orchestrate contacts with individual trustees who are at least willing to listen to our concerns. I want to emphasize my choice of the words "initiate" and "orchestrate." Trustees should not be approached on the same topic by numerous individuals; they will rightly see it as a waste of their time. In the short story (Chapter 6), Jason's comment at the end of the meeting that he was going to see the president the next morning represents the kind of unscripted act that should not occur. As a group, we should outline a strategy for approaching individual board members and the board itself. We should also consider how to initiate such contacts. Some individuals will resent being contacted at home, for example, and we are not advancing our cause when we unthinkingly pick up the phone and decide to give a trustee or president a piece of our minds. It is also not a bad idea to keep board members regularly informed about our work, our actions, and our goals. Discussion should be ongoing and systematic rather than sporadic and stopgap.

Trustees are also political animals. They should hear about the abuse that we often have to put up with when we make our arguments for a nondiscrimination clause, a fair housing policy, or a domestic partners agreement. However, we should also point out to them that the political issue will not go away until they accept our arguments. As I noted in Part I, some years ago, we had a pitched battle at Penn State over implementing a nondiscrimination clause. The board of trustees was, as expected, quite conservative, but a handful of fair-minded individuals at least took the time to talk to a small group of us. By the time we met with the board, we had become extremely well organized. We emphasized that we would not give up. We also made reference to the board's recent decision to divest itself of stocks in South Africa. This issue of divestment had consumed a great deal of their time, and it had been quite divisive. We encouraged those board members with whom we spoke to get the issue of sexual orientation behind them—if they approved the inclusion of the clause in the policy, they would not be bound in knots the way they had been for more than two years with regard to South Africa. The comment made political sense to those with whom we spoke, and the strength of our group convinced them that we would not give up. Ultimately, the administration and liberal board members used this argument successfully to persuade their conservative counterparts to approve the clause. The issue had moved in their minds from one that might have been morally right but politically inappropriate, to one that was politically expedient if they wanted to get on with other issues.

Suggestions of this kind are entirely in keeping with what I mean by cultural politics. We interpret the university as a culture and seek to decenter the norms that constrain us, recognize the importance of changing the discourse about our identity construction, and engage in work that we see as intellectual, existential and strategic. To think of work as only intellectual will point us to defeat. Alternatively, to think only in terms of strategy, as Jason did, robs our work of its moral structure.

Know the Rules. If we understand the structure in which the institution is embedded, then we also need to understand how policies get approved. Such an understanding necessitates that we comprehend the formal and informal structure of the institution. Again, taking an issue to a college president or a vice president of student affairs and saying that we want them to approve it shows a counterproductive lack of understanding on our part that can be used against us. For example, at Penn State, when we said that we wanted a sexual orientation clause, the initial argument used against us was that such a clause was impossible because it would lead to a lawsuit. Because none of us was a lawyer, we believed what they said; over time, however, we realized that, at a minimum, the administration was mistaken and, at worst, was lying so that it would not have to deal with us. A lawsuit could not have been used against the university if they had implemented a sexual orientation clause.

When we understand how the legislative process works, we can then manage the system. We need to know, for example, how the student government conducts its work and, more important, how members of faculty deal with issues. Individuals who understand the faculty senate can be quite helpful when we ask for their support on issues such as a domestic partners policy. Indeed, we also need to understand who has the authority to make decisions. As I mentioned with regard to a housing policy, we should not inflate some issues into being greater than they actually are. If a similar issue can be decided by a recommendation of the faculty senate and approval of the provost, then that is what we should demand as well. There is nothing to be gained when we try to receive the highest approval possible on every issue; as I noted in regard to the board of trustees in general, the more often we have to deal with them, the less likely it is that our initiatives will be passed.

We also need to comprehend the informal decision-making structure of the institution. There are always groups on campus that function as a kitchen cabinet. They do not have formal authority and they do not vote, but they exercise a significant degree of influence in the daily workings of the institution. At Penn State, there is a council of academic deans, and, at the University of Southern California, there is a dean's council. Every president also has a small group of close personal advisers. The ability to influence such groups can go a long way in moving the legislative process along. At Penn State, we talked informally with the council of academic deans about the sexual orientation clause; as with the board of trustees, we informed them that the topic would not dissolve and we would continue to press the issue until it was successfully resolved. The deans had their own issues that they wanted the administration to consider, but they realized that as long as the institution was preoccupied with the issue of a sexual orientation clause, they would have to delay making decisions on other matters. They took no vote in support of the clause, but they also communicated privately to different individuals in the faculty senate and the administration that they wanted the issue resolved, and, if that meant passage of a clause, then so be it. Once again, their input on the matter had little, if anything, to do with their moral support for the rights of queers; instead, they voiced a parochial political concern.

Know the Players. Each step I am suggesting here relates to and refines the previous steps so that they form a comprehensive strategy for action. If we know the formal and informal structures of the organization, then we should also fill in the blank faces in those structures to acquaint ourselves with those we will be engaging politically. Such a tactic is important for promoting any initiative aimed at organizational change, but it is even more critical with regard to queer-related struggles. Some individuals may have such a religious bias against us that any degree of discussion will be useless. Other individuals will have relatives who are lesbian, gay or bisexual and may want to help as a sign of support. Most lamentably, a few individuals will be closeted and have so much internalized homophobia that they will go out of their way to speak against us so that the mainstream does not think they are one of us. And quite often, many individuals have an honest desire to learn more, but they are waiting to be asked or engaged; they will not take the first step either because of other demands on their time or because they do not want to appear intrusive. Ultimately, however, the most important group we can tap is ourselves. We need to be constantly vigilant about how we orchestrate a movement so that it is broadly based and inclusive, rather than a closet full of activists, so to speak. One of the main points the interviewees raised in Chapter 5 was the lack of role models in graduate school and on campus. We need concerted action to provide space for closeted individuals gradually to speak up and come out.

Knowing who is homophobic is helpful on two levels. First, it is important to know who is lined up against us. Second, when we know which opponents are bigoted, then we do not need to waste time or effort engaging them in endless conversation that will ultimately prove useless. As with queers, homophobes come in all shapes, sizes, and personae. Those who have an honest religious conviction and express themselves with sincerity are certainly more convincing to the mainstream than those who seek to denigrate or smear us for their own warped purposes. When the faculty senate at Penn State, for example, finally had a debate about the sexual orientation clause, a fellow took to the senate floor to read a prepared statement that was so slanderous of lesbian and gay people that the chair ruled him out of order, to the applause of many senators. Another person who was against the measure stood up to state that he completely disavowed himself from the position that had just been presented. Slanderous commentary often helps our cause when fair-minded individuals see it in the light of common day.

At the same time, some people's minds remain closed on this matter. Our propensity for making moral arguments when discussing sexual orientation often suggests that we want to persuade people that they are mistaken. Underlying such a dialogue is the conviction that ultimately we will be able to persuade them through the logic, passion, and humanity of our argument. Think again. We are not a debating society. An understaffed and underfinanced group trying to create a specific kind of change needs to stay focused. Some people will simply not change their minds, and it is a waste of breath and effort to try to make them. We are ultimately involved in reframing the culture of our society; we must realize that such change will have to take place within a specific framework of cultural politics.

As I mentioned in a previous chapter, the media often presents us as beholden to the straight world. How we are represented today may a little more positive than it was in the past, but what hasn't changed is that we are still consistently being defined by the straight world. Our battles should not be handed over to other people to fight for us; such action would only reconfirm the prejudice that we ourselves are not strong enough to fight our enemies. But at the same time, we should actively welcome and accept the support of our straight allies. Ultimately, individuals like those represented by Brian, the fictional dean in "Ashes," turn out to be good people; we should work with them and support them. During our fight for a sexual orientation clause at Penn State, an individual whose brother was gay was extremely helpful to us. He never made the issue a factor—indeed, he never mentioned it—but his support was critical. Sometimes we mistakenly think that we do not need the help of others. It is not a sign of weakness to accept an offer of support. In doing so, we demonstrate to the broader community that we have outside support and are able to work with others; we also learn ourselves that we are not alone and we lay the foundation for agape and community.

Indeed, there will always be individuals in colleges and universities willing to support us, but they often do not know how to. They are not homophobic; they are simply fearful of intruding, or they think their help or advice may not be wanted. Sadly, their fears may sometimes be well-founded. In general, however, these concerns turn out to be groundless. The main problem is that we are not well organized enough to tap into these other areas of support. All church ministers are not like Pat Robertson or Jerry Falwell of the homophobic religious right. Countless religious people are individuals of conscience who, through their ministry, know about the harassment and discrimination we face and are willing to help us. A minister at Penn State, for example, was extremely persuasive when she testified to the faculty senate in favor of a sexual orientation clause. She demonstrated to many people that although the religious right was lined up against us, it was still possible to be religious and support lesbian and gay rights.

Liberals in politically sensitive administrative positions may also hesitate to speak up by themselves on our behalf. A dean may not want to be the sole administrator speaking to the president about a domestic partners policy. But when a significant portion of faculty members requests action, a fair-minded liberal dean more often than not will speak up. Resident assistants in the dorms who are straight may have firsthand knowledge of the problems that we face, but they do not have the time or wherewithal to orchestrate their knowledge into a unified statement. Given the well-organized attacks against us, it is incumbent on us to organize groups such as resident assistants.

And finally, we need to deal with ourselves. Over the past few years, a brouhaha has taken place over the idea of outing major personalities. Although it is certainly interesting and often useful to know that rabid right-wingers like Roy Cohn and J. Edgar Hoover were closeted homosexuals or that a major spokesperson for the antigay U.S. Department of Defense today is closeted, such knowledge does nothing directly to influence my institution's implementing a domestic partners policy. However, it always deeply concerns me when we who are involved in queer politics find that one of the major persons speaking against us is closeted. I have no qualms about outing such an individual. I need to be entirely clear. Some individuals are often closeted to everyone, leading lives of quiet desperation, to use Thoreau's phrase. I may feel sad for them and regret their decision, but I believe it is unconscionable for anyone to out them in the interests of furthering a cause. However, if that same individual's internalized homophobia is enacted by publicly speaking out against us, then two steps are necessary.

First, we should privately inform the person that we find such comments particularly offensive and that, second, we will have no option but to publicly out the person unless he or she stops immediately. I am suggesting zero tolerance for anyone who is lesbian or gay or bisexual and seeks to hide his or her sexual orientation by promoting homophobia. Rarely is an issue so cut and dried for me. If the person says he or she will not publicly speak against us but then signs a letter to the president against a progay initiative, then he or she should be outed. I also have no problems with honest individuals who have differences of opinion. It is possible, for example, that a gay man may have a philosophical position against the domestic partners policy we are promoting. We need to listen to his argument and acknowledge it.

Fortunately, most closeted people in our colleges and universities are not academic Roy Cohns. However, many queer individuals do not know how to make themselves useful in a campaign to change the institution.

Even more than straight supporters, the lesbian and gay community contains a vast wealth of positive energy waiting to be tapped. Such an effort for change can be difficult in an elite institution. Faculty members are not used to talking to secretaries as peers. Students are often hesitant to think they could assume a leadership role in an organization that includes faculty members. Staff worry about their jobs. Younger untenured faculty members have qualms about how to interact with older senior faculty members. Some men and women may not know how to talk and work together.

No rules exist for helping members of such a diverse group to work productively together, but an awareness of potential trouble can help to resolve potential conflict. Indeed, the idea of agape again frames our work so that we realize we cannot succeed if we silence others. Such an operating principle may be effected by forming a coordinating council that includes representatives from each constituency. Putting an equal number of men and women in a decision-making group would also help. The simple point here is that to overlook our friends and colleagues is philosophically wrong and strategically foolhardy. Every queer may not be willing to spend 20 hours a week trying to implement a fair housing policy, but few individuals would be unwilling to spend some amount of time working in support of such an issue. The key lies in coordination and an honest willingness to engage one another in dialogues of respect.

Alliances. In Chapter 4, I wrote about trying to understand the differences and similarities we have with other oppressed groups. If we accept the premises presented in that chapter, then we have two strategic actions to develop. First, we must create an arena for making it possible for other groups to understand our problems and concerns, and second, we must make an active effort to understand other groups' issues and provide support to them when they ask us. Creating ongoing dialogues might take any number of formats—a broad-based coalition that meets periodically, a tightly knit group of multicultural coordinators, multiple groups that work together within specific categories (faculty, students, etc.), and so on. The key is for dialogue to occur so that we are able to understand one another's concerns and support each other when the need arises.

We will need to spell out what such support will actually entail. Because issues and institutions vary, what we ask of others will change according to time and circumstance. On one topic we may need a resolution passed by a multicultural group. At another time we may need the group's physical presence at a meeting with the president, and, at yet another moment, we may need little more than a letter of support.

Support is a two-way street. I am troubled when we ask for support without having shown any of our own for another group's struggles. We must educate ourselves about the issues that other oppressed groups confront. I am always frustrated when straight friends say that they have read a book or watched a television show with a gay character and think they know the challenges I face. They do not. Understanding my life takes more of an engagement than simply watching *Tales of the City,* the TV adaptation of Armistead Maupin's novel about gay life in San Francisco. Similarly, I am bothered at times that we do not do enough in our community to engage those who are different from us. Men claim solidarity with women but do little to comprehend the reality of women. White gays claim that they are oppressed like African Americans and are engaged in a joint struggle for civil rights, but they often do not do enough to understand the lives of straight and gay African Americans. I wrote this text during the year that Californians passed the anti-immigrant measure, Proposition 187. When we first arrived in California, Barry and I went to a meeting sponsored by the American Civil Liberties Union to oppose Proposition 187. At the meeting were representatives from a remarkable array of community groups—the National Association for the Advancement of Colored People, the Mexican American Legal Defense and Education Fund, the California Teachers Association, the National Organization for Women. No representative from a California gay and lesbian group was in attendance. (Barry and I were new to town and unaffiliated.) A queer absence at such a meeting is lamentable. On a political and moral level, we should not ask of others what we do not demand of ourselves. On a philosophical level, our absence signals our misunderstanding of what it means to exist in a multicultural world according to the principle of agape. Gay activists are leaders in a multicultural world and we must live by example. Although I argued that lesbian and gay people should not be included in affirmative action statements, for example, it is imperative that we join straight women and people of color in actions to protect and extend affirmative action.

Break the Rules. All of the strategies for change that I have offered here operate within the system. However critical it is to understand the structure, rules, and players with whom we will work, we should also not fool ourselves into thinking that if we simply play by the rules, we will get what we want. The rules have been made to exclude us. We can certainly use our knowledge of the rules to succeed occasionally in creating change, but we should also recognize that sometimes we need to break the rules.

Some years ago when I returned from a sabbatical, I made the rounds at Penn State to let people know that I had returned. A vice president mentioned in passing that no one had made the president angrier throughout his tenure at the university than I. I have already mentioned that during the struggle over a sexual orientation clause, I had a meeting with the president where my Irish temper got the better of me. He shouted at me, and I shouted back. I see that incident as an accomplishment. Perhaps he should have been made angrier sooner, because he dragged his feet on every queer-related issue that he confronted.

We are working on important issues. We should get angry. The discourse of the academy seems to require that we always be polite and cordial. Sometimes, however, being polite does not work. Sometimes, it will be necessary to demonstrate in front of the board of trustees to let them know that we are serious. Sometimes, going through the appropriate channels will not get us what we want. There are times when, in the words of a friend, we should not be shushed. If that takes raising our collective voice, so be it.

Consequently, I am suggesting that we must understand the system and work within it, but at times, we should also disrupt it. These involve matters of timing and alliances. We must not make empty threats. Queer Chicken Littles who proclaim at every turn that someone had better give us what we want or the sky will fall retard the movement. Administrators will dismiss such comments as overblown threats we cannot carry out. Similarly, we should always protect free speech. Lavender fascism is no better than any other form. Breaking the rules does not mean that we should infringe on someone else's rights, but if the administration will not work with us in good faith, it should be made to understand that we will protest and demonstrate. One of the main reasons that the administration at Penn State gave in to us over the sexual orientation clause was that they realized we were well organized and capable of pulling off a major demonstration that would have encircled the entire administration building. Queer tactics are sometimes needed to highlight the absurdity of a particular policy. The simple point here is that when all avenues have been exhausted and the administration asks us to wait for some unknown right moment to enact our agenda, we have to say that our patience has worn thin, we are tired of waiting, and that this moment—now—is the only right time to implement a new policy, or we will be forced to use other nonviolent tactics. We will not be denied.

Finally, throughout our struggle, we need to ensure that we do not demonize one another or our opponents. It is to everyone's benefit that we speak with individuals and groups on an ongoing basis. Our work is dialogical. People need to see us in the fullness of who we are. Yes, I am a gay man. I am also an academic who writes about decision making and strategy. I am also a mountain climber. We should not pigeonhole anyone or let ourselves be stereotyped and cordoned off. To cut off all dialogue on all issues because you and I disagree on a specific issue is not helpful. To demonize the other person is to fall into a trap of our own making.

And if it's not a good idea to make our opponents into enemies, we ought not make our allies into enemies either. We need to allow ourselves to get angry with one another and still continue to work with one another. Rather than avoid obnoxious individuals like the character Jason in "Ashes," we need to speak with them about our discomfort concerning their strategies and styles. Community of the kind that I have discussed here assumes that we will disagree, that we will have arguments about the nature of the institution and our strategies for changing it. We want to foment dialogue. To do so will sometimes entail getting angry, but we will always need to keep talking about the full range of issues that confront us in academic life. A diverse community will always disagree; an academic community should always keep talking.

What I have outlined is not a fixed blueprint for change because contingencies, personalities, and history will change what we need to do. At a minimum, I have counseled that we think strategically about what specifically we want to accomplish, and how we can set out to achieve our goals. Although we should work within the system, we should also at times break the rules when necessary. All of these suggestions are framed by the ideas of cultural politics and agape. In what follows, I conclude with a discussion of what the queer university might look like if we extend this structural agenda into the realm of curriculum, pedagogy, knowledge, and power.

Looking Back,
Looking Ahead

What Gay Men Do in the Dark

When I listen to conservative Christian ministers speak about the sins of homosexuality, I am often as surprised at their interest in what gay men purportedly do in the dark as I am repulsed by their lies. They paint pictures of activities that presumably all gay men indulge in, but I know I have not participated in any of them. Here's one portrait of what Barry and I have done in the dark:

We spent my sabbatical from Penn State in Costa Rica. I had a Fulbright to do research and Barry taught high school math. One night we went to a movie in downtown San Jose—*Las Guardaespaldas*. The movie starred Whitney Houston and Kevin Costner, having finally reached Central America six months after its appearance in the United States as *The Bodyguard*. I remember the theater being packed with people; there was a good deal of noise throughout the movie. Although the spoken lines were dubbed in Spanish, the songs were in English. When Whitney Houston broke out with that tune "I Will Always Love You," I felt Barry's hand reach over to mine and grab it. He held it there in the movie in the dark, and I felt all those things that two people in love feel for one another—passion, safety, devotion, intensity. I was one lucky queer.

Thirty years ago, Hollister Barnes (1958) wrote an article titled "I am glad I am homosexual" (p. 6). What is remarkable about his title and the accompanying article is not so much his statement but that this kind of comment has been seen as confrontational throughout this century and remains so today. For someone to utter "I am homosexual" has been enough of a problem, but to add happiness to the statement has turned the phrasing from a problem to an affirmation, from shame to pride, from acquiescence to confrontation.

In many respects, this text has been about these movements—from shame to pride, from submission to confrontation and from a stigma to a source of strength. We recognize today, however, that even the use of the word homosexual involves a normalization that can no longer be tolerated. Instead, we have kept in step with our homosexual ancestors by saying that we are queer. As Michael Warner (1993) has noted, the use of the word queer, "rejects a minoritizing logic of toleration or simple political-interest representation in favor of a more thorough resistance to regimes of the normal" (p. xxvi). As researchers, then, I have argued that we are academic outlaws intellectually and morally concerned with subverting those structures and processes that seek to keep people on the margins, voiceless and silenced.

What I have struggled to come to terms with in this book is how the idea of knowledge and the academy has been desexualized so that what we have come to define as normal is actually heterosexual privilege. How we structure our texts and who we decide to populate them with—our wives, husbands, children and long-time companions—are political decisions that either reaffirm or destabilize sexual relations in the academy and ultimately in society as well. Our definition of how we should act frames more than simply good table manners; we either leave pictures of our partners in our desk drawers along with our earrings, or we display them as significations of who we are in much the same way that individuals call on other cultural artifacts to define who they are. We seek to understand the power of the norm and how our sexual identities differ from those of other oppressed groups, or we avoid discussions of difference altogether and try to fit into the norm by counterfeiting our identities.

To outline the argument, I called on three varied uses of data. Case study interviews offered a view of what it means to be a closeted academic today and what it meant yesterday. Such qualitative data are relatively straightforward (no pun intended!) and acceptable in the academic world of the late 20th century. However, I have also tried to locate myself in the text by drawing on incidents from my own public and private life to highlight and personalize the struggles and challenges that queer people face. My purpose in framing the text in this manner was twofold. First, in a postmodern age it has become commonplace to speak of an author's "subject position." Far too often what we mean by such a term is little more than a simpleminded recitation of who we are, as if presenting our credentials to readers will define our epistemological and ontological standpoints. However, to say that the author is an educated, white, gay male would include a panoply of individuals having little in common with what I have written. Instead, I have tried to point out who I am in a fuller manner than I have done in other academic texts by describing my life. Admittedly, such a description is one-sided, subjective, and partial. I have also not written an autobiography; rather, I have used my life as a point of departure and reference point to expand on my own ideas about cultural studies and queer theory.

And second, I have tried to make less use of academic jargon, hoping to invoke the passion that I often feel with regard to creating change in academe. In doing so, I have consciously avoided the cool logic used, ironically, both by the current esoteric devotees of postmodernism and the logical positivists of a previous age. By offering a text invoking the first person singular and using examples from my own life, I by no means intend to imply that all texts should be written in a similar vein. However, I have tried using this discursive manner to highlight what I mean by normalizing relations. Structures—organizational, textual—do not determine outcomes, but they help define how we raise questions and what answers we will find. This book's textual structure, then, has sought to portray academic life in a manner different from that of standard academic prose, which seeks to remove (or hide) the author from the text. As an agent for political change, I thought it inappropriate to assume a position of objective detachment or neutrality.

And finally, I have used a short story as part of the data. Foucault (1973) has written, "I am well aware that I have never written anything but fictions. I do not mean to say that the truth is therefore absent. It seems to me the possibility exists for fiction to function in truth, and for bringing it about that a true discourse engenders or 'manufactures' something that does not yet exist, that is, it fictions it" (p. 43). Aside from my discomfort with Foucault's typically obtuse style, I find myself in agreement with what he has written. I certainly do not believe that all empirical questions escape scientific reason; however, as with Foucault, I have tried to offer a short story that "functions in truth." Thus, Chapter 6 experiments with presenting ideas in such a way that readers gain insights into the argument different from those they would receive by reading a more scientific and objective text. Such a chapter also calls for reading a text in a way that is different from the way in which the other chapters are read; one intent has been to highlight the multiple public and private selves we inhabit as readers, authors, narrators.

In this concluding chapter, I summarize and bring together the various strands of thought touched on throughout the text. I extrapolate on the need for cultural studies and queer theory to move in tandem toward an understanding of the specificity of social relations at work in academe. I do not so much intend that we become antiscientific or subjective but that we develop a sense of knowledge production and identity that is dramatically different from what we have previously seen in the academy. In doing so, I acknowledge our discursive and political relationship to our homosexual predecessors and map strategies for the future.

Cultural Identity and Power

We have made much of identity politics over the past generation. Our understanding that multiple and conflicting identities exist in relation to norms has aided our understanding of how constructs such as race and sexual orientation have been defined. In many respects, the debates fueled between essentialists and social constructionists have helped clarify what we even mean by identity. Nonetheless, a danger exists that by reifying identity we reproduce a cheery liberalism that assumes that if we just accept people for who they are, then everything will be okay.

To be sure, I want a world where homophobia is abolished and the fear of violence against lesbian and gay people is eradicated. But the assumption at work throughout this text has been that merely inaugurating suggestions such as those made in the previous chapter—however helpful and necessary they are—will be insufficient if we do not investigate the structure of cultural identities and their codes of power. Chantal Mouffe (1988) is helpful here:

> Relations of authority and power cannot completely disappear, and it is important to abandon the myth of a transparent society, reconciled with itself, for that kind of fantasy leads to totalitarianism. A project of radical and plural democracy requires the existence of multiplicity, of plurality, and of conflict. (p. 41)

Identities, then, of contestation and regulation exist within culture. I have argued for analyses that are based on a cultural politics so that we link identity formation to institutional practices. I am also suggesting more than simply that identities exist within groups. Instead of queer people organizing as yet another ethnic minority, I have argued that we—and other marginalized groups—might locate our investigations in a study of the structure of institutional cultures in general and in the case represented here, of academe in particular. From this perspective, identity becomes a cultural matter of group signification based on historically specific social relations.

At this point, cultural studies and queer theory come together and call on Foucaultian notions of power. We move away from the idea that one person or group has power and another does not. Instead, power is a structural activity; our challenge is to decode the mechanisms of power. Critics have suggested that Foucault's analysis delegitimizes political action; we come to believe that change is impossible and we are all helpless victims. That is not my reading of Foucault. In my view, he has rightly challenged the utopian notions of liberalism, but he has not fallen into the nihilistic trap that we find with other French cognoscenti—Baudrillard and Lyotard perhaps most prominently. Instead, Foucault offers the possibility for individual and group resistance and explains the contingencies of power. He argues for the necessity of a micropolitics in which multiple groups contend for power; we have moved away from a simplistic and deterministic Marxian dialectic of struggle, with the state located in economic structures. Most important, Foucault (1974) speaks of institutions such as colleges and universities in the following manner:

> It seems to me that the real political task in a society such as ours is to criticize the working of institutions which appear to be both neutral and independent; to criticize them in such a manner that the political violence

which has always exercised itself obscurely through them will be unmasked, so that one can fight them. (p. 171)

This argument's ramifications for queer theory, cultural studies and the academy are multiple. One point is to redefine and reclaim our past. Texts such as *Queering the Renaissance* (Goldberg, 1994) and *The Invention of Heterosexuality* (Katz, 1995) are helpful examples of works that reassess different historical moments and, in doing so, reframe our present. History is no longer seen as a linear path but as a series of trajectories and displacements instead. The idea of identity itself takes on new meanings as we create from the past alternative interpretations of what it meant, for example, to be a gay academic 50 years ago.

An additional point is the reformulation of what is meant by *intellectual*. As opposed to someone who develops totalizing discourses about knowledge from a removed perspective, we seek an agent for change who advises and assists local initiatives. The academic should no longer simply speak and think on behalf of an anonymous mass but should instead become involved in localized, daily struggles. The queer academic, then, uses theory to change structures on campus.

Language, the way it is used and by whom, becomes a central object of analysis within and across institutions. Discourse is power. As Best and Kellner (1991) note, "The rules determining discourse enforce norms of what is rational, sane, or true, and to speak from outside these rules is to risk marginalization and exclusion" (p. 58). At the same time, it should be possible to develop counterdiscourses that provide marginalized groups with forms of resistance. In one sense, texts such as Goldberg's and Katz's are examples of historical counterdiscourses. The activities of groups like Queer Nation are an attempt at creating current-day counterdiscourses. And as I noted with regard to this text, another important discursive activity is analyzing the production, reception and varied uses of texts; their relation to power in terms of how they are used to define social relations, values, and notions of community and identity bears investigation so that we can develop alternative discourses. Simply stated, if we have no understanding or analyses, we will be unable to resist. The challenge is to disrupt normalized relations.

Thus, rather than seeing knowledge as neutral and objective as modernists do, or as capable of emancipation as Marxists once argued, knowledge and its production become indissociable from regimes of power (Foucault, 1980). Identity becomes shaped within the definition of what is acceptable. Although Foucault used multiple examples of how institutions and their practices—prisons, hospitals, asylums—functioned as mechanisms of power, what is most pertinent here is a deconstructive attempt to see how homosexuality has been defined and redefined so that knowledge has functioned as a vehicle for social control.

The idea of liberation—a utopian moment—is eschewed, and large-scale revolution is seen merely as the displacement of one totalitarian code of power for another. As noted by Foucault (1977),

> Humanity does not gradually progress from combat to combat until it arrives at universal reciprocity, where the rule of law finally replaces warfare; humanity installs each of its violences in a system of rules and thus proceeds from domination to domination. (p. 151)

Such an idea—regardless of whether one agrees or disagrees—may seem far removed from the ivy walls of academe, but it has a direct relationship to our understanding of the nature of reality and identity. For if liberation is possible, then we accept the modernist notion that identities are stable and all a community need do is accept the range of diversities that exist. What I am suggesting here, however, is that we need to interrogate how it is that we accept some diversities and not others. What are the relations that get us, in effect, to the table?

I want to reiterate that by moving beyond modernism, I am not rejecting all of its premises out of hand. Indeed, I could not have written the previous chapter if I believed that ostensibly rational action in an organization is useless. Modernity has made significant advances in liberty, law and our understanding of democracy and equality. However, a reconstruction of modernist politics should now recognize the theoretical contributions that individuals such as Foucault have made.

In sum, then, I am suggesting that cultural identities are never provided in advance, out of whole cloth; rather, they are constant reconstructions that occur over time and place. The challenge is to create the conditions for enablement where our multiple identities can be decoupled from overarching norms. Such a view speaks for the need of pluralities rather than singular norms. The struggle becomes one of cultural politics over the discursive conditions of identity formation. Rather than see the duality in terms of minority/majority, as if all minorities were similar, we seek multiple voices and try to make sense of where differences and similarities lie.

In Chapter 2, I outlined a scaffolding for cultural studies and queer theory as cultural politics that bears repeating at this point:

1. It is historicist in that it seeks to understand sexual identity over time.
2. It seeks to uncover norms and decode ideological practices.
3. It is confrontational and disruptive rather than consensual.
4. It understands sexual identity in terms of more than simply a sexual act.
5. It sees all of culture as interpretive and political.

I offered these propositions as a way to formalize admittedly abstract comments about the nature of knowledge, identity and culture. I then suggested that we face three challenges in dealing with these propositions: *intellectual, existential,* and *strategic.* In the previous chapter, I offered the *strategic challenges* that might be dealt with in the academy. The *existential challenge* refers to the conditions we create so that individuals and groups have the means not merely to grasp cultural capital but to produce it. Within the academy this suggests dramatic new configurations of how we position ourselves vis-à-vis knowledge production and one another. Indeed, the emergence of electronically mediated forms of communication in all spheres of everyday intellectual and artistic life moves the grounds of scholarship away from traditional disciplines and toward alternative configurations. As critical intellectuals, academics become agents who produce knowledge and assume responsibility for creating dialogic spaces in the larger culture.

And finally, the *intellectual challenge* returns us to discussions about structure. On an academic level, issues such as departmental configuration and faculty appointments come into question. How is knowledge organized and what does it mean in the institution if someone undertakes queer analyses? Do we professionalize lesbian, gay and bisexual studies so that we have our own journals, conferences and subgroups within other associations? Where does political action fit in? On an administrative level, how we organize and orchestrate groupings such as lesbian, gay and bisexual students or queer alumni comes in for investigation. Do we seek to assimilate groups? If subcultures are modalities of the overriding organizational culture, then what does it mean to encourage the creation of anticultural groups? How do we handle activism and voice? These are the kinds of questions that the intellectual challenge raises for us based on what has been discussed in the text. Thus, cultural studies and queer theory point us toward four reconfigurations within the academy.

The Critical Intellectual. The claim made here follows from several suggestions made throughout the book. The modernist has viewed the intellectual as an individual disengaged from the give-and-take of everyday life; the Marxist has seen the intellectual as an enlightened soul leading the masses. Academics have taken on the purest form of this kind of intellectual. They study particular phenomena and posit hypotheses or answers that they hope will improve the general welfare of society. Again, one ought not to draw caricatures of such people; they have often found cures for diseases, made breakthroughs in understanding many puzzles, or created new ways of thinking about and acting in the world. Computer circuitry, a cure for polio, and a better comprehension of why dinosaurs vanished from the earth are all attributable to such academic work in one way or another.

However, I am suggesting that a social theorist of the kind needed today should be engaged in daily struggles and challenges. Such theorists would refute the objectivity of knowledge and bring their own pedagogical authority into question in the classroom. Thus, as Henry Giroux (1994) notes, such intellectuals "reject the traditional notion of teaching as a technique or set of neutral skills and argues that teaching is a social practice that can only be understood through considerations of history, politics, power, and culture" (p. 280). In this light, educators develop a critical language through which to examine issues such as sexual orientation.

Specifically, such a suggestion means that lesbian and gay intellectuals and straight intellectuals have multiple tasks to undertake. Queers will certainly be open about who we are, but we will have to do more than simply come out. In accepting the political and cultural ramifications of such an act, we acknowledge that we have particular responsibilities to speak out and act on our campuses in support of our constituencies and in solidarity with other groups. We should also not revert to the stance of the disengaged intellectual. I am arguing that queer theory is inevitably political.

Similarly, the new role of the straight intellectual will be to come to terms with what it means to be lesbian or gay on campus and think about how all of us might create an environment that honors difference rather than marginalizes it. Pedagogical examples range from the kind of descriptions we use in our classes—do we always speak of married couples in examples in a math class? Does a history class ever touch on the lives of queer people?—to the creation of different curricular configurations.

The Task of Theory. Social theorists work to understand the various levels of social reality and how power operates throughout them. As with Best and Kellner (1991), I am suggesting that a theory of this kind is multidimensional, nonreductive and dialectical:

> It conceptualizes the connections between the economic, political, social, and cultural dimensions of society and refuses to reduce social phenomena to any one dimension. A dialectical theory describes the mediation, or interconnections, that relate social phenomena to each other and the dominant mode of social organization. (p. 263)

A dialectical study of sexual orientation, for example, analyzes how the economy over time has helped define categories such as gay, lesbian, queer, or invert. We also investigate the cultural aspects of life to see not merely economic structures but also those symbolic and discursive codes that relate to what I have defined as cultural capital. We analyze the politics of how queers have been silenced or have seized voice. We investigate how queers are marginalized and fixed as specific entities as well as how they destabilize relations when they come out and speak up. Dialectical analysis, then, relates microlevel phenomena to the larger social forces at work in society. We investigate the larger structural forces in society and consider the interplay of those forces with the more microscopic aspects of everyday life.

Just as the intellectual becomes an agent for change, so the task of social theory is not simply to illuminate different conceptual puzzles but to develop critiques that help individuals and groups to come together to effect change. We develop new ways of seeing so that categories of silence change—individuals are able to come out without the fear or consequences that currently exist, and the conceptualization of what we mean by gay or queer also changes. In effect, theory enables individuals to gain control over the means of cultural production.

Departments and Compartmentalization. It will come as no surprise that I believe the idea of professionalizing knowledge through departmental structures ought to be changed. Departments stymie interdisciplinary dialogue. Proponents of cultural studies and queer theory seek theoretical insights across academic areas. Analyses of sexual orientation need to take place beyond merely one academic area. Departments professionalize knowledge in such a way, for instance, that English department members work only with their colleagues in areas of study, and those in psychology do likewise. Colleges and universities need to expand the discourse so that previously cordoned-off arenas of knowledge evolve into interdisciplinary sites where dialogues across professional affiliation take place. As noted by Roland Barthes,

> Interdisciplinary work . . . is not about confronting already constituted disciplines (none of which, in fact, is willing to let itself go). To do something interdisciplinary, it's not enough to choose a "subject" (a theme) and gather around it two or three sciences. Interdisciplinarity consists in creating a new object that belongs to no one. (quoted in Clifford & Marcus, 1986, p. 1)

Similarly, I urge queers not to professionalize queer studies by creating for ourselves yet another set of academic departments. Conferences, articles and academic discussion groups that exclude the general citizenry contradict the kind of focus I have suggested for queer theory. If we assume that the structures of knowledge in part have defined normalized relations that have excluded homosexuals, then we need to break those structures rather than merely reinvent them for ourselves. Queer theory and cultural studies of the kind I am suggesting here are inherently concerned with the advancement of democracy. Democracy is ideally participatory and inclusive rather than passive and exclusive. To the extent that academics have set off their areas of inquiry from the general public, we make an intellectual, existential and strategic blunder. We misinterpret how structures define knowledge; we overlook the call for engaged intellectuals; and we mistakenly assume that only those who hold the cultural capital can understand theoretical formulations.

Cultural Citizenship and Agape. All of this text focuses on the relationships we have with one another and how we need to honor the differences and connections within community. Agape is not a cure-all for the problem posed by Rodney King's famous question after the Los Angeles riots in 1992—"Why can't we all get along?" However, at a time when dialogue across differences seems impossible, I am suggesting that as academics, we might point out, we must point out, alternative possibilities.

When I travel to my campus in Los Angeles, I take city streets that wind through various ethnic neighborhoods. I invariably must stop at a red light on Alvarado Street. Waiting at the light, I read a billboard that has the same sentence in three languages. Sorry to say, I cannot read the Chinese. But a year in Central America has enabled me to stumble through the meaning of the Spanish sentence—"Mantiene vive la esperanza." Keep hope alive.

In an age when many of us think our elected leaders and institutions have failed us, a feeling of paralysis creeps in—we feel unable to create change. For academics, one response is to retreat to our corner offices and develop obscure theories that will not challenge or disrupt the status quo but will help us gain academic reward and tenure. A conservative response is to overwhelm society with calls for reinstalling norms. Keep immigrants out. Do not offer remedial education to college students. Overturn affirmative action. And keep queers at the margins. One reflex for queer academics is to withdraw to our own sanctuaries and study our topics in isolation, or to form isolated networks so that we need not bother with the daily battles in society and on our campuses. However, those of us involved in education have an obligation to deal with the idea of cultural citizenship. One of our central tasks is to help foster active, engaged, citizens who will function productively in the 21st century and deal with the myriad of problems confronting us. Through agape, we engage in the creation of hope. Hope's creation in a democracy will be noisy because people will disagree with one another. Cultural studies and queer theory demand communication and talent. Those of us who subscribe to these values need to encourage voice, to encourage disagreement.

Our colleges and universities need to be noisier—in the sense that honest dialogue that confronts differences is good. To be sure, we must not drown out other voices. Yet it is of concern to me when we assume that we cannot argue and disagree with one another. We must work harder at developing dialogues of respect. Our arguments are good ones; they are about the future of our society. Queer theory, then, does not pertain only to queers, and cultural studies does not only entail an academic debate. If we can reconceptualize what we mean by sexual orientation, ultimately all of society will change. These struggles are about moments when men and women can express affection for their partners without fear, and a straight person can understand—through agape—the connections we have with each another. Agape enables us to see our differences, but it also helps us understand our similarities. In doing so, we keep hope alive.

References

Abelove, H., Barale, M. A., & Halperin, D. M. (Eds.). (1993). *The lesbian and gay studies reader*. New York: Routledge.

Agger, B. (1992). *Cultural studies as critical theory*. Washington, DC: Falmer.

Barnes, H. (1958, August). I am glad I am homosexual. *One Magazine*, 6-9.

Baudrillard, J. (1983a). Ecstasy of communication. In H. Foster (Ed.), *The antiaesthetic: Essays on postmodern culture* (pp. 126-134). Port Townsend, WA: Bay Press.

Baudrillard, J. (1983b). *Simulations*. New York: Semiotext.

Bawer, B. (1993). *A place at the table: The gay individual in American society*. New York: Poseidon.

Bennett, T. (1992). Putting policy into cultural studies. In L. Grossberg, C. Nelson, & P. A. Treichler (Eds.), *Cultural studies*. New York: Routledge.

Best, S., & Kellner, D. (1991). *Postmodern theory: Critical interrogations*. New York: Guilford.

Bloland, H. G. (1995). Postmodernism and higher education. *The Journal of Higher Education, 66*(5), 521-559.

Boswell, J. (1981). *Christianity, social tolerance, and homosexuality: Gay people in Western Europe from the beginning of the Christian era to the fourteenth century*. Chicago: University of Chicago Press.

Bourdieu, P. (1977). Systems of education and systems of thought. *International Social Science Journal, 19*(3), 338-358.

Britzman, D. P. (1995). Is there a queer pedagogy? Or, stop reading straight. *Educational Theory, 45*(2), 151-165.

Chauncey, G. (1994). *Gay New York: Gender, urban culture, and the making of the gay male world, 1890-1940*. New York: Basic Books.

Chesebro, J. W. (1981). Views of homosexuality among social scientists. In J. W. Chesebro (Ed.), *Gayspeak*. New York: Pilgrim Press.

Clifford, J., & Marcus, G. E. (Eds.). (1986). *Writing culture: The poetics and politics of ethnography*. Berkeley: University of California Press.

Collins, P. H. (1991). *Black feminist thought: Knowledge, consciousness, and the politics of empowerment*. New York: Routledge.

Cosson, S. (1991). Queer. *OUT/LOOK, 11*, 16.

Crapanzano, V. (1992). *Hermes' dilemma and Hamlet's desire: On the epistemology of interpretation.* Cambridge, MA: Harvard University Press.

Crew, L. (Ed.). (1978). *The gay academic.* Palm Springs, CA: ETC.

D'Augelli, A. R. (1991). Teaching lesbian and gay development: A pedagogy of the oppressed. In W. G. Tierney (Ed.), *Culture and ideology in higher education: Advancing a critical agenda.* New York: Praeger.

De Lauretis, T. (1991). Queer theory: Lesbian and gay sexualities an introduction. *Differences: A Journal of Feminist Cultural Studies, 3*(2), iii-xviii.

Doty, A. (1993). *Making things perfectly queer: Interpreting mass culture.* Minneapolis: University of Minnesota Press.

Epstein, S. (1987). Gay politics, ethnic identity: The limits of social constructionism. *Socialist Review, 17*(3), 9-54.

Foucault, M. (1973). *The order of things.* New York: Vintage.

Foucault, M. (1974). Human nature: Justice versus power. In F. Elders (Ed.), *Reflexive water: The basic concerns of mankind.* London: Souvenir.

Foucault, M. (1977). *Language, counter-memory, practice.* Ithaca, NY: Cornell University Press.

Foucault, M. (1979). *Discipline and punish.* New York: Vintage.

Foucault, M. (1980). *The history of sexuality.* New York: Vintage.

Freire, P. (1970). *Pedagogy of the oppressed* (M. B. Ramos, Trans). New York: Seabury.

Fuss, D. (1989). *Essentially speaking: Feminism, nature, and difference.* New York: Routledge.

Giroux, H. A. (1993). *Living dangerously: Multiculturalism and the politics of difference.* New York: Peter Lang.

Giroux, H. A. (1994, Fall). Doing cultural studies: Youth and the challenge of pedagogy. *Harvard Educational Review, 64*(3), 278-308.

Goldberg, D. T. (1993). *Racist culture: Philosophy and the politics of meaning.* Cambridge, MA: Blackwell.

Goldberg, J. (Ed.). (1994). *Queering the renaissance.* Durham, NC: Duke University Press.

Guillory, J. (1993). *Cultural capital: The problem of literary canon formation.* Chicago: University Of Chicago Press.

Hall, S. (1990). Cultural identity and diaspora. In J. Rutherford (Ed.), *Identity: Community, culture, difference.* London: Lawrence & Wishart.

Harbeck, K. M. (1992). *Coming out of the classroom closet: Gay and lesbian students, teachers, and curricula.* New York: Harrington Park.

Haver, W. (in press). Queer research. *East Asian Studies.*

Hennessy, R. (1995). Queer visibility in commodity culture. In L. Nicholson & S. Seidman (Eds.), *Social postmodernism: Beyond identity politics.* New York: Cambridge University Press.

Hill, P. J. (1991). Multiculturalism: The crucial philosophical and organizational issues. *Change, 23*(4), 38-47.

hooks, b. (1981). *Ain't I a woman: Black women and feminism.* Boston: South End.

hooks, b. (1989). *Talking back: Thinking feminist Black.* Boston: South End.

hooks, b. (1990). *Yearning: Race, gender, and cultural politics.* Boston: South End.

hooks, b. (1992). *Black looks: Race and representation.* Boston: South End.

Katz, J. N. (1995). *The invention of heterosexuality.* New York: Dutton.

Kennedy, L. E., & Davis, M. D. (1993). *Boots of leather, slippers of gold: The history of a lesbian community.* New York: Routledge.

King, M. L., Jr. (1958). *Stride toward freedom: The Montgomery story*. New York: Harper & Row.

Kritzman, L. D. (Ed.). (1988). *Michel Foucault: Politics, philosophy, culture*. New York: Routledge.

Lorde, A. (1984). *Sister outsider: Essays and speeches*. Freedom, CA: Crossing Press.

Lorde, A. (1985). *I am your sister: Black women organizing across sexualities*. Latham, NY: Kitchen Table, Women of Color Press.

Lyotard, J. F. (1984). *The postmodern condition*. Minneapolis: University of Minnesota Press.

McDermott, R., & Varenne, H. (1995). Culture as disability. *Anthropology and Education Quarterly, 26*(3), 324-348.

McLaren, P. (1989). *Life in schools: An introduction to critical pedagogy in the foundations of education*. New York: Longman.

McLaren, P. (1995). *Critical politics and predatory culture: Oppositional politics in a postmodern world*. New York: Routledge.

McLaughlin, D., & Tierney, W. G. (Eds.). (1993). *Naming silenced lives: Personal narratives and the process of educational change*. New York: Routledge.

Mohanty, C. T. (1989-1990). On race and voice: Challenges for liberal education in the 1990s. *Cultural Critique, 14,* 179-208.

Monette, P. (1994). *Last watch of the night: Essays too personal and otherwise*. New York: Harcourt Brace.

Mouffe, C. (1988). Radical democracy: Modern or postmodern? In A. Ross (Ed.), *Universal abandon? The politics of postmodernism*. Minneapolis: University of Minnesota Press.

Newton, E. (1993). *Cherry Grove, Fire Island: Sixty years in America's first gay and lesbian town*. Boston: Beacon.

Omi, M., & Winant, H. (1994). *Racial formation in the United States from the 1960s to the 1990s* (2nd ed.). New York: Routledge.

Omi, M., & Winant, H. (1993). On the theoretical concept of race. In C. McCarthy & W. Crichlow (Eds.), *Race, identity, and representation in education*. New York: Routledge.

Patton, C. (1993). Tremble, hetero swine! In M. Warner (Ed.), *Fear of a queer planet: Queer politics and social theory*. Minneapolis: University of Minnesota Press.

Phelan, S. (1989). *Identity politics: Lesbian feminism and the limits of community*. Philadelphia: Temple University Press.

Rosaldo, R. (1994). Whose cultural studies? *American Anthropologist, 96*(3), 524-529.

Rutherford, J. (1990). A place called home: Identity and the cultural politics of difference. In J. Rutherford (Ed.), *Identity: community, culture, difference*. London: Lawrence & Wishart.

Sedgwick, E. K. (1990). *Epistemology of the closet*. Berkeley: University of California Press.

Seidman, S. (1993). Identity and politics in a postmodern gay culture: Some historical and conceptual notes. In M. Warner (Ed.), *Fear of a queer planet: Queer politics and social theory*. Minneapolis: University of Minnesota Press.

Seidman, S. (1995). Deconstructing queer theory or the under-theorization of the social and the ethical. In L. Nicholson & S. Seidman (Eds.), *Social postmodernism: Beyond identity politics*. New York: Cambridge University Press.

Signorile, M. (1993). *Queer in America: Sex, the media, and the closets of power*. New York: Random House.

Slagle, R. A. (1995, Spring). In defense of queer nation: From identity politics to a politics of difference. *Western Journal of Communication, 59,* 85-102.

Smith, B., & Smith, B. (1981). Across the kitchen table: A sister to sister dialogue. In C. Moraga & G. Anzaldua (Eds.), *This bridge called my back: Writings by radical women of color.* Watertown, MA: Persephone.

Steele, S. (1990). *The content of our character: A new vision of race in America.* New York: St. Martin's.

Sullivan, A. (1995). *Virtually normal: An argument about homosexuality.* New York: Knopf.

Tierney, W. G. (1992). *Official encouragement, institutional discouragement: minorities in academe—The Native American experience.* Norwood, NJ: Ablex.

Tierney, W. G. (1993). *Building communities of difference: Higher education in the twenty-first century.* Westport, CT: Bergin & Garvey.

Tierney, W. G. (1994). On method and hope. In A. Gitlin (Ed.), *Power and method.* New York: Routledge.

Tierney, W. G. (1995a). Cultural politics: Theory and practice. *Review of Higher Education, 18*(3), 345-355.

Tierney, W. G. (1995b). (Re)presentation and voice. *Qualitative Inquiry, 1*(4), 379-390.

Tierney, W. G. (1996). Understanding domestic partner benefits. *The Diversity Factor, 5*(1), 27-30.

Tierney, W. G., & Bensimon, E. M. (1996). *Promotion and tenure: Culture and socialization in academe.* Albany: SUNY Press.

Tierney, W. G., & Dilley, P. (in press). Constructing knowledge: Educational research and gay and lesbian studies. In W. Pinar (Ed.), *Queer theory in education.* Mahwah, NJ: Lawrence Erlbaum.

Tierney, W. G., & Lincoln, Y. S. (1997). *Representation and the text: Reframing the narrative voice.* Albany: SUNY Press.

Tierney, W. G. et al. (1992). *Enhancing diversity: Toward a better campus climate.* University Park, PA: Committee on Lesbian and Gay Concerns, Pennsylvania State University.

Waller, W. (1961). *The sociology of teaching.* New York: Russell & Russell. (Original work published 1932).

Warner, M. (Ed.). (1993). *Fear of a queer planet: Queer politics and social theory.* Minneapolis: University of Minnesota Press.

Weeks, J. (1995). *Invented moralities: Sexual values in an age of uncertainty.* New York: Columbia University Press.

West, C. (1990). The new cultural politics of difference. *October, 53,* 93-109.

Williams, W. L. (1992). *The spirit and the flesh: Sexual diversity in American Indian culture.* Boston: Beacon.

Woods, J. D., & Lucas, J. H. (1994). *The corporate closet: The professional lives of gay men in America.* New York: Free Press.

Index

181

About the Author

William G. Tierney is Professor and Director of the Center for Higher Education Policy Analysis at the University of Southern California. Prior to going to USC, he was Professor of Education and Senior Scientist in the Center for the Study of Higher Education at Pennsylvania State University. Dr. Tierney received a master's degree from Harvard University and holds a PhD from Stanford University in administration and policy analysis. His research interests pertain to faculty productivity, decision making, organizational reengineering, and issues of equity. The results of his research have appeared in higher education and anthropological journals. Some of his previous books include *Curricular Landscapes, Democratic Vistas: Transformative Leadership in Higher Education* (1989); *Official Encouragement, Institutional Discouragement: Minorities in Academe—The Native American Experience* (1992); *Building Communities of Difference: Higher Education in the 21st Century* (1993); and, with Estela Bensimon, *Promotion & Tenure: Culture and Socialization*

in Academe (1996), which pertains to the problems and challenges junior faculty face in academe. He is currently involved in a two-year study of faculty productivity, funded by the Pew Endowment. He has received funding for his research from the Lilly Endowment, the Ford Foundation, Teacher's Insurance and Annuity Association College Retirement Equities Fund (TIAA-CREF), and the U.S. Department of Education. He teaches graduate courses on curricular theory, organizational behavior, and qualitative methodology. Tierney brings with him both administrative experience as an academic dean at a Native American community college in North Dakota and cross-cultural insight from Peace Corps work in Morocco, as well as a year in Central America as a Fulbright Scholar.